OSAT

School Counselor (139) Secrets Study Guide

DEAR FUTURE EXAM SUCCESS STORY

First of all, **THANK YOU** for purchasing Mometrix study materials!

Second, congratulations! You are one of the few determined test-takers who are committed to doing whatever it takes to excel on your exam. **You have come to the right place.** We developed these study materials with one goal in mind: to deliver you the information you need in a format that's concise and easy to use.

In addition to optimizing your guide for the content of the test, we've outlined our recommended steps for breaking down the preparation process into small, attainable goals so you can make sure you stay on track.

We've also analyzed the entire test-taking process, identifying the most common pitfalls and showing how you can overcome them and be ready for any curveball the test throws you.

Standardized testing is one of the biggest obstacles on your road to success, which only increases the importance of doing well in the high-pressure, high-stakes environment of test day. Your results on this test could have a significant impact on your future, and this guide provides the information and practical advice to help you achieve your full potential on test day.

Your success is our success

We would love to hear from you! If you would like to share the story of your exam success or if you have any questions or comments in regard to our products, please contact us at **800-673-8175** or **support@mometrix.com**.

Thanks again for your business and we wish you continued success!

Sincerely,
The Mometrix Test Preparation Team

Need more help? Check out our flashcards at:
http://MometrixFlashcards.com/CEOE

Copyright © 2023 by Mometrix Media LLC. All rights reserved.
Written and edited by the Mometrix Exam Secrets Test Prep Team
Printed in the United States of America

Table of Contents

Introduction

Thank you for purchasing this resource! You have made the choice to prepare yourself for a test that could have a huge impact on your future, and this guide is designed to help you be fully ready for test day. Obviously, it's important to have a solid understanding of the test material, but you also need to be prepared for the unique environment and stressors of the test, so that you can perform to the best of your abilities.

For this purpose, the first section that appears in this guide is the **Secret Keys**. We've devoted countless hours to meticulously researching what works and what doesn't, and we've boiled down our findings to the five most impactful steps you can take to improve your performance on the test. We start at the beginning with study planning and move through the preparation process, all the way to the testing strategies that will help you get the most out of what you know when you're finally sitting in front of the test.

We recommend that you start preparing for your test as far in advance as possible. However, if you've bought this guide as a last-minute study resource and only have a few days before your test, we recommend that you skip over the first two Secret Keys since they address a long-term study plan.

If you struggle with **test anxiety**, we strongly encourage you to check out our recommendations for how you can overcome it. Test anxiety is a formidable foe, but it can be beaten, and we want to make sure you have the tools you need to defeat it.

Copyright © Mometrix Media. You have been licensed one copy of this document for personal use only. Any other reproduction or redistribution is strictly prohibited. All rights reserved.
This content is provided for test preparation purposes only and does not imply an endorsement by Mometrix of any particular political, scientific, or religious point of view.

Secret Key #1 – Plan Big, Study Small

There's a lot riding on your performance. If you want to ace this test, you're going to need to keep your skills sharp and the material fresh in your mind. You need a plan that lets you review everything you need to know while still fitting in your schedule. We'll break this strategy down into three categories.

Information Organization

Start with the information you already have: the official test outline. From this, you can make a complete list of all the concepts you need to cover before the test. Organize these concepts into groups that can be studied together, and create a list of any related vocabulary you need to learn so you can brush up on any difficult terms. You'll want to keep this vocabulary list handy once you actually start studying since you may need to add to it along the way.

Time Management

Once you have your set of study concepts, decide how to spread them out over the time you have left before the test. Break your study plan into small, clear goals so you have a manageable task for each day and know exactly what you're doing. Then just focus on one small step at a time. When you manage your time this way, you don't need to spend hours at a time studying. Studying a small block of content for a short period each day helps you retain information better and avoid stressing over how much you have left to do. You can relax knowing that you have a plan to cover everything in time. In order for this strategy to be effective though, you have to start studying early and stick to your schedule. Avoid the exhaustion and futility that comes from last-minute cramming!

Study Environment

The environment you study in has a big impact on your learning. Studying in a coffee shop, while probably more enjoyable, is not likely to be as fruitful as studying in a quiet room. It's important to keep distractions to a minimum. You're only planning to study for a short block of time, so make the most of it. Don't pause to check your phone or get up to find a snack. It's also important to **avoid multitasking**. Research has consistently shown that multitasking will make your studying dramatically less effective. Your study area should also be comfortable and well-lit so you don't have the distraction of straining your eyes or sitting on an uncomfortable chair.

The time of day you study is also important. You want to be rested and alert. Don't wait until just before bedtime. Study when you'll be most likely to comprehend and remember. Even better, if you know what time of day your test will be, set that time aside for study. That way your brain will be used to working on that subject at that specific time and you'll have a better chance of recalling information.

Finally, it can be helpful to team up with others who are studying for the same test. Your actual studying should be done in as isolated an environment as possible, but the work of organizing the information and setting up the study plan can be divided up. In between study sessions, you can discuss with your teammates the concepts that you're all studying and quiz each other on the details. Just be sure that your teammates are as serious about the test as you are. If you find that your study time is being replaced with social time, you might need to find a new team.

Copyright © Mometrix Media. You have been licensed one copy of this document for personal use only. Any other reproduction or redistribution is strictly prohibited. All rights reserved.
This content is provided for test preparation purposes only and does not imply an endorsement by Mometrix of any particular political, scientific, or religious point of view.

Secret Key #2 – Make Your Studying Count

You're devoting a lot of time and effort to preparing for this test, so you want to be absolutely certain it will pay off. This means doing more than just reading the content and hoping you can remember it on test day. It's important to make every minute of study count. There are two main areas you can focus on to make your studying count.

Retention

It doesn't matter how much time you study if you can't remember the material. You need to make sure you are retaining the concepts. To check your retention of the information you're learning, try recalling it at later times with minimal prompting. Try carrying around flashcards and glance at one or two from time to time or ask a friend who's also studying for the test to quiz you.

To enhance your retention, look for ways to put the information into practice so that you can apply it rather than simply recalling it. If you're using the information in practical ways, it will be much easier to remember. Similarly, it helps to solidify a concept in your mind if you're not only reading it to yourself but also explaining it to someone else. Ask a friend to let you teach them about a concept you're a little shaky on (or speak aloud to an imaginary audience if necessary). As you try to summarize, define, give examples, and answer your friend's questions, you'll understand the concepts better and they will stay with you longer. Finally, step back for a big picture view and ask yourself how each piece of information fits with the whole subject. When you link the different concepts together and see them working together as a whole, it's easier to remember the individual components.

Finally, practice showing your work on any multi-step problems, even if you're just studying. Writing out each step you take to solve a problem will help solidify the process in your mind, and you'll be more likely to remember it during the test.

Modality

Modality simply refers to the means or method by which you study. Choosing a study modality that fits your own individual learning style is crucial. No two people learn best in exactly the same way, so it's important to know your strengths and use them to your advantage.

For example, if you learn best by visualization, focus on visualizing a concept in your mind and draw an image or a diagram. Try color-coding your notes, illustrating them, or creating symbols that will trigger your mind to recall a learned concept. If you learn best by hearing or discussing information, find a study partner who learns the same way or read aloud to yourself. Think about how to put the information in your own words. Imagine that you are giving a lecture on the topic and record yourself so you can listen to it later.

For any learning style, flashcards can be helpful. Organize the information so you can take advantage of spare moments to review. Underline key words or phrases. Use different colors for different categories. Mnemonic devices (such as creating a short list in which every item starts with the same letter) can also help with retention. Find what works best for you and use it to store the information in your mind most effectively and easily.

Copyright © Mometrix Media. You have been licensed one copy of this document for personal use only. Any other reproduction or redistribution is strictly prohibited. All rights reserved.
This content is provided for test preparation purposes only and does not imply an endorsement by Mometrix of any particular political, scientific, or religious point of view.

Secret Key #3 – Practice the Right Way

Your success on test day depends not only on how many hours you put into preparing, but also on whether you prepared the right way. It's good to check along the way to see if your studying is paying off. One of the most effective ways to do this is by taking practice tests to evaluate your progress. Practice tests are useful because they show exactly where you need to improve. Every time you take a practice test, pay special attention to these three groups of questions:

- The questions you got wrong
- The questions you had to guess on, even if you guessed right
- The questions you found difficult or slow to work through

This will show you exactly what your weak areas are, and where you need to devote more study time. Ask yourself why each of these questions gave you trouble. Was it because you didn't understand the material? Was it because you didn't remember the vocabulary? Do you need more repetitions on this type of question to build speed and confidence? Dig into those questions and figure out how you can strengthen your weak areas as you go back to review the material.

Additionally, many practice tests have a section explaining the answer choices. It can be tempting to read the explanation and think that you now have a good understanding of the concept. However, an explanation likely only covers part of the question's broader context. Even if the explanation makes perfect sense, **go back and investigate** every concept related to the question until you're positive you have a thorough understanding.

As you go along, keep in mind that the practice test is just that: practice. Memorizing these questions and answers will not be very helpful on the actual test because it is unlikely to have any of the same exact questions. If you only know the right answers to the sample questions, you won't be prepared for the real thing. **Study the concepts** until you understand them fully, and then you'll be able to answer any question that shows up on the test.

It's important to wait on the practice tests until you're ready. If you take a test on your first day of study, you may be overwhelmed by the amount of material covered and how much you need to learn. Work up to it gradually.

On test day, you'll need to be prepared for answering questions, managing your time, and using the test-taking strategies you've learned. It's a lot to balance, like a mental marathon that will have a big impact on your future. Like training for a marathon, you'll need to start slowly and work your way up. When test day arrives, you'll be ready.

Start with the strategies you've read in the first two Secret Keys—plan your course and study in the way that works best for you. If you have time, consider using multiple study resources to get different approaches to the same concepts. It can be helpful to see difficult concepts from more than one angle. Then find a good source for practice tests. Many times, the test website will suggest potential study resources or provide sample tests.

Copyright © Mometrix Media. You have been licensed one copy of this document for personal use only. Any other reproduction or redistribution is strictly prohibited. All rights reserved.
This content is provided for test preparation purposes only and does not imply an endorsement by Mometrix of any particular political, scientific, or religious point of view.

Practice Test Strategy

If you're able to find at least three practice tests, we recommend this strategy:

Untimed and Open-Book Practice

Take the first test with no time constraints and with your notes and study guide handy. Take your time and focus on applying the strategies you've learned.

Timed and Open-Book Practice

Take the second practice test open-book as well, but set a timer and practice pacing yourself to finish in time.

Timed and Closed-Book Practice

Take any other practice tests as if it were test day. Set a timer and put away your study materials. Sit at a table or desk in a quiet room, imagine yourself at the testing center, and answer questions as quickly and accurately as possible.

Keep repeating timed and closed-book tests on a regular basis until you run out of practice tests or it's time for the actual test. Your mind will be ready for the schedule and stress of test day, and you'll be able to focus on recalling the material you've learned.

Copyright © Mometrix Media. You have been licensed one copy of this document for personal use only. Any other reproduction or redistribution is strictly prohibited. All rights reserved.
This content is provided for test preparation purposes only and does not imply an endorsement by Mometrix of any particular political, scientific, or religious point of view.

Secret Key #4 – Pace Yourself

Once you're fully prepared for the material on the test, your biggest challenge on test day will be managing your time. Just knowing that the clock is ticking can make you panic even if you have plenty of time left. Work on pacing yourself so you can build confidence against the time constraints of the exam. Pacing is a difficult skill to master, especially in a high-pressure environment, so **practice is vital**.

Set time expectations for your pace based on how much time is available. For example, if a section has 60 questions and the time limit is 30 minutes, you know you have to average 30 seconds or less per question in order to answer them all. Although 30 seconds is the hard limit, set 25 seconds per question as your goal, so you reserve extra time to spend on harder questions. When you budget extra time for the harder questions, you no longer have any reason to stress when those questions take longer to answer.

Don't let this time expectation distract you from working through the test at a calm, steady pace, but keep it in mind so you don't spend too much time on any one question. Recognize that taking extra time on one question you don't understand may keep you from answering two that you do understand later in the test. If your time limit for a question is up and you're still not sure of the answer, mark it and move on, and come back to it later if the time and the test format allow. If the testing format doesn't allow you to return to earlier questions, just make an educated guess; then put it out of your mind and move on.

On the easier questions, be careful not to rush. It may seem wise to hurry through them so you have more time for the challenging ones, but it's not worth missing one if you know the concept and just didn't take the time to read the question fully. Work efficiently but make sure you understand the question and have looked at all of the answer choices, since more than one may seem right at first.

Even if you're paying attention to the time, you may find yourself a little behind at some point. You should speed up to get back on track, but do so wisely. Don't panic; just take a few seconds less on each question until you're caught up. Don't guess without thinking, but do look through the answer choices and eliminate any you know are wrong. If you can get down to two choices, it is often worthwhile to guess from those. Once you've chosen an answer, move on and don't dwell on any that you skipped or had to hurry through. If a question was taking too long, chances are it was one of the harder ones, so you weren't as likely to get it right anyway.

On the other hand, if you find yourself getting ahead of schedule, it may be beneficial to slow down a little. The more quickly you work, the more likely you are to make a careless mistake that will affect your score. You've budgeted time for each question, so don't be afraid to spend that time. Practice an efficient but careful pace to get the most out of the time you have.

Copyright © Mometrix Media. You have been licensed one copy of this document for personal use only. Any other reproduction or redistribution is strictly prohibited. All rights reserved.
This content is provided for test preparation purposes only and does not imply an endorsement by Mometrix of any particular political, scientific, or religious point of view.

Secret Key #5 – Have a Plan for Guessing

When you're taking the test, you may find yourself stuck on a question. Some of the answer choices seem better than others, but you don't see the one answer choice that is obviously correct. What do you do?

The scenario described above is very common, yet most test takers have not effectively prepared for it. Developing and practicing a plan for guessing may be one of the single most effective uses of your time as you get ready for the exam.

In developing your plan for guessing, there are three questions to address:

- When should you start the guessing process?
- How should you narrow down the choices?
- Which answer should you choose?

When to Start the Guessing Process

Unless your plan for guessing is to select C every time (which, despite its merits, is not what we recommend), you need to leave yourself enough time to apply your answer elimination strategies. Since you have a limited amount of time for each question, that means that if you're going to give yourself the best shot at guessing correctly, you have to decide quickly whether or not you will guess.

Of course, the best-case scenario is that you don't have to guess at all, so first, see if you can answer the question based on your knowledge of the subject and basic reasoning skills. Focus on the key words in the question and try to jog your memory of related topics. Give yourself a chance to bring the knowledge to mind, but once you realize that you don't have (or you can't access) the knowledge you need to answer the question, it's time to start the guessing process.

It's almost always better to start the guessing process too early than too late. It only takes a few seconds to remember something and answer the question from knowledge. Carefully eliminating wrong answer choices takes longer. Plus, going through the process of eliminating answer choices can actually help jog your memory.

Summary: Start the guessing process as soon as you decide that you can't answer the question based on your knowledge.

Copyright © Mometrix Media. You have been licensed one copy of this document for personal use only. Any other reproduction or redistribution is strictly prohibited. All rights reserved.
This content is provided for test preparation purposes only and does not imply an endorsement by Mometrix of any particular political, scientific, or religious point of view.

How to Narrow Down the Choices

The next chapter in this book (**Test-Taking Strategies**) includes a wide range of strategies for how to approach questions and how to look for answer choices to eliminate. You will definitely want to read those carefully, practice them, and figure out which ones work best for you. Here though, we're going to address a mindset rather than a particular strategy.

Your odds of guessing an answer correctly depend on how many options you are choosing from.

Number of options left	5	4	3	2	1
Odds of guessing correctly	20%	25%	33%	50%	100%

You can see from this chart just how valuable it is to be able to eliminate incorrect answers and make an educated guess, but there are two things that many test takers do that cause them to miss out on the benefits of guessing:

- Accidentally eliminating the correct answer
- Selecting an answer based on an impression

We'll look at the first one here, and the second one in the next section.

To avoid accidentally eliminating the correct answer, we recommend a thought exercise called **the $5 challenge**. In this challenge, you only eliminate an answer choice from contention if you are willing to bet $5 on it being wrong. Why $5? Five dollars is a small but not insignificant amount of money. It's an amount you could afford to lose but wouldn't want to throw away. And while losing $5 once might not hurt too much, doing it twenty times will set you back $100. In the same way, each small decision you make—eliminating a choice here, guessing on a question there—won't by itself impact your score very much, but when you put them all together, they can make a big difference. By holding each answer choice elimination decision to a higher standard, you can reduce the risk of accidentally eliminating the correct answer.

The $5 challenge can also be applied in a positive sense: If you are willing to bet $5 that an answer choice *is* correct, go ahead and mark it as correct.

Summary: Only eliminate an answer choice if you are willing to bet $5 that it is wrong.

Copyright © Mometrix Media. You have been licensed one copy of this document for personal use only. Any other reproduction or redistribution is strictly prohibited. All rights reserved.
This content is provided for test preparation purposes only and does not imply an endorsement by Mometrix of any particular political, scientific, or religious point of view.

Which Answer to Choose

You're taking the test. You've run into a hard question and decided you'll have to guess. You've eliminated all the answer choices you're willing to bet $5 on. Now you have to pick an answer. Why do we even need to talk about this? Why can't you just pick whichever one you feel like when the time comes?

The answer to these questions is that if you don't come into the test with a plan, you'll rely on your impression to select an answer choice, and if you do that, you risk falling into a trap. The test writers know that everyone who takes their test will be guessing on some of the questions, so they intentionally write wrong answer choices to seem plausible. You still have to pick an answer though, and if the wrong answer choices are designed to look right, how can you ever be sure that you're not falling for their trap? The best solution we've found to this dilemma is to take the decision out of your hands entirely. Here is the process we recommend:

Once you've eliminated any choices that you are confident (willing to bet $5) are wrong, select the first remaining choice as your answer.

Whether you choose to select the first remaining choice, the second, or the last, the important thing is that you use some preselected standard. Using this approach guarantees that you will not be enticed into selecting an answer choice that looks right, because you are not basing your decision on how the answer choices look.

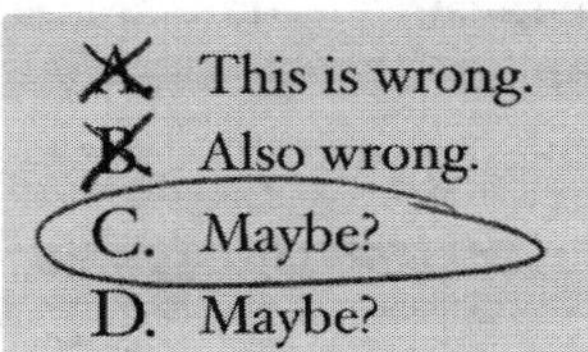

This is not meant to make you question your knowledge. Instead, it is to help you recognize the difference between your knowledge and your impressions. There's a huge difference between thinking an answer is right because of what you know, and thinking an answer is right because it looks or sounds like it should be right.

Summary: To ensure that your selection is appropriately random, make a predetermined selection from among all answer choices you have not eliminated.

Copyright © Mometrix Media. You have been licensed one copy of this document for personal use only. Any other reproduction or redistribution is strictly prohibited. All rights reserved.
This content is provided for test preparation purposes only and does not imply an endorsement by Mometrix of any particular political, scientific, or religious point of view.

Test-Taking Strategies

This section contains a list of test-taking strategies that you may find helpful as you work through the test. By taking what you know and applying logical thought, you can maximize your chances of answering any question correctly!

It is very important to realize that every question is different and every person is different: no single strategy will work on every question, and no single strategy will work for every person. That's why we've included all of them here, so you can try them out and determine which ones work best for different types of questions and which ones work best for you.

Question Strategies

✓ Read Carefully

Read the question and the answer choices carefully. Don't miss the question because you misread the terms. You have plenty of time to read each question thoroughly and make sure you understand what is being asked. Yet a happy medium must be attained, so don't waste too much time. You must read carefully and efficiently.

✓ Contextual Clues

Look for contextual clues. If the question includes a word you are not familiar with, look at the immediate context for some indication of what the word might mean. Contextual clues can often give you all the information you need to decipher the meaning of an unfamiliar word. Even if you can't determine the meaning, you may be able to narrow down the possibilities enough to make a solid guess at the answer to the question.

✓ Prefixes

If you're having trouble with a word in the question or answer choices, try dissecting it. Take advantage of every clue that the word might include. Prefixes can be a huge help. Usually, they allow you to determine a basic meaning. *Pre-* means before, *post-* means after, *pro-* is positive, *de-* is negative. From prefixes, you can get an idea of the general meaning of the word and try to put it into context.

✓ Hedge Words

Watch out for critical hedge words, such as *likely*, *may*, *can*, *sometimes*, *often*, *almost*, *mostly*, *usually*, *generally*, *rarely*, and *sometimes*. Question writers insert these hedge phrases to cover every possibility. Often an answer choice will be wrong simply because it leaves no room for exception. Be on guard for answer choices that have definitive words such as *exactly* and *always*.

✓ Switchback Words

Stay alert for *switchbacks*. These are the words and phrases frequently used to alert you to shifts in thought. The most common switchback words are *but*, *although*, and *however*. Others include *nevertheless*, *on the other hand*, *even though*, *while*, *in spite of*, *despite*, and *regardless of*. Switchback words are important to catch because they can change the direction of the question or an answer choice.

Copyright © Mometrix Media. You have been licensed one copy of this document for personal use only. Any other reproduction or redistribution is strictly prohibited. All rights reserved.
This content is provided for test preparation purposes only and does not imply an endorsement by Mometrix of any particular political, scientific, or religious point of view.

⊘ Face Value

When in doubt, use common sense. Accept the situation in the problem at face value. Don't read too much into it. These problems will not require you to make wild assumptions. If you have to go beyond creativity and warp time or space in order to have an answer choice fit the question, then you should move on and consider the other answer choices. These are normal problems rooted in reality. The applicable relationship or explanation may not be readily apparent, but it is there for you to figure out. Use your common sense to interpret anything that isn't clear.

Answer Choice Strategies

⊘ Answer Selection

The most thorough way to pick an answer choice is to identify and eliminate wrong answers until only one is left, then confirm it is the correct answer. Sometimes an answer choice may immediately seem right, but be careful. The test writers will usually put more than one reasonable answer choice on each question, so take a second to read all of them and make sure that the other choices are not equally obvious. As long as you have time left, it is better to read every answer choice than to pick the first one that looks right without checking the others.

⊘ Answer Choice Families

An answer choice family consists of two (in rare cases, three) answer choices that are very similar in construction and cannot all be true at the same time. If you see two answer choices that are direct opposites or parallels, one of them is usually the correct answer. For instance, if one answer choice says that quantity x increases and another either says that quantity x decreases (opposite) or says that quantity y increases (parallel), then those answer choices would fall into the same family. An answer choice that doesn't match the construction of the answer choice family is more likely to be incorrect. Most questions will not have answer choice families, but when they do appear, you should be prepared to recognize them.

⊘ Eliminate Answers

Eliminate answer choices as soon as you realize they are wrong, but make sure you consider all possibilities. If you are eliminating answer choices and realize that the last one you are left with is also wrong, don't panic. Start over and consider each choice again. There may be something you missed the first time that you will realize on the second pass.

⊘ Avoid Fact Traps

Don't be distracted by an answer choice that is factually true but doesn't answer the question. You are looking for the choice that answers the question. Stay focused on what the question is asking for so you don't accidentally pick an answer that is true but incorrect. Always go back to the question and make sure the answer choice you've selected actually answers the question and is not merely a true statement.

⊘ Extreme Statements

In general, you should avoid answers that put forth extreme actions as standard practice or proclaim controversial ideas as established fact. An answer choice that states the "process should be used in certain situations, if…" is much more likely to be correct than one that states the "process should be discontinued completely." The first is a calm rational statement and doesn't even make a definitive, uncompromising stance, using a hedge word *if* to provide wiggle room, whereas the second choice is far more extreme.

Copyright © Mometrix Media. You have been licensed one copy of this document for personal use only. Any other reproduction or redistribution is strictly prohibited. All rights reserved.
This content is provided for test preparation purposes only and does not imply an endorsement by Mometrix of any particular political, scientific, or religious point of view.

⊘ BENCHMARK

As you read through the answer choices and you come across one that seems to answer the question well, mentally select that answer choice. This is not your final answer, but it's the one that will help you evaluate the other answer choices. The one that you selected is your benchmark or standard for judging each of the other answer choices. Every other answer choice must be compared to your benchmark. That choice is correct until proven otherwise by another answer choice beating it. If you find a better answer, then that one becomes your new benchmark. Once you've decided that no other choice answers the question as well as your benchmark, you have your final answer.

⊘ PREDICT THE ANSWER

Before you even start looking at the answer choices, it is often best to try to predict the answer. When you come up with the answer on your own, it is easier to avoid distractions and traps because you will know exactly what to look for. The right answer choice is unlikely to be word-for-word what you came up with, but it should be a close match. Even if you are confident that you have the right answer, you should still take the time to read each option before moving on.

General Strategies

⊘ TOUGH QUESTIONS

If you are stumped on a problem or it appears too hard or too difficult, don't waste time. Move on! Remember though, if you can quickly check for obviously incorrect answer choices, your chances of guessing correctly are greatly improved. Before you completely give up, at least try to knock out a couple of possible answers. Eliminate what you can and then guess at the remaining answer choices before moving on.

⊘ CHECK YOUR WORK

Since you will probably not know every term listed and the answer to every question, it is important that you get credit for the ones that you do know. Don't miss any questions through careless mistakes. If at all possible, try to take a second to look back over your answer selection and make sure you've selected the correct answer choice and haven't made a costly careless mistake (such as marking an answer choice that you didn't mean to mark). This quick double check should more than pay for itself in caught mistakes for the time it costs.

⊘ PACE YOURSELF

It's easy to be overwhelmed when you're looking at a page full of questions; your mind is confused and full of random thoughts, and the clock is ticking down faster than you would like. Calm down and maintain the pace that you have set for yourself. Especially as you get down to the last few minutes of the test, don't let the small numbers on the clock make you panic. As long as you are on track by monitoring your pace, you are guaranteed to have time for each question.

⊘ DON'T RUSH

It is very easy to make errors when you are in a hurry. Maintaining a fast pace in answering questions is pointless if it makes you miss questions that you would have gotten right otherwise. Test writers like to include distracting information and wrong answers that seem right. Taking a little extra time to avoid careless mistakes can make all the difference in your test score. Find a pace that allows you to be confident in the answers that you select.

Copyright © Mometrix Media. You have been licensed one copy of this document for personal use only. Any other reproduction or redistribution is strictly prohibited. All rights reserved.
This content is provided for test preparation purposes only and does not imply an endorsement by Mometrix of any particular political, scientific, or religious point of view.

⊘ Keep Moving

Panicking will not help you pass the test, so do your best to stay calm and keep moving. Taking deep breaths and going through the answer elimination steps you practiced can help to break through a stress barrier and keep your pace.

Final Notes

The combination of a solid foundation of content knowledge and the confidence that comes from practicing your plan for applying that knowledge is the key to maximizing your performance on test day. As your foundation of content knowledge is built up and strengthened, you'll find that the strategies included in this chapter become more and more effective in helping you quickly sift through the distractions and traps of the test to isolate the correct answer.

Now that you're preparing to move forward into the test content chapters of this book, be sure to keep your goal in mind. As you read, think about how you will be able to apply this information on the test. If you've already seen sample questions for the test and you have an idea of the question format and style, try to come up with questions of your own that you can answer based on what you're reading. This will give you valuable practice applying your knowledge in the same ways you can expect to on test day.

Good luck and good studying!

Copyright © Mometrix Media. You have been licensed one copy of this document for personal use only. Any other reproduction or redistribution is strictly prohibited. All rights reserved.
This content is provided for test preparation purposes only and does not imply an endorsement by Mometrix of any particular political, scientific, or religious point of view.

Copyright © Mometrix Media. You have been licensed one copy of this document for personal use only. Any other reproduction or redistribution is strictly prohibited. All rights reserved.
This content is provided for test preparation purposes only and does not imply an endorsement by Mometrix of any particular political, scientific, or religious point of view.

Human Development, Learning, and Diversity

Human Growth and Development

Piaget's Theories of Development of Students in Early Childhood

According to **Piaget**, students in early childhood (the years between 2 and 6, spanning preschool to kindergarten) generally are incapable of grasping **abstract concepts**, such as those dealing with time and space. They are developing **motor skills**, usually through play, as well as language skills and the ability to imitate events. These skills will grow and develop during the early childhood years, which will be reflected in improved use of language, increased motor skills, and the appearance of more concreteness in their drawings. During this time, children are egocentric; however, they are also **developing social skills** as well as the ability to regulate some of their own emotional responses. Counselors will be well served to engage a child's imaginative skills in the session, as well as to consider some of the theoretical concepts of childhood experts like Piaget.

Carl Rogers's Contribution to Counseling

Rogerian therapy assumes that counseling clients become healthier when therapists provide them with human acceptance rather than "expert" guidance. Earlier psychotherapy saw the client as someone to be acted upon: Rogers used the therapeutic relationship to create a medium of **unconditional positive regard**. Therapists use empathy (or empathic understanding) to reach out to and nurture clients and teach self-acceptance.

Rogers believed that therapists should be as transparent or genuine as possible; a departure from earlier ideas of therapy that positioned the therapist as unknowable, unflappable, and an expert on the client's "problem." Rogerian therapy takes the client as the expert on him/herself, and counselors are careful not to provide interpretation, advice, or didactic training but to simply be there with the client, attending to the growing relationship, considered the central place of healing in client-centered therapy.

In Rogerian counseling, therapists teach clients to lead the process, asking perhaps for the first time in their lives, "What do *I* want? What matters to *me*?" Rogerian therapists model genuineness and congruence in their relationships with clients, who, it may be argued, suffered from a lack of congruence in early family life that perpetuates mental suffering in adult life.

Erik Erikson's Stages of Early Childhood Development

In **Erikson's** theoretical paradigm, the years of early childhood development are defined by a **series of crises** which result in **positive or maladaptive behaviors**. Each developmental stage is preceded by a crisis that ideally is resolved through positive development of skills and behaviors. For instance, ego development may be prompted by the crisis of self-promotion being perceived as counter to the obligation to others: that is, the drive to grow and develop being tempered by a sense of guilt. Refining the balance between these two directives (incorporating self-worth, imagination and sometimes gender) contributes to the child's self-discovery. Counselors should encourage students to explore positive behaviors or actions that may be out of the student's normal realm, in the interest of developing new skills. In addition, increases in language and motor skills tends to encourage self-promotion and self-discovery. Opportunities for developing these skills should be seized in the counseling setting.

Copyright © Mometrix Media. You have been licensed one copy of this document for personal use only. Any other reproduction or redistribution is strictly prohibited. All rights reserved.
This content is provided for test preparation purposes only and does not imply an endorsement by Mometrix of any particular political, scientific, or religious point of view.

Play-Time Setting

For children between the ages of 2 and 6, play is an integral part of development. Children often **express emotions, describe events, and project their desires in a play setting**. In the counseling session, a good strategy is for the counselor to interact with the child in play-time settings, using such manipulatives as dolls, toys, puppets, art projects, or other favorites. The play-time setting can be a wonderful opportunity for children to explore not only their environment, but also their own capabilities and skills. The counseling session will be best served if the child is allowed sufficient and reasonable latitude for exploring the boundaries of self-discovery, self-confidence, and emotional self-regulation. The play setting provides an environment for developing and regulating skills and behaviors. Counselors can provide such media as dolls, animals, art supplies, and animals, through which children can express themselves.

Developmental Stage of Middle Childhood

Middle childhood, generally associated with the ages between 7 and 11, is most easily distinguished by the ability to **think logically, read and write more skillfully, and mentally reverse actions**. While they are still unable to grasp many abstract ideas, students in this age group are nonetheless increasingly able to manipulate concrete information. They are able to generalize about their actions or their environment based on this information. The development of logical thinking allows children in this age group to interact more cooperatively, in part because they are more able to recognize intentionality and are becoming less egocentric. Counselors working with this age group can use such strategies as exploration, manipulation of information, and action. Sessions are best served if the counselor remains aware that students in this age group are generally able to reason logically, based on concrete information. For this reason, middle childhood is often called the concrete operational stage.

Erik Erikson's 8 Stages of Psychosocial Development

Each of **Erik Erikson's eight developmental stages** contains a psychosocial crisis, the positive resolution of which results in attainment of a basic virtue. Erikson's theory posits that people move through stages in order, with each stage being resolved positively or negatively. The more stages whose outcomes are healthy, the healthier the personality.

The school ages (between 5 and 12 and 12 and 18) are stages of Industry versus Inferiority and Identity versus Role Confusion. Adolescence is characterized by the identity crisis, in which students explore and create a unique self.

Although some developmental stages may not be positively resolved the first time around, Eriksonian theory says that they can be returned to later in life and successfully worked through.

Psychosocial Crisis	Basic Virtue	Age
Trust vs. Mistrust	Hope	0-1.5 years old
Autonomy vs. Shame	Will	1.5-3 years old
Initiative vs. Guilt	Purpose	3-5 years old
Industry vs. Inferiority	Competency	5-12 years old
Identity vs. Role Confusion	Fidelity	12-18 years old
Intimacy vs. Isolation	Love	18-40 years old
Generativity vs. Stagnation	Care	40-65 years old
Ego Integrity vs. Despair	Wisdom	65+ years old

Copyright © Mometrix Media. You have been licensed one copy of this document for personal use only. Any other reproduction or redistribution is strictly prohibited. All rights reserved.
This content is provided for test preparation purposes only and does not imply an endorsement by Mometrix of any particular political, scientific, or religious point of view.

B. F. Skinner's Behavior Modification Theory

Skinner believed that behavior was **created and reinforced by the environment**. In his theory of operant conditioning, a stimulus generates a response, and behavior is learned by experiencing the outcome of one's behavior as positive or negative. Behaviors that create an unpleasant outcome (punishment) are avoided, and those creating a pleasant outcome (reward) are repeated. Behavior can be reinforced or extinguished by applying different outcomes, and the challenge is to discover why an outcome that one person might find rewarding (recognition by the teacher in front of the whole class) might be a punishment for someone else.

In **behavior modification**, reinforcements may be positive or negative, meaning that the reinforcement may occur after the response (positive reinforcement) or may be taken away after the response (negative reinforcement). For example, if a child misbehaves while playing a game, he/she may be put in time-out. Removing the child from the game is a negative reinforcement and should diminish the misbehavior. On the other hand, if the misbehavior goes unchallenged and the child wins the game, the misbehavior would be positively reinforced by winning. Skinner's model also posits that behaviors can be increased or decreased by planned repetition, or schedules of reinforcement.

Robert Havighurst's Theory of Psychosocial Development

Like Erikson, **Robert Havighurst** identified stages of development based on chronological age and the resolution of specific developmental tasks throughout the life span. Havighurst proposed a six-stage model of human development:

Tasks:

- **Infancy/early childhood, age birth to 6 years**—learning to crawl, talk, and walk; being potty trained, knowing gender
- **Middle childhood, age 6 to 12**—learning social roles, values, morality, and relational skills; learning about one's self; becoming independent.
- **Adolescence, age 13 to 18**—growing independence, handling physical changes of puberty and sexuality, and beginning to work
- **Early adulthood, age 19 to 30**—becoming a mate, a spouse, and/or a parent; finding an occupation; becoming socially responsible
- **Middle age, age 30 to 60**—finding satisfaction at work, exploring outside interests (hobbies), experiencing the start of aging, and caring for parents
- **Later maturity, age 60+**—changing living situations, experiencing and coping with the physical changes of aging, and retiring and handling the changes of income and social life that retirement brings

Sigmund Freud's Theory of Psychosexual Development

Freud's three parts of the personality, which drive behavior, he labeled id, ego, and superego. The id, or pleasure principle, is primitive and unconcerned with morality or rationality. The ego, logical and stable, is concerned with higher thought processes. The superego contains or inhibits antisocial behavior.

Stages of Psychosexual Development:

- **Oral, birth to 1 year**—Everything goes into the mouth! The child gets primary satisfaction from biting, chewing, and sucking. Frustration at this stage may cause overeating or smoking habits, nail biting, or talking too much.

Copyright © Mometrix Media. You have been licensed one copy of this document for personal use only. Any other reproduction or redistribution is strictly prohibited. All rights reserved.
This content is provided for test preparation purposes only and does not imply an endorsement by Mometrix of any particular political, scientific, or religious point of view.

- **Anal, age 1 to 3 years**—The primary focus is on potty training. Harsh parental attitudes around toileting may cause children to grow up overinhibited and obsessed with cleanliness: permissive parenting can create messy, sloppy, "over-expressive" adults.
- **Phallic, age 3 to 6 years**—Freud identified two complexes that he believed accompanied children's growing awareness of the opposite sex and sexual feelings. The Oedipus Complex and the Electra Complex, he thought, defined the attraction children felt for the other-gendered parent.
- **Latent, age 6 to 11 years**—The superego reigns: children learn to delay gratification. Friendships and peer groups gain importance. Sexuality temporarily recedes.
- **Genital, age 11 to 18**—With puberty, sexuality reassumes its importance in the life cycle and people begin to engage in mature sexual relationships.

POSITIVE FEEDBACK FOR STUDENTS IN MIDDLE CHILDHOOD

Middle childhood is distinguished by a developing, yet often fragile **sense of competency**. This sense of competency is particularly dependent on external feedback, from friends, family, and authority figures. A sense of competency is also encouraged by the student's own success in accomplishing increasingly challenging tasks, though it can also be discouraged by failure. Counselors working with this age group need to be sensitive to this fragility, and respond by providing manageable tasks that the student is more likely to succeed in. Positive, encouraging feedback is also very beneficial to students in this age group. Both **positive feedback** and opportunities for success provide valuable buffers against the development of feelings of inadequacy in students in middle childhood, including self-fulfilling behaviors that validate a sense of incompetence and failure.

ENCOURAGING PEER RELATIONSHIPS FOR MIDDLE CHILDHOOD STUDENTS

During this time of competency development, peer interaction is particularly important for the student in middle childhood for a number of reasons. Not only is peer feedback important, but peer interaction provides an opportunity for students to see their peers in a similar balance of success and failure, which validates their position and allows for the development of empathy for others' positions. Likewise, students in this age group develop a sense of understanding and tolerance for differing appearances and behaviors through healthy peer interaction. A counselor can provide opportunities for peer interaction by holding group counseling sessions, as well as by encouraging healthy friendships for students in this age group. Often, significant friendships are formed. These friendships can be pivotal to the development of a student's sense of self-competency and significance among their peers.

CHARACTERISTICS OF THE STAGES OF ADOLESCENCE

Adolescence is a time of breakthrough transition between childhood and adulthood, and is generally divided into three sub-stages. Although the stages are very individualized, the years between ages 11 to 14 are usually called adolescence, 15 to 18 middle adolescence, and 18 and above late adolescence. The accomplishments realized during these three stages affect **physical appearance, social interaction, and thinking processes**. The physical changes are known collectively as puberty. Students in this age group develop a more comprehensive understanding of social roles and relationships. Furthermore, thinking processes evolve from concrete to formal, resulting in an increased ability to think abstractly. Counselors working with this age group need to be mindful of both the stage at which a student is operating and the next phase of development, so that they can provide opportunities for that development.

Copyright © Mometrix Media. You have been licensed one copy of this document for personal use only. Any other reproduction or redistribution is strictly prohibited. All rights reserved.
This content is provided for test preparation purposes only and does not imply an endorsement by Mometrix of any particular political, scientific, or religious point of view.

Therapeutic Strategies for Working with Adolescents

Adolescent students are increasingly able to apply **abstract thinking** to possible solutions and scenarios of situations. Counselors working with this age group can take advantage of this abstract thinking by soliciting the student's collaboration in generating and implementing solutions to problems. The beginning of this process could be asking a student to view a situation differently, allowing for a larger spectrum of possible solutions. Adolescent students are also able to think reflectively, allowing for a better sense of responsibility for actions. Students in this age group are also increasingly egocentric and **less dependent on external feedback**, sometimes resulting in reckless behavior. They are more **self-conscious**, particularly with students of their age group. Counselors are best served by facilitating the student's ability to balance these feelings with increased social awareness and abstract thinking skills. Counselors can also provide students in this age group with opportunities for the development and implementation of alternate approaches to problem solving.

Effects of Puberty on Adolescent Students

The onset and progress of **puberty** complements and often perpetuates role confusion for the adolescent student. Adolescence is a pivotal time, in which students refine self-concepts of worth, value in the larger society, and life goals. This self-definition is often validated by peer interaction. The counselor should work with students in this age group by encouraging them to develop goals and values of their own, not necessarily those of their peer group. Counselors can assist students in developing their own senses of identity and worth, separate from social cliques or idolized hero symbols. Students in this age group begin to understand that their actions and beliefs form an integral part of their role and their value system. Counselors can positively facilitate this connection when working with adolescents. It is important that counselors endorse the idea of the worth and significance of every individual.

Peer Relationships for Adolescent Students

Adolescent students are simultaneously developing a sense of self-worth and self-identity and developing close ties with their peer groups. It is important for the counselor to assist the student in balancing the significance of **peer relationships** with the evolution of his or her own self-definition. Students in the adolescent age group often develop a sense of ethnic identity before they develop a sense of self-identity. While the role of a peer group can bolster and validate a student's ethnic or cultural identity, it is also important for the student to develop personal and individual goals. Counselors can work with adolescent students to help them identify personal goals as well as ideas and perceptions that diverge from the group identity. The influence of community beliefs and behaviors can hinder the development of individuality. Nonetheless, because peer relationships are very important to adolescents, counselors should also encourage and endorse healthy relationships.

Copyright © Mometrix Media. You have been licensed one copy of this document for personal use only. Any other reproduction or redistribution is strictly prohibited. All rights reserved.
This content is provided for test preparation purposes only and does not imply an endorsement by Mometrix of any particular political, scientific, or religious point of view.

Student Diversity

NEED FOR SENSITIVITY TO DIVERSITY OF CULTURE

As America becomes more **culturally diverse**, schools will be increasingly comprised of a mix of different races, religions, and socioeconomic levels. Counselors need to be aware of the significance of these factors in the learning environments of students. Certain ethnic groups may be victims of social and economic hierarchies, which can affect the availability of technology and other education-related amenities. Counselors can act as non-judgmental liaisons for students if they are sensitive to some of the situational differences defined by race. They can also work with groups of students on such issues as assertiveness and empowerment. A counselor should also consider the problems faced by second-language learners, as well as the religious and cultural factors that may affect academic and social success.

BECOMING MORE CULTURALLY AWARE

The first step in becoming more **culturally aware** is to recognize the need to do so. Counselors who work with a diversity of races and socioeconomic groups should invest the time and attention to understand the roots and ramifications of the differences. There are cultural sensitivity training sessions available, often through the school district. Although cultural sensitivity training is becoming more commonplace and is even required in some districts, counselors and their programs will be best served by a proactive approach. Some counselors reach beyond the school district to surrounding cultural enclaves, to further their understanding of a particular culture. Some counselors take further action by becoming involved in addressing policy and practices that better the overall academic achievement of a particularly underserved group, although the effectiveness of this has not been clearly demonstrated.

PROMOTING CULTURAL SENSITIVITY IN THE SCHOOL ENVIRONMENT

Cultural sensitivity helps counselors recognize culturally based differences within the school environment. Counselors observe interactions affected by cultural differences, and then address any problems while maintaining sensitivity to both the minority and the majority cultures. Counselors can involve school staff and counselors in discussions regarding the methods and policies for addressing cultural differences and conflicts among students, as well as between teachers and students. Certain school practices can lead to an appreciation and celebration of these differences. These practices can include talking with students and parents and actively learning about different cultures. Increasing cultural awareness within a school environment can lead to a rich, dynamic community, and can improve the value of a well-designed counseling program.

PROFESSIONAL SKILLS AND COMPETENCIES RELATED TO CULTURAL AWARENESS

Counselors striving to attain an **environment of cultural sensitivity** can begin the process by first presenting a professional demeanor toward all students and other members of the school community. It is important to recognize that cultural and socioeconomic differences can affect behavior and appearance, and to avoid responding negatively or differently to these manifestations. It is also important to remember that every person, including the counselor, lives with certain presuppositions, and to be cognizant of these presuppositions while developing an increased understanding of cultural differences and misunderstandings. Some of the bases for these misunderstandings include racism, stereotyping, socioeconomic oppression, and discrimination. Additionally, cultural differences could be gender-based, belief-based, or based on other distinguishing characteristics. Being aware of these cultural layers and learning to respond with dignity and respect can provide a healthy example for the school community.

Copyright © Mometrix Media. You have been licensed one copy of this document for personal use only. Any other reproduction or redistribution is strictly prohibited. All rights reserved.
This content is provided for test preparation purposes only and does not imply an endorsement by Mometrix of any particular political, scientific, or religious point of view.

Limitations of Language When Addressing Issues of Cultural Diversity

Counselors who have been sensitized to cultural differences, and trained in strategies for addressing these differences in the school environment, may still experience difficulty finding the right words when communicating with school staff, counselors, students and the rest of the school community. There is no one way to solve this problem; however, counselors should recognize that cultural differences can stem from historical traditions, racial or ethnic classifications, economic status, or cosmology. These differences can affect how people view and respond to life experiences, and can often divide populations into groups of similar experience and perception. Awareness of some of the roots of cultural diversity and cultural bias can help the counselor develop terminology for addressing issues of diversity and integrating cultural sensitivity into various aspects of the counseling program.

Components of Culture

Before broaching the subject of culture, counselors should first define culture and describe its influence. Listed below are some of the **key components of culture**:

- Beliefs or belief systems that define one's place in society, the world, and the cosmos. These beliefs can become assumptions and practices regarding social status, personal empowerment, and relation to material wealth.
- Perception of life experiences and how those experiences can affect life choices.
- Value systems including family, career, and education
- Religious beliefs and practices
- Definitions and circumstances relating to belief in life's purpose
- Accepted behaviors for self-validation

It is also important to remember that cultural distinctions are often rooted in historical tradition, supported by generations of practice and affirmation. Working with a culturally diverse population is best approached by recognizing and respecting the roots of culture.

Race and Segregation in the School Environment

Race can also be defined by biogenetic factors, socioeconomic grouping, distinctive traits and behaviors, language, traditions, and rituals. Individually or as an aggregate, these factors often play a part in racial discrimination and segregation. **Segregation** also may be based on economic status, academic achievement, level of fluency in English, or disability. In this sense, race can be viewed as a political and psychological concept. Counselors working in the school community to dissipate cultural biases and misunderstandings will be well served to recognize that race is a concept defined primarily by these behavioral and economic factors.

Parameters of Ethnicity

In contrast to race, **ethnicity** is rooted in **national origin and/or distinctive cultural patterns**. In other words, ethnicity is based on more easily identifiable factors. Groups of students with the same ethnicity share the same general ancestral background. A group that shares ethnicity will often share religious beliefs; attitudes toward family, school and career; and customs, traditions and rituals. These beliefs and traditions are often reinforced by the fact that individuals who share an ethnicity tend to socialize together, providing a continuum of culture. However, counselors should be sensitive to the fact that individuals can present degrees of assimilation, developing practices and beliefs that differ from their ethnic origins. Ethnicity is generally associated with family, although it can also be defined by religion, race, and cultural history.

Copyright © Mometrix Media. You have been licensed one copy of this document for personal use only. Any other reproduction or redistribution is strictly prohibited. All rights reserved.
This content is provided for test preparation purposes only and does not imply an endorsement by Mometrix of any particular political, scientific, or religious point of view.

Oppression

Although **oppression** may be rooted in cultural or racist biases, and is usually expressed through inequities of power or benefits. The general psychological basis for oppression is a fallacious assumption by one group that another group is intrinsically inferior or incapable of a particular quality of life. Unfortunately, these misperceptions often are perpetuated by the conditions that result from them. Individuals or groups who possess the power or benefits (e.g. better paying jobs, better access to technology, and better access to transportation) inherently define oppressed individuals as inferior by their lack of these quality of life indicators. **Oppressed groups** may internalize this definition, further perpetuating the oppression and exploitation. Oppressed individuals or groups will often accept their subservient position in the school or work environment because they do not feel empowered to challenge the dominant group. **Oppressive tactics** include exploitation, intimidation, and violence.

Types

The **forms of oppression** can be placed into five general categories. The first category is **individualized oppression**, which encompasses oppression stemming from assumptions of inferiority in another person based on race or culture. This process extrapolated to the group level becomes **cultural oppression**, which is comprised of actions or attitudes toward a cultural group that result in the targeted group changing its behavior. **Systemic or institutional oppression** is hierarchical practices that inherently discriminate against certain groups in the distribution of resources. Oppression that is internalized by the targeted group is insidious because the oppressed group believes and perpetuates its own perceived inferiority. Conversely, **external oppression** describes actions or beliefs targeting a particular group because they are perceived by others as inferior. Instances of oppression may fall into more than one category.

Multicultural Counseling

While developing a counseling relationship with a student or students, it is important to recognize whether multicultural factors obtain. **Multicultural counseling** occurs when the race or ethnicity of the students is different from that of the counselor. The multicultural counseling relationship will necessarily involve two sets of expectations, perceptions, social environments, beliefs and backgrounds, often beyond the usual disparities between two people. Sensitivity to culturally-based differences can be helpful in communication and setting expectations. The five major cultural groups identified by the Association of Multicultural Counseling and Development (AMCD) are African/Black, Asian, Caucasian/European, Hispanic/Latino/a, and Native American. Other cultural groups can pertain to gender, sexual orientation, religious beliefs, etc. A counselor should try to remain aware of multicultural counseling without falling into a biased taxonomy.

Forms of Oppression That Can Affect Distribution of Resources

The terms below identify **oppressive belief systems** targeting specific groups. Often, public schools and other societal entities distribute resources unfairly based on these perceptions:

- Ableism – targeting persons identified by different abilities/disabilities
- Ageism – targeting persons younger than 18 or older than 50
- Beautyism – targeting persons who are obese or otherwise fall outside of expected appearance norms
- Classism – targeting persons based on income level or socioeconomic class
- Familyism – targeting persons whose family falls outside of expected norms, such as single parents, same gender parents, or foster families

Copyright © Mometrix Media. You have been licensed one copy of this document for personal use only. Any other reproduction or redistribution is strictly prohibited. All rights reserved.
This content is provided for test preparation purposes only and does not imply an endorsement by Mometrix of any particular political, scientific, or religious point of view.

- Heterosexism and Transgenderism – targeting persons who are homosexual, lesbian, bisexual, two-spirit, intersex, or transgender
- Linguicism – targeting persons because they do not speak the dominant language, or do so with a marked accent
- Racism – targeting persons of another color or of mixed race
- Religionism – targeting persons who do not practice the dominant religion
- Sexism – targeting persons of a different sex

Ensuring That Counselors are Competent in Multicultural Environments

Counselors who will be working with different cultural or ethnic groups are best served by not only receiving initial training in multicultural counseling, but also by attending workshops and other instruction in the field on an ongoing basis. Many schools and districts with a diverse student body require this of school counselors. Counselors who receive ongoing training in multicultural counseling will be less likely to impose their own belief systems and cultural insensitivity on the counseling relationship, and more likely to consider cultural differences when communicating and setting goals with students. School counselors and counselors can usually recognize when they are incorporating cultural sensitivity in their counseling methods by assessing the success of the sessions. If a counselor or counseling program is operating with multicultural competence, there should be no significant differentiation between success rates with students of different cultural backgrounds.

Levels of Multicultural Counseling

Multicultural counseling incorporates three distinct levels of competence. The initial, foundational level is that of **awareness**. Counselors can begin to build multicultural competence by first becoming aware of the effects of culture on worldview, behaviors, etc. It is also a good first step for counselors to be aware of their own preconceived notions about cultures, as well as aspects of their value system that are culturally based. Building on this, counselors can come to knowledge, respect, and understanding of other cultures, realizing that cultural assimilation is not always the recommended course of action for students. **Cultural sensitivity** includes refraining from imposing dominant beliefs and attitudes, unless appropriate. Balancing social protocol with cultural expression is a valuable skill that counselors can teach to students. Lastly, counselors can develop **skills** that enable them to implement effective and appropriate strategies when working with students from diverse cultures.

Types of Knowledge About Different Cultures That Will Enrich Multicultural Sensitivity

Counselors working with diverse cultures can increase and enrich their sensitivity by understanding the concepts and terminology of a particular culture, as well as by learning developmental theories related to that culture. In order to understand a culture, a counselor needs a working knowledge of the history, traditions, strengths, needs, and resources of it. Counselors can act as consultants and liaisons by assisting students who are misunderstood and misrepresented by school staff, students, public media, etc. Understanding the semantics and terminology of specific cultures can be particularly helpful in mediating between cultural groups, as well as in encouraging communication and sensitivity between groups. Counselors who approach diversity with a fundamental knowledge of specific cultures and the impact of culture can provide role models for dynamic multicultural understanding and communication in the school environment. Understanding the impact of culture in particular can lay a strong foundation for multicultural sensitivity, as counselors, students, and school personnel begin to recognize the cultural basis of many misunderstandings.

Copyright © Mometrix Media. You have been licensed one copy of this document for personal use only. Any other reproduction or redistribution is strictly prohibited. All rights reserved.
This content is provided for test preparation purposes only and does not imply an endorsement by Mometrix of any particular political, scientific, or religious point of view.

Counseling Skills That Indicate Multicultural Sensitivity

Counselors who are sensitive to cultural differences will more likely develop strategies and hypotheses that are free of **cultural biases**. Developing hypotheses that are not culturally slanted will allow counselors to more objectively plan and implement intervention strategies. **Multicultural sensitivity** enables counselors to design and deliver lesson plans that are free from stereotypical icons or remarks; it also helps them decide when and how to generalize instructions for diverse groups of students. With increased sensitivity, counselors can design activities and strategies that are inclusive of diverse cultures or that are individualized for different cultures. An example of an inclusive activity is eliciting student responses about a recent event on campus. An individualized activity could be asking students to write about holiday traditions in their home, which would allow students to respond from a cultural perspective.

Areas of the School System Positively Impacted By Multiculturally Competent Counselors

Cultural and ethnic diversity in the school environment often results in disparities in peripheral areas, particularly if issues of **oppression** and **bias** are not addressed. Some of the peripheral areas that can be impacted by culturally-based hierarchies include academic achievement, literacy competence, AP course participation, career planning, and, most significantly, disparities in standardized test results, which can negatively affect college opportunities and eventual income level. Counselors who operate with multicultural sensitivity can significantly mitigate these disparities by acting as a liaison between the student body and school officials. In this capacity, counselors can act on students' behalf when there is a culturally-based misunderstanding, as well help students develop strategies for bridging cultural gaps. Counselors can also help school staff and officials pinpoint practices that may inherently pose a disadvantage for certain cultural groups.

Need for Multicultural and Anti-Oppression Training in Counseling Programs

Traditional school counseling programs reflect long-practiced curricular parameters based on Western European culture and history. Consequently, practice and discussions tend to be non-inclusive of other cultures, particularly in regard to diversity and multicultural counseling issues. Counselors who have been trained in a traditional Western European program are usually inadequately prepared to address issues associated with multicultural identities, especially the practices and environments of oppression. Without infusing additional multicultural training into a counseling program, counselors often unknowingly perpetuate the Western paradigm. Counselors and the programs they create will then lack an understanding of oppression, cultural history, cultural identity, and the acquisition of multicultural competency. This is why the onus is usually on the counselor to obtain ongoing multicultural training, and to invest in research about multiculturalism and oppression, in order to bring a more comprehensive perspective into the school environment.

Social Justice

Social justice incorporates awareness of inequalities based on cultural, race or ethnicity, and the ability to redistribute resources. Counselors who work with diverse student groups should know when and if those groups have been historically oppressed. This historical oppression usually reveals practices and attitudes that have been accepted and ingrained in the larger community as well as the school environment. Counselors can systematically and diplomatically address these practices and attitudes, in the interest of creating social environments that support social justice. Examples of these practices and attitudes include testing that does not allow for second language learners, and lesson plans that use examples that are only familiar to certain cultural groups.

Copyright © Mometrix Media. You have been licensed one copy of this document for personal use only. Any other reproduction or redistribution is strictly prohibited. All rights reserved.
This content is provided for test preparation purposes only and does not imply an endorsement by Mometrix of any particular political, scientific, or religious point of view.

Counselors can work with students, school staff, and the surrounding community to establish an environment of social justice.

Helping Students Become Empowered

The idea of **empowerment** includes the distribution of resources, but is rooted in a larger context of social relationships and dynamics. **Culturally-based oppression** often depends on acceptance from both the dominant culture and the oppressed culture. Historically oppressed cultures sometimes adopt ways of thinking and behaving that originally were enforced by violence or other extreme means, but have continued because of cultural identity. Likewise, historically dominant cultures adopt ways of thinking and behaving that perpetuate a false sense of superiority. Counselors can help students develop personal empowerment by encouraging them to recognize that individuals, and groups of individuals, often share many similarities and are connected at a fundamental level. This kind of thinking transcends historical relationships and forges new interpersonal connections, giving empowerment to previously disenfranchised groups.

Development of Consciousness and Self-Image Through Empowerment

There are several key areas of personal dynamics and self-image that are impacted by empowerment:

- Individuals begin to relate to others based on commonalities of experience and belonging, rather than on preconceived notions of difference.
- Individuals begin to recognize social dynamics objectively, rather than internalizing them and view them in a subjective sense.
- A sense of empowerment and recognition of social dynamics can reverse students' thinking, from that of victim to that of change agent for social justice.
- Once individuals understand that social dynamics, and not any inherent inferiority, determine their social status, the implications for personal growth can be exponential.

Counselors who work with students toward empowerment are giving them back the power that taken by culturally-based beliefs, attitudes and practices. Empowerment should be understood as being not hierarchical, such that the oppressed group is now the dominant group, but rather as egalitarian, ensuring fair distribution of resources and opportunity.

Strategies for Helping Students Feel Empowered

Counselors can **help students feel empowered** by pointing out their membership in the larger community and helping them to develop ownership and responsibility for their actions. Counselors can begin by discussing the parameters of group membership, noting that each of us belongs to several groups. Students must recognize that they belong to groups based on their occupation, community, culture, gender, etc. This recognition enables students to transcend limits of identity. Counselors can then point out that social dynamics involve the whole community, affecting individuals in myriad ways. This allows students to broaden their understanding of social processes. Students should also be encouraged to take personal responsibility for their academic progress, as well as for other actions and behaviors. Counselors can help students develop new behaviors that reflect a stronger self-confidence, a perception of membership in the larger community, and a realization that they can positively contribute to that community.

Skill-Building and Developing an Increased Knowledge Base While Promoting Empowerment

Counselors working with students toward empowerment can first provide them with the knowledge and perspective that will allow them to approach their goals and circumstances

Copyright © Mometrix Media. You have been licensed one copy of this document for personal use only. Any other reproduction or redistribution is strictly prohibited. All rights reserved.
This content is provided for test preparation purposes only and does not imply an endorsement by Mometrix of any particular political, scientific, or religious point of view.

differently. Even though students can understand their community membership in theory, often particular events or circumstances become a discouraging validation of the status quo. Counselors can partner with students to confront these circumstances, addressing them on a problem-specific basis, from an enlightened and empowered perspective. A good problem-solving strategy includes the following key steps:

- Identify the problem.
- Work together to set a goal that will mitigate or solve the problem.
- Develop incremental actions toward the goal.
- Identify available resources for achieving the goals.

Counselors can also provide support and encouragement, reminding students of their strengths, their desire to change their circumstances, and the support and resources available.

Need for Additional Multicultural Training in Individual Counseling Sessions

As with developing counseling programs, counselors who conduct **individual counseling sessions** can sometimes suffer from a dearth of multicultural knowledge, at least in part because of the limited scope of their training. This can affect counselors' interactions with students, as well as the strategies used to address problems. Many graduate programs fail to address cultures other than those with a Western European perspective. This can be a handicap for counselors working with a diverse student body, since they would lack an understanding of different cultural beliefs, terminology, historical oppression, and other factors. Understandably, their approach in counseling might be irrelevant or even offensive. Counselors working with a diverse student body should obtain multicultural training, develop relevant strategies for individual counseling, and collaborate with other counselors or school staff as appropriate.

Effects of Culture on Students' Perception and Participation in Counseling Process

There are numerous **cultural factors that can affect the counseling relationship**. One of the primary factors is the difference between group-oriented cultures and individual-oriented cultures. Students who come from a culture that values the group above the individual will approach communication, goal-setting, and decision-making from a completely different perspective than those who comes from a culture that values the individual above the group (such as traditional Western culture). Culture can determine whether the student perceives the counselor as a helper or an intruder. Students from some cultural backgrounds may communicate more with body language than words, and could perceive the counselor's communication similarly. Culture can affect students' time orientation, sense of self, and ability to make decisions. This is particularly significant when counselors are working with students from a historically oppressed culture. Counselors can develop appropriate strategies for developing a student's sense of empowerment in harmony with his or her cultural values.

Composing Group Sessions with Multicultural Students

The dynamics of **group sessions** can be particularly influenced by cultural factors. Understanding how different cultural groups respond to stereotypes, oppression, discrimination, and prejudice can assist the counselor in forming groups. Likewise, **student perceptions of the counselor** as facilitator or authority can affect the group dynamics. Although the recommendation is not necessarily to limit groups to similar cultures, and in fact in some cases it might be valuable to blend cultures, it is up to the counselor to be sensitive to the ramifications of multicultural dynamics. It is worth noting that culture can include gender, religion, and other criteria. Counselors

Copyright © Mometrix Media. You have been licensed one copy of this document for personal use only. Any other reproduction or redistribution is strictly prohibited. All rights reserved.
This content is provided for test preparation purposes only and does not imply an endorsement by Mometrix of any particular political, scientific, or religious point of view.

should refer to literature, research, and other resources regarding considerations and practices related to cultural diversity.

Facilitating Multicultural Understanding in Group Sessions

Although multicultural groups can benefit from the richness of blended cultures, these groups may be more susceptible to misunderstandings and conflicts as a result of the differences in perspectives. The counselor can provide valuable leadership by encouraging the interchange of ideas about such topics as self-identity, self-worth, oppression, and responsibility to society. Likewise, if there is conflict in the group, the counselor who has been trained in multicultural sensitivity can better recognize if the conflict is culturally based, and can take the opportunity to intervene and work with the students to develop strategies for resolution. It may be possible for the group to work as a whole on culturally-based conflict resolution, allowing other members to contribute newly learned skills or perspectives. Multicultural counseling groups can provide fertile ground for teaching multicultural sensitivity.

Importance of Multicultural Sensitivity When Consulting with Parents and Teachers

Sensitivity to cultural differences can be especially important when consulting with parents and teachers on a student matter, particularly when the student's family is from a different culture than the teacher or counselor. Often, the consulting/discussion group will be comprised of the student, his or her parents, the counselor, the teacher, and a school counselor. Counselors need to be especially sensitive to the following key factors:

- A parent who lives in a culturally isolated household or neighborhood
- A student who is bi-cultural
- The culture of the teacher/counselor
- The culture of the counselor

Counselors should create an environment that allows comfortable communication and input from all parties. Counselors should be sensitive to the cultural significance and perception of the issue at hand, as well as to the best ways to address the problem within the cultural contexts represented.

Addressing Cultural Biases or Stereotypes in Consulting Arrangements

In the process of facilitating a discussion among parents, student, teachers, and other parties in a consulting discussion, counselors may find that one or more individuals may be communicating or acting from a paradigm of **bias** or **stereotyping**. This may develop into a resistance to resolution, particularly if the problem is culturally based. Counselors may need to challenge the individuals by pointing out the specific words or behaviors that perpetuate stereotypes and the negative effect that these actions have on the intervention process. Counselors can remind the group of the shared desire for resolution, and how stereotyping can detract from the purpose of the gathering. They can remind participants that the well-being of the student will be best served by collaboration and by refraining from expressions of cultural bias and stereotyping.

Assessing Students from Diverse Cultural Backgrounds

In most school environments, there are a number of standardized tests that are administered to assess academic achievement and aptitude. Counselors can provide a valuable service to the school and its students by determining if tests are inherently culturally biased, and by suggesting **alternate assessment methods** as appropriate. Some of the aspects of testing that should be reviewed are references to events or individuals that are specific to particular cultures and language-based assessment that does not allow for second language learners. It may be appropriate

Copyright © Mometrix Media. You have been licensed one copy of this document for personal use only. Any other reproduction or redistribution is strictly prohibited. All rights reserved.
This content is provided for test preparation purposes only and does not imply an endorsement by Mometrix of any particular political, scientific, or religious point of view.

for the counselor to help school counselors develop alternative testing methods, or to work one-on-one with students from disadvantaged cultures. Counselors should obtain training and use outside resources to identify **culturally biased testing** and to choose alternative methods. It is also important to understand how to communicate testing results to families of students from diverse cultures.

Avoiding Cultural Bias When Conducting Assessment

Counselors should be particularly vigilant about any personal biases that could obscure the assessment process. In other words, if a test is designed to assess student readiness for academic promotion, and half of the students perform at the readiness level, while the other half perform below the readiness level, the initial reaction might be that the test was successful, and that half of the class is ready for promotion. However, if a counselor finds that lines of success or failure fall in a quasi-line progression toward eliminating or isolating a particular cultural group, he or she should avoid the assumption that the test validates cultural differences, and instead should review the test and the testing process for cultural biases. Not only can these cultural biases negatively affect individual students, but the continued use of a **culturally skewed test** can be used to fallaciously document poor achievement by particular cultures, and further perpetuate academic oppression.

Making Tests Available in Languages Other Than the Dominant Language

Assessment vehicles that are language based, such as math word problems or reading comprehension tests, may intrinsically put second-language learners at a disadvantage. Counselors should be sensitive to this disadvantage, and should offer students alternate testing methods. These methods may include written tests in the student's native language or the presence of an interpreter. Translators may also be on hand to present the questions in both the **dominant language** and the **student's native language**, in order to assist the student in making associations between the two. It is important that the test be presented in a way that is comfortable, allows ample time for translation, and does not contain any implications of inferiority about second-language learners. Assessment of second-language learners should fairly and accurately test students' aptitudes, skills, and abilities.

Using Curriculum Lessons to Address Multicultural Sensitivity

Often, counselors are required to deliver **lesson plans regarding multicultural awareness and sensitivity** to diverse groups of students. Counselors can improve the cultural climate in a school setting by promoting multicultural sensitivity and educating students about best practices for positive diversity. They can begin by defining and identifying cultural differences, as well as appropriate language and behaviors for addressing these differences. A lesson plan about multicultural sensitivity can first identify that culture may include or refer to race, ethnicity, gender, sexual orientation, different levels of ability, etc. Counselors can illustrate how culturally-biased behaviors and attitudes can lead to oppression and conflict, whereas avoidance of these behaviors can contribute to the richness of a diverse student body. Counselors should also remind students of the negativity engendered by practicing and promoting oppressive behaviors among their families and other members of their own culture.

Lesson Plan Topics on Positive Diversity and Multicultural Sensitivity

Counselors wishing to educate students on **positive diversity and multicultural sensitivity** can include both informational and reflective elements in their lesson plans. Informational elements can encompass the correct usage of multicultural terminology, identification of oppression and oppressive practices, and identification of cultural differences and how they can affect interaction. Counselors can explain culturally-based differences of world view and value systems. Reflective exercises can include group discussions, testimonies of personal experience, or journal exercises

Copyright © Mometrix Media. You have been licensed one copy of this document for personal use only. Any other reproduction or redistribution is strictly prohibited. All rights reserved.
This content is provided for test preparation purposes only and does not imply an endorsement by Mometrix of any particular political, scientific, or religious point of view.

exploring personal biases and assumptions. Counselors can also include examples of racism, ageism, ableism, etc., to identify cultural bias and illustrate its negative impact. Students could be asked to identify cultural bias in historical texts. The class can also discuss ideas for addressing oppressive beliefs and practices throughout the world. Lesson plans can alternate between informational lecture and reflective discussion to best engage the students in the topic.

Including the Surrounding Community in Building Multicultural Sensitivity

Counselors can offer their expertise and act as **liaisons to the surrounding community** by including parents and neighbors in discussions and events promoting multicultural sensitivity. It is usually the responsibility of the counselor to coordinate this community outreach, which can take many forms. Counselors can develop peer mediation services, family counseling services, or hold workshops in the community to discuss cultural diversity. One of the common goals of a community outreach program is to increase multicultural sensitivity and communication, not only within the community, but also in the area surrounding the school campus. Since school campuses are often diverse, and the neighborhoods often culturally isolated, school counselors can be the vehicle for transcending cultural differences and encouraging multicultural understanding. Another method for involving the surrounding community is to hold programs, such as talent shows, on campus and invite the parents and neighbors.

Developing Relationships with the Surrounding Multicultural Community

Because students are in many ways required to **assimilate** the dominant culture, counselors may be only vaguely aware of the unique expectations, belief systems, and practices of a **student's native culture**. By developing and maintaining relationships with members of the surrounding community, counselors can be exposed to cultural practices and assumptions that are more pronounced because neighborhoods tend to be culturally isolated. In this way, counselors may gain insight about cultural identity from adults in the neighborhood. Students may be less likely to reveal some information, partly because of inherent role dynamics between the adult counselor and the adolescent student. Counselors can also find out about cultural holidays, traditions, and events in the neighborhood.

Significance of Data Collection and Sharing

Counselors can make a significant contribution to both the efficacy and the equity of a school's curriculum by **collecting and sharing data** related to the academic performance of the student body. This data can be invaluable in identifying chronic achievement inequities among racial, ethnic, and/or socioeconomic groups. Counselors should work with school staff and counselors to identify these inequities and to implement strategies to rectify the disparities. This may result in changes to course offerings or changes to the counseling program itself. Data collection may also identify strategies or courses of study that are successful. Since decisions related to curriculum are often made by committee, including school boards, clear and accurate presentation of the information is vital. Therefore, interpretation of the data is particularly important and should be conducted in collaboration with school counselors and staff.

Areas for Student Data Collection

The first area to focus on when **collecting data** is that of academic achievement. Sources include standardized test scores, grade point averages, other academic-based scores or results, and retention and graduation rates. Secondly, academic participation can be quantitatively assessed by looking at data related to course enrollment, discipline referrals, suspension rates, incidents involving illegal substances, parent participation, homework completion, and extracurricular participation. It should be noted that retention/drop-out rates can form part of both the achievement and the participation data bases. The third major area of focus for student data

Copyright © Mometrix Media. You have been licensed one copy of this document for personal use only. Any other reproduction or redistribution is strictly prohibited. All rights reserved.
This content is provided for test preparation purposes only and does not imply an endorsement by Mometrix of any particular political, scientific, or religious point of view.

collection is the set of graduation-readiness competencies. These competencies include the number of students with four-year plans on file and the number of students who have participated in workshops related to career-planning, job-shadowing, and conflict resolution. Students who have completed their academic goals also form part of the graduation-readiness competency data.

Collecting Data on Multicultural Students

It is important to have appropriate variables when using data collection to determine inequities based on race, culture, ethnicity, and socioeconomic status. While there may be significant conclusions to be drawn by comparing results divided by gender, race, socioeconomic status, second-language learners, and other major categories, more useful information may be gained by comparing results in different areas within cultural groups. For instance, the results of second-language learners who perform well on aptitude tests that are number based, but poorly on those that are language based, should be assessed to determine if the testing and/or the curriculum inherently results in a cultural inequity. This kind of data gathering can identify which programs, courses, and strategies are most and least effective for diverse students, and adjustments can be made accordingly. In addition, if students do well on standardized tests, and poorly in the classroom assignments and tests, this may be an indication of poor participation in the classroom.

Importance of Personal Research and Reflection in Multicultural Counseling

For counselors to be competent in multicultural counseling, it is important for them to develop a sensitivity to the significance of the distinguishing characteristics of culture. A good foundation for this sensitivity is **self-investigation and self-reflection** on the counselor's own cultural background. Counselors can develop an understanding of how their cultural and ethnic background has contributed to their value system, their traditions and rituals, their view of the individual's place in the larger society, and many other personal traits. Likewise, cultural history can reveal how particular cultures or cultural traits have played a part in social hierarchy. Counselors who are aware of their own ties to culture will be better able to understand the significance of culture for students who come from a different cultural background. A counselor with this valuable foundation can be an important liaison for students who need to balance tradition with assimilation.

Ongoing Workshops and Seminars for Maintaining Multicultural Competence

The issues of diversity in the counseling and school environment are complex and multidimensional. As a society, our collective knowledge of diverse cultures and multiculturalism is continually evolving. Therefore, it is advisable for counselors to periodically attend **workshops and seminars** on the subject. Each workshop or seminar will help to **expand a counselor's sensitivity to diverse cultures**. From these events, counselors will learn how to work better with students and their families in the school counseling environment. They will learn strategies and terminology that reflect sensitivity and understanding of the scope of culture in general, as well as of the specifics of particular cultures. Fortunately, many professional organizations are aware of the need for ongoing training in multiculturalism and will usually offer numerous opportunities for the school counselor.

Value of Organizations That Work on Multicultural Competence

The knowledge base formed from attending workshops and seminars can be greatly added to by meeting with other counselors on a regular basis or by joining organizations dedicated to increasing cultural sensitivity. The knowledge gained during periodic attendance at workshops can sometimes dissipate in an environment where it is not necessarily reinforced. Meeting with peers can repeat and validate this knowledge and can also provide the opportunity to implement and revise strategies. The combined expertise of the group can allow for **shared ideas and strategies** toward multicultural competency. Also, as a group, an organization of peers can collaborate on

Copyright © Mometrix Media. You have been licensed one copy of this document for personal use only. Any other reproduction or redistribution is strictly prohibited. All rights reserved.
This content is provided for test preparation purposes only and does not imply an endorsement by Mometrix of any particular political, scientific, or religious point of view.

methods and strategies for combating oppression in the school and surrounding community through school counseling curricula and programs. These professional organizations include Counselors for Social Justice and the Association for Multicultural Counseling and Development.

Reading Literature About Multiculturalism to Increase Knowledge and Sensitivity

The ability to read, analyze, and critically explore issues of cultural diversity through a written medium offers benefits not necessarily present in a seminar, workshop, or organizational meeting. Literature about cultural diversity can explore **historical and current events** through the eyes and **perspectives of several cultural groups**, especially when the written text is the culmination of research and interviews. Reading these texts, counselors can gain a comprehensive understanding of the historical factors and impact of events in relation to race, socioeconomic class, culture, gender, and the histories of other groups who have been oppressed or victimized because of culture. A good book dealing with these issues is Howard Zinn's *A People's History of the United States*, which contains personal testimonies and anecdotes about the subject. These personal stories allow for a first-person perspective on issues of social justice, giving the counselor a sense of empathy to bring to the multicultural counseling environment.

Benefits of Continued Reading of Literature on Multiculturalism

The benefits of reading **literature that addresses issues of multiculturalism** are generally two-fold: for one thing, literature on the subject of multiculturalism is always evolving, reflecting current research and other input. As with organizational meetings, literature dealing with cultural diversity is a compilation of the experiences and expertise of a number of people from a variety of perspectives. Counselors should become cognizant of this evolving expertise, in multiculturalism as well as other aspects of counseling. Secondly, teaching or counseling in isolation from the continued input of others increases the risk of personal biases and perspectives coloring the curriculum. Any one individual inherently has a limited worldview, and no individual or group of individuals could possibly know all there is to know about other cultures. Consequently, continued exposure to viewpoints and perspectives beyond their own horizon allows counselors to respond appropriately to a diverse student body.

Importance of a Checklist in Determining Own Multicultural Competence

A **checklist** can provide a rubric for counselors to assess their own level of multicultural awareness, sensitivity, and competence. For counselors commencing their own edification in multicultural sensitivity, or those who are relatively new and beginning the process of multicultural training, checklists can provide a set of goals to attain in the process of becoming more aware of multicultural issues. Counselors can see which issues or concerns are in need of further work, and can take advantage of the available resources for development in these areas. Once these goals are attained, counselors can periodically review the checklist to ascertain that they are continuing to incorporate the guidelines and strategies represented by the checklist, and can again refer to outside resources if indicated. The Association for Multicultural Counseling and Development, as well as other agencies, publishes appropriate checklists that address such issues as behavior, knowledge, sensitivity, and awareness.

IDEIA

The **Individuals with Disabilities Education and Improvement Act (IDEIA)** was enacted to ensure that eligible school-aged students receive the opportunity for a reasonable education. Eligible students are defined as those students who exhibit any single or combination of 13 identified disabilities. Reasonable education is distinguished as allowing students to make reasonable educational progress, not necessarily to achieve their highest possible performance.

Copyright © Mometrix Media. You have been licensed one copy of this document for personal use only. Any other reproduction or redistribution is strictly prohibited. All rights reserved.
This content is provided for test preparation purposes only and does not imply an endorsement by Mometrix of any particular political, scientific, or religious point of view.

Eligible students can receive a **free appropriate public education (FAPE)** under IDEIA. The Act stipulates that these eligible students receive an education that is designed around their intellectual and physical levels. It is also mandated that the delivery of the curriculum be specially designed to meet the particular requirements of students. If the disability presented by the child has a minimal or non-negative effect on learning, then the student may not be eligible for IDEIA resources, but may be eligible for reasonable accommodations under Section 504.

Autism, Deaf-Blindness, Deafness, and Hearing Impairment Per IDEIA Criteria

Autism is a disability that affects social interactions as well as verbal and nonverbal communications. It can manifest in repetitive activities, stereotyped movements, resistance to changes in routine or environment, and unusual responses to stimuli. Most autism is evident in children before the age of 3. Academic performance may be mildly or severely impacted by autism, depending on the range and intensity of the symptoms.

Deaf-blindness refers to significant impairment in both hearing and vision. The combined impairments can result in severe suppression of development, learning, and communication, well beyond that which would result from deafness or blindness alone.

Deafness refers to a hearing impairment that is sufficient to affect the processing of linguistic information through hearing, with or without amplification. Academic participation and performance are affected accordingly.

Hearing impairment refers to a permanent or fluctuating condition that adversely affects the educational performance but does not qualify as deafness.

Developmental Delay, Emotional Disturbance, and Intellectual Disabilities Per IDEIA Criteria

Developmental delay refers to a significant cognitive lapse between ages 3 and 9 that cannot be accounted for by any other identified disability.

Emotional disturbance refers to a spectrum of symptoms that encompass a general inability to cope or learn which presents over a long period of time and to a marked degree. Symptoms include an unexplainable inability to learn, inappropriate behaviors or feelings under normal circumstances, a tendency to develop physical symptoms or fears that correlate with personal or academic problems, the inability to foster satisfactory interpersonal relationships with peers or teachers, and a general mood of unhappiness or depression. This condition adversely affects educational performance accordingly. IDEIA includes schizophrenia in this category.

"Intellectual disabilities" *refers to a significantly sub-average intellectual* functioning that may exist alongside deficits in adaptive behavior and may manifest during the developmental period.

Implementing Special Education Appropriation for Students

Generally, the steps involved in **appropriating special education accommodations** for a student include:

- Student will be recommended as needing special accommodations or additional instruction by parents/guardians, the school system, school personnel, or a state agency.
- History of student learning problems will be reviewed with parents/guardians, school counselors, school educators/special educators.
- Counselor should request written consent from parents/guardians to conduct further formal assessment.

Copyright © Mometrix Media. You have been licensed one copy of this document for personal use only. Any other reproduction or redistribution is strictly prohibited. All rights reserved.
This content is provided for test preparation purposes only and does not imply an endorsement by Mometrix of any particular political, scientific, or religious point of view.

- Students is formally assessed through tests administered by psychologists, special educators, specialists such as audiologists, etc., to determine the specific special needs and the extent of the special needs.
- Student eligibility for special accommodations is determined from results of assessment.
- If student is eligible, counselor will develop an individualized education plan (IEP) that will address student needs.
- Counselor will implement an FAPE in the least restrictive environment (LRE), as determined by the parents/guardians and educators.

Review Video: 504 Plans and IEPs
Visit mometrix.com/academy and enter code: 881103

Copyright © Mometrix Media. You have been licensed one copy of this document for personal use only. Any other reproduction or redistribution is strictly prohibited. All rights reserved.
This content is provided for test preparation purposes only and does not imply an endorsement by Mometrix of any particular political, scientific, or religious point of view.

Promoting Academic, Social/Emotional, and Career Development

Academic Advisement and Career Planning

Advantages of Evidence-Based Curricula in Helping Students Meet Sequenced Outcome Goals

Counselors can facilitate students in **meeting short-term and long-term goals** by using either curricula they have developed, commercially available curricula, or a combination of both. There are several advantages of using commercially available curricula, the first of which is that they are usually evidence-based, having been developed and revised in response to professional research and tracked success rates. Counselors using **evidence-based curricula** experience the added benefit of more widespread institutional support for an established, evidence-based curricular model. Counselors can collaborate with school staff and administration to select an appropriate commercial curriculum, and from there identify pedagogy that best addresses student outcomes. When a commercial curriculum is selected and adopted, outcomes can be matched with appropriate pedagogical methods. Often these evidenced-based curricula provide both students and school faculty with the confidence and efficacy that result from utilizing established pedagogy.

Contributing to Academic Achievement While Targeting Personal and Social Development

Counselors can best serve their students and the school system as a whole by continually **integrating developmental goals with academic goals**. Since students mature and move through the graded school system simultaneously, counselors should maintain a conscientious awareness of achievement standards in the areas of academic development, personal-social development, and career development. These areas are inherently interdependent, and an effective counselor will consciously integrate them toward the holistic development of his or her students. The ASCA identifies three key strategies for this integration:

- Counselors should be aware of the academic content and schedule of classes, and should tailor counseling sessions to the academic needs of the students.
- Counselors should refer to the school documents and personnel for explicit and implicit goals and competency standards for the students.
- Counselors should be proactive in enriching certain academic areas for students.

Addressing Career Development with Students in Grades K to 5

For young students, **career awareness** is the primary goal of career development. Children can be made aware of the different kinds of jobs, and it's to their long-term benefit if that learning also addresses the idea that they need not feel limited by gender, socioeconomic status, or ethnic background—or even the attitudes of their family members. In early school years, career awareness can be facilitated by field trips to places where people do interesting work, by having adults come to the classroom to talk about and demonstrate their work, by playing games and creating stories about different kinds of work, and by watching videos and reading books about occupations. Children can be encouraged to notice how their favorite activities might relate to work. Reporting on the work their parents and other family members do can be another way to engage the curiosity and awareness of the world of work. Craft fairs or farmers' markets, where children make (or grow) and sell their work are another way of showing children that they can

Copyright © Mometrix Media. You have been licensed one copy of this document for personal use only. Any other reproduction or redistribution is strictly prohibited. All rights reserved.
This content is provided for test preparation purposes only and does not imply an endorsement by Mometrix of any particular political, scientific, or religious point of view.

work for themselves in ways that they might not otherwise consider if they've grown up in a corporate-focused work culture.

Career Counseling for Middle School Students

Middle school students should be encouraged to explore careers, investigating how their interests and strengths could lead to satisfying work. Students might go with their parents to work, might interview other adults about their occupations, and might read about unusual career choices. At this time of life, grades will begin to impact the options children have regarding college: it's also a time for career counselors to assist students whose life paths might lead them to the trades, to entrepreneurial activities, to the arts, or to other nontraditional vocations. Students whose families have traditionally been involved in particular professions might be discovering that they're well-suited to the tradition or that they will need support in pursuing other interests. Part-time jobs after school give students a little spending money, a feeling for what makes a strong work ethic, and a taste of what it's like to work in a particular occupation. Volunteering is another way that students can explore potential interests and gain skills.

Career Counseling for High School Students

Career counselors may administer **career inventorie**s to help students identify personal strengths and interests associated with particular occupations. Students will need guidance in choosing high school courses relevant to their future paths in college, trade school, or business. Preparing for college entrance exams and locating funding for training are parts of student career development work that may require the help of a school counselor, especially when students' families are not familiar with the course of the students' proposed occupational fields.

Students from disadvantaged background should be helped to take courses, prepare for exams, and locate scholarships that will help them overcome those disadvantages. Personal encouragement and locating mentors or guides are valuable strategies because building hope will increase the student's motivation to use the tools. Without hope and support from a trusted advisor, students whose social/familial environment does not support their career paths can be overwhelmed by the process and mired in pessimism.

Helping Students When Career Interests Don't Match Career Assessment

Career assessments measure interests, but many factors contribute to career choices. For example, a student with a **Holland code** of artistic-entrepreneurial-social (AES) may state the determination to become an engineer. The counselor can discuss with the student how the AES code doesn't seem to match up with the student's ambition and explore possible reasons for the incongruence without telling the student that "you're wrong." It's possible that the student's parents have raised their child to take up a "solid occupation," and the student is either trying to please the parents or has other personal goals. Perhaps the student isn't aware of potential careers available for the Holland codes and needs to explore.

Perhaps, the student is **multiskilled**, wants the security of a higher-paying job, and plans to keep art on the side while becoming a consulting engineer (satisfying the entrepreneurial tendencies.) The main purpose of the counselor in the situation is not to force the student to see "reality" but to support the student, using the discrepancy in the test to fully explore, actively choose, and fully prepare for the chosen career.

Copyright © Mometrix Media. You have been licensed one copy of this document for personal use only. Any other reproduction or redistribution is strictly prohibited. All rights reserved.
This content is provided for test preparation purposes only and does not imply an endorsement by Mometrix of any particular political, scientific, or religious point of view.

Promoting a Healthy School Environment

Benefits of Establishing a Relationship over a Number of Counseling Sessions

Foremost in the school counseling model is the **establishment of a trust relationship between counselor and student**. Trust and cooperation sometimes needs to be established over a period of several visits, and is augmented by a strict policy of confidentiality by the counselor, which further contributes to the perception of a safe environment. The process of identifying and addressing key or underlying issues can be much more productive when the relationship between the counselor and student is fully established over a number of sessions. An added benefit of numerous sessions can be the student's increased receptiveness to the counselor's recommendations.

Contributing to Academic Development in Classrooms

Since school counselors are primarily concerned with personal issues that affect academic performance, they are often expected to devote a percentage of their time to developing programs that deliver guidance and instruction to all students. Incorporated in these programs are strategies that address such topics as academic performance, career planning, and social skills. Counselors may also be asked to contribute to curriculum implementation. **School counselors are expected to contribute significant resources to teaching**. Although the guidelines for counselor contributions to curriculum implementation may differ between schools, there are generally understood percentages, based on age groups. In elementary school settings, 35 to 45 percent of the counseling program should be devoted to curriculum implementation. In the middle school milieu, the percentage is 25 to 35 percent. High schools generally expect 15 to 25 percent of the counseling program to be devoted to curriculum implementation.

Counselors as Teachers

School counselors can have a positive influence on classroom instruction, specifically in the areas of personal and social growth related to academic performance. Although in the past guidance counseling was often an added role for teachers, students are now able to benefit from the expertise of trained guidance counselors, both in and out of the classroom environment. One of the benchmark criteria for **classroom instruction by school counselors** is empowering students to be productive members of society. Throughout their school years, counselors can assist students in such areas as study skills, time management, social skills, and career planning. The American School Counselor Association (ASCA) is a strong proponent of school counselors contributing their expertise to the classroom environment. Counselors can also assist students with preparation for standard-based testing and other academic goals set by the school.

Classroom Guidance

Benefits

The **benefits of classroom guidance** are found to be extraordinary and exponential. Results show that students who have experienced classroom guidance are significantly more successful academically and socially than those who have not had classroom guidance. This seems to be the case across the board, regardless of school district or even geographic area. In terms of academic success, these students fare noticeably better in attendance, test success, and overall grade-point average. Socially, their in-class behaviors improve markedly, and they are better able to cope with personal issues. Finally, students who have had the benefit of classroom guidance are more likely to attend college and to participate in career planning.

Copyright © Mometrix Media. You have been licensed one copy of this document for personal use only. Any other reproduction or redistribution is strictly prohibited. All rights reserved.
This content is provided for test preparation purposes only and does not imply an endorsement by Mometrix of any particular political, scientific, or religious point of view.

Assessing Effectiveness

As with any counseling strategy, it is important to both qualitatively and quantitatively **assess the success of classroom guidance**. It is important to establish a rubric that includes such criteria as grades, test scores, and graduation rates. Both pre- and post-intervention surveys are recommended. There can also be a qualitative appraisal of the effectiveness of intervention strategies in the classroom, delineating changes in behavior or classroom tenor. Note that demographic information can be valuable in assessing classroom strategies, but that it should not be included in pre- or post- intervention surveys. In other words, data gathering (grades, etc.) needs to be free of demographic categories, whereas ethnicity, gender, socioeconomic status and other demographics may be included on final evaluative reports. A significant added caution is that all data gathered should be confidential, with little or no reference to identifiable specifics.

Student Response Evaluation Methodology for Measuring Content

Counselors may want to assess student perceptions and **student responses** in order to qualitatively evaluate the effectiveness of classroom guidance content. The approach should be informal, gearing the evaluation in a way that is not readily perceived as an assessment. Younger children may respond well to a fill-in-the-blank cartoon; older students may be able to write or complete narratives that allow them to express their feelings about academic success, their role in the classroom or society, or other relevant perceptions. Other recommendations include scaled devices to self-report feelings, or another spectrum-like instrument, so long as they are user-friendly and informal. Counselors will generally want to assess the effect of classroom strategies on behavior, motivation, increased coping skills, and interest in planning. As with quantitative assessments, these more informal qualitative assessments should be administered both pre- and post-intervention, to more effectively assess the effect of the interventions.

Student Response Evaluation Methodology for Measuring Process

Process evaluation is necessarily more focused and formal, since it is administered to solicit feedback on specific components of the classroom guidance strategies. This type of evaluation is particularly valuable when developing or introducing a new strategy, since it provides a kind of rating system to assess the value of the strategy. The format for this type of evaluation should be more formal and quantitative than an evaluation of content acquisition. Surveys can be administered with rating systems, using terms like extremely helpful, helpful, not helpful, etc. It is also a good idea to include a comments section that will provide qualifiers for the rated responses. In other words, if a strategy was not particularly well received, what about it could be changed, if anything? This type of evaluation is often administered during the first classroom sessions using a strategy, providing valuable feedback for refining and revising the strategy in subsequent class meetings.

Adhering to an Overall Theory of Counseling

According to the tenets of an overarching theory of counseling. School counselors should be familiar with a number of theorists and models, in order to select one that is applicable to the school setting. Human development theories can serve as a viable foundation for many program designs, as can peripheral models of developmental phases within age groups. However, not all counseling sessions or students will necessarily be well served by same theoretical paradigm, so counselors should be watchful that a particular approach will address the situation or student group appropriately. Counselors should consider age levels and other defining factors in each counseling situation.

Copyright © Mometrix Media. You have been licensed one copy of this document for personal use only. Any other reproduction or redistribution is strictly prohibited. All rights reserved.
This content is provided for test preparation purposes only and does not imply an endorsement by Mometrix of any particular political, scientific, or religious point of view.

Sequential Nature of Strategies Based on Developmental Stages

Counselors need to be cognizant of developmental stages as they implement strategies for different age groups and developmental levels. A recommended approach is to dovetail a particular **developmental theory** with sequential task order as it is standardized in the K-12 curriculum. Certain learned life skills and levels of awareness may be negated if a student encounters significant life changes after the strategy is implemented, or if the strategy is implemented too early. By incorporating the K-12 model with the particular developmental theory, counselors can build a comprehensive model of guidance that introduces sequential skills in a meaningful order. It is important for counselors to be aware of students' developmental level before introducing a task or awareness that is beyond the student's capability or understanding. A good reference is the Adlerian-based framework of five key stages:

- Understanding self and others
- Development of empathy
- Ability to communicate
- Ability to cooperate
- Responsibility

Delivering Curriculum Through Consultation

School counselors are in the valuable position of liaison between students and school staff. They work with students on personal and academic issues, and collaborate with school personnel on appropriate strategies to facilitate student learning and development. Although counselors may directly design curriculum or deliver guidance in a classroom setting, often they will act as consultants to school staff in curriculum design, program development, or other related issues. **Collaboration** seems to work best when teachers follow a standardized curriculum and counselors solicit and assess student feedback. The counselors will advise the teachers, who will in turn implement the curricular changes. Counselors can infuse personal guidance and development into standardized curriculum to create a much richer program for students.

Delivering Curriculum Through Collaboration

In some cases, the best model for curriculum delivery that incorporates counseling guidelines is a partnership between the counselor and teacher. The particular value of this model lies in the fact that each partner is able to contribute his or her expertise in curriculum delivery. An example of this is teaching social skills through role playing, which can be designed around a historical setting. In this particular model, the counselor would contribute a set of guidelines for social skills, based on the agea and developmental levels of the students. A history teacher would plan the lesson around the historical period indicated by the grade level, and a drama teacher could contribute expertise regarding performance and role playing. This **collaboration** would culminate in a lesson addressing different modes of learning, while delivering curriculum and honoring counseling guidelines.

Delivering Curriculum Through Direct Teaching

Counselors who work according to the **direct-teaching** model function much like regular instructors, although they deliver a different type of information. While standard instruction focuses on information-based academic areas, direct teaching by school counselors focuses on life and social skills. Referring to appropriate topics for each age and grade level, counselors can plan and deliver the lessons that are most useful for specific developmental levels. Elementary students might benefit from a lesson on friendship or independence, while middle school students may need lessons on anger management, conflict resolution, or stress management. For high school students,

Copyright © Mometrix Media. You have been licensed one copy of this document for personal use only. Any other reproduction or redistribution is strictly prohibited. All rights reserved.
This content is provided for test preparation purposes only and does not imply an endorsement by Mometrix of any particular political, scientific, or religious point of view.

these lessons could expand to incorporate planning for the future. Some topics under this umbrella could be college preparation skills, career planning, and goal setting. Other topics appropriate for high school students fall in the categories of relationships and responsibility.

Delivering Curriculum That Addresses Career Planning and Conflict Resolution

One of the qualities that differentiates school counselors from teachers is their training and knowledge base, both in areas pertinent to school-age children and in appropriate expectations for each age and grade level. Although **conflict resolution** is a valuable skill to learn at any age, the delivery method and context will differ greatly between age levels. Counselors are particularly knowledgeable about this. One example of this is teaching young children how to get along with their friends through a puppet lesson; for high school students, an example is role-playing to address relationships with parents. It is important that high school students be given a wealth of information about career and college planning, which is an area of expertise for school counselors. Counselors can talk to high school students about setting goals, researching options, and planning for the future.

Role of Seating Arrangements in Classroom Guidance Lessons

Seating arrangements can be very important in establishing tone and expectation, as well as in contributing to the efficacy of a guidance lesson in the classroom. Counselors can choose other seating arrangements that are most conducive to the planned activity or lesson. Just the process of rearranging the established seating in a classroom can signal a change in the group dynamic. If students are asked to break into small groups, the expectation is that group discussion will occur. Counselors can implement this seating arrangement to address interpersonal skills. An added benefit to this kind of seating arrangement is that student groups can address different topics. Conversely, if the activity is one that requires the group of students to listen to the counselor, the chairs and desks would all face the front of the classroom.

Implications of Various Types of Seating Arrangements

Two key **areas influenced by seating arrangements** are formality and communication, specifically whether communication is one-sided or open and interactive. At one end of this spectrum is an arrangement in which seats are all facing one direction, toward a speaker or screen. This arrangement inherently discourages interaction, and implies one-way communication by the person or event at the front of the room. At the other end of the spectrum is an arrangement of small groups, in which the participants face each other. This arrangement allows for a great deal of interpersonal dialogue, and relegates the counselor to the role of facilitator. The gradations in between include U-shaped seating, which encourages discussion with a speaker; seats in a circle, which encourages discussion without a speaker; and seating around a table. Counselors should consider how much participation, if any, is appropriate for a given session when looking at seating arrangements.

Encouraging Positive Perception of Role Among School Teachers

School counselors run the risk of being perceived as disruptive and counter-productive to the class. One of the ways to mitigate this negative perception, besides conversation and collaboration with teachers, is to understand and respect certain aspects of the classroom dynamic. Particularly when working with younger children, maintaining routine is important to the continuity of the class. The counselor should strive for a role that is complementary and not disruptive. It is also important for counselors to understand and respect the established rules and behavior standards in classrooms. By recognizing that classroom dynamics have been established and providing a continuum,

Copyright © Mometrix Media. You have been licensed one copy of this document for personal use only. Any other reproduction or redistribution is strictly prohibited. All rights reserved.
This content is provided for test preparation purposes only and does not imply an endorsement by Mometrix of any particular political, scientific, or religious point of view.

counselors can fulfill the role of facilitator and gain the respect and trust of teachers and other school staff.

Mitigating Classroom Disturbances

Managing classroom tone and behavior is best accomplished by developing appropriate lessons and incorporating dynamic content, vocal and body signals in lesson delivery. It is important to develop lesson plans that are challenging yet manageable for the age and developmental level of the students. In addition, counselors can incorporate words of encouragement and validation in lessons, giving students a sense of connection to the classroom discussion and activities. Counselors can add a bit of humor to maintain interest and to pique students' creativity. In addition, utilizing changes in voice pitch, moving around the room, and making eye contact with different students can add to a counselor's ability to manage the tenor of a classroom. Not only does this contribute to the credibility of counselors in the classroom, but also greatly improves the efficacy of the lesson.

Role of Smooth Lesson Development

Giving students not only interesting and informative classroom content is another pivotal factor in mitigating the occurrences and opportunity for **classroom disturbance**. It is important for counselors to provide a consistent flow of content and interaction with students in order to keep the class focused on the lesson at hand and away from any possible distractions. This consistent flow also provides a standard backdrop of activity, so that any distracting activities are easily noticed; whereas if a lesson includes lulls or unfocused time, distractions can not only occur more easily, but also can occur relatively unnoticed and pave the way for increased distractive activities. Practices for developing sufficient classroom content include good preparation as well as familiarity with the lesson content. During the lesson, no matter how well planned, the counselor should continue to be watchful for any classroom disturbance, and should bring students back into focus as appropriate.

Addressing Classroom Disturbances When There Are Extraneous Factors

If a counselor feels that a **classroom disturbance** is rooted in a relationship outside of the classroom or the personal issues of one student, he or she may be able to restore the learning environment in the classroom and provide empathy at the same time. In the process of reminding a student or students to support the classroom learning environment, counselors may discover that there are underlying issues feeding the disturbance. It is important to approach each situation from a position of mutual respect and group consideration, so as to not be perceived as an unsympathetic, top-down authority. On the contrary, a counselor wants to be perceived as a knowledgeable person whose concern is the well-being of all students. A counselor can serve as a sounding board and resource expert for students who are experiencing problems that interfere with their learning experience.

Addressing Individual Discipline Issues

In order to manage with empathy, a counselor should maintain his or her role as authority while conveying a message of accessibility and expertise. When first approaching students, counselors should try to establish a kind of partnership, allowing students to participate in addressing issues that are disruptive to their learning environment. Students who feel they can participate in this resolution are less likely to feel isolated and singled out. However, counselors need to maintain the students' respect for the counselor's role. Not only does this prevent disruptions from becoming more pronounced, it also serves to give students confidence in the counselor's expertise. In the process of **working with a disruptive student**, counselors can suggest to the student underlying problems that may be fueling the disruption, providing an effective, holistic response to a classroom disturbance.

Copyright © Mometrix Media. You have been licensed one copy of this document for personal use only. Any other reproduction or redistribution is strictly prohibited. All rights reserved.
This content is provided for test preparation purposes only and does not imply an endorsement by Mometrix of any particular political, scientific, or religious point of view.

Addressing Attention-Seeking Behavior

Because of the When a student exhibits **attention-seeking behavior**, it is important that counselors do not reward the behavior with undue attention while disciplining the student. Counselors can develop consistent consequences for disruptive, attention-seeking behavior, and make these consequences known to students when first beginning work with them. Counselors may want to work with teachers and other staff to develop and communicate these consequences to students. Consequences should be directly related and proportional to the behavior. The effect of implementing these consequences should validate a perception that the counselors and teachers are interested in ensuring a calm and productive classroom environment for all students. Disciplinary actions should be free of anger or other emotional volatility. It is also important for counselors to remain objective, and to not infuse personal or moral assessments into their discipline. All of this will serve to downplay and neutralize attention-seeking behaviors in the classroom.

Expectations for Students

A counselor should set high **expectations** regarding students. However, it is important for the counselor to remember that every student is different and that expectations should be set accordingly. One of the first considerations to take is the student's developmental level. A counselor needs to be aware if the student has any learning disabilities or is developmentally slow. Another factor to consider is the instructional level for the students. Expectations should not be set so high that they go beyond the instructional level. A kindergartener cannot be expected to perform on the same level as a sixth grader. The opposite is also true; expectations should not be set too low that the students will be performing below grade level and unmotivated to achieve anything higher than that.

Awareness of National Perspective Concerning Education

It is vital that counselors are aware of the **national perspective concerning education**. They need to know what is expected of them, their staff, and their school. Counselors should know what the expectations are and make sure they are trying everything to meet those standards. The nation has certain goals that they expect schools to achieve, and counselors need to know what is expected of them and ensure their school is moving in that direction. When a counselor knows what the national expectation is, they can look at their school and ask whether they have the means to achieve those expectations. If they do not then they will know what their educational needs are and find the means to achieve those goals.

Selecting a Conflict Management Technique

In most cases, when a counselor is deciding which technique is the most appropriate to resolve conflict, they will choose a contingency approach, meaning that they choose the technique based on the nature of the situation. However, a counselor should also consider the individual personal needs of the staff when selecting a conflict management technique. Other important factors to consider are the people involved in the conflict, how serious the situation is to them, the type and intensity of the conflict, and the authority that the individuals possess. A counselor is likely to encounter several different types of conflicts and therefore there will be a number of alternative techniques from which to choose. One technique will not be suitable in all situations.

Gaining Support for Change

There are certain groups that will be affected the most when there is change: the faculty, the students, the parents, the school board, the counselor's superiors, and the state department of public instruction. These groups can also provide the most support or the most resistance to

Copyright © Mometrix Media. You have been licensed one copy of this document for personal use only. Any other reproduction or redistribution is strictly prohibited. All rights reserved.
This content is provided for test preparation purposes only and does not imply an endorsement by Mometrix of any particular political, scientific, or religious point of view.

change. Counselors must remember that every group will have their opinions, and the most professional thing to do is respect, listen, and accept those opinions, even if they are not agreed upon. One of the most important groups a counselor needs to consider during the change process is the faculty. It is crucial to get the faculty involved, because if the faculty does not understand why there needs to be a change, there will be less support, and in return, an implementation of a new program might not be successful.

Adoption of an Innovation

The first stage a counselor will go through is the awareness stage, which is becoming aware of a **new innovation**, but not having enough information about it. Many times, a counselor may not even have a strong enough interest to find out more information about the subject. During the interest stage, a counselor is beginning to show signs of wanting to gather more information, and may even begin to develop negative or positive feelings. At the mental stage, the counselor has decided this is something worth trying and is evaluating the innovation and deciding how it will be implemented. They may also ask respected members of the school community to assess it. During the trial stage, the innovation is implemented on a limited basis. Next is the adoption stage, the point when the innovation is implemented fully. The last stage is the integration stage, in which the innovation has become a routine.

Use of Referent Influence to Change a Person's Behavior

If a counselor possesses a **referent influence**, this means others are able to identify with the counselor as a person. Certain characteristics that others can identify with are a strong character, an outspoken personality, and a compelling leadership style. Characteristics like these may enable a counselor to gain cooperation from others even if teachers, parents and students question the decisions made by the counselor. However, there are no particular character traits that have a positive impact on everyone. While some groups respond positively to certain traits, others may view them as a sign of weak leadership. Another issue with referent influence is that if a counselor is in a position of leadership, their authenticity has already been established; if certain traits are not there, the probability of them developing is small.

Use of Reward Influence to Change a Person's Behavior

A counselor is said to have **reward influence** when he or she provides incentives for individuals who act and obey the rules of the program. One issue with this type of influence it that a counselor may not have enough rewards to be able to distribute equally. There may occasionally be a time when rewards may be offered to an individual or group without the same reward being distributed to others. This may seem like preferential treatment, which is not viewed favorably in the education field. Another problem that may arise is that the counselor may receive very little reward to give from the school board and other bureaucratic agencies. Although these problems may occur, a counselor can develop their own unique rewards. These rewards can include a free period, an additional lunch break, or support for a new activity a teacher wants to implement.

Copyright © Mometrix Media. You have been licensed one copy of this document for personal use only. Any other reproduction or redistribution is strictly prohibited. All rights reserved.
This content is provided for test preparation purposes only and does not imply an endorsement by Mometrix of any particular political, scientific, or religious point of view.

Student Assessment

Importance of Assessment

Assessment of both the student and the situation in any counseling sessions is very important, in that it serves to provide the counselor with both treatment and methodology for that treatment. A counselor will consider each student's developmental stage and environment to determine the best method for approaching a particular circumstance or problem. In addition, school or district policy can affect the counselor's methods, as for instance whether to use formal methods or to be more informal and flexible in developing a treatment for a particular student. Assessment can be formal or informal, and can be rather individualized among counselors. A comprehensive assessment of student needs, the precipitating event or situation, and a careful choice of approaches and actions based on this assessment are very important factors in the success of a counseling relationship.

Distinguishing Characteristics of Effective Assessment Methods in Academic Setting

In contrast to the **assessment methods** used in a mental health institution, assessment in an academic setting is less formal and more geared toward establishing a trusting and collaborative relationship with the student. In a mental health setting, the counseling session might be well served if the counselor asks direct questions to the client, in order to assess the problems. However, in an academic setting, an effective counseling relationship depends not only on the student's cooperation, which is facilitated by a less direct approach to assessment, but also on the incorporation of student needs not readily divulged. A counselor in an academic setting needs to be aware of, for instance, a student's body language when assessing and treating the student. It is important for a counselor in an academic setting to listen and observe carefully, and to engage in non-intrusive inquiry.

Information Obtained During Assessment

Although a counselor may discover information over a period of time and through different methods, in the context of the counseling relationship he or she should strive to obtain the following information:
Precipitating situation or event: specifically the duration, intensity, manifestation, and triggers

- Developmental and environmental factors: for instance, socioeconomic and cultural settings, medical and emotional background, physical and emotional development, etc. This information can often be obtained from parents, teachers, and other people connected to the student.
- Relationship specifics: specifically relationships with family, classmates, and teachers, and how the student behaves in these relationships
- Academic performance: what are the student's successes and failures in school? Does the student have difficulty in particular subjects? Does the student have an identified learning disability?
- Personal attributes and affinities: favorite activities, favorite subjects, talents, and strengths, and how these are incorporated in the student's daily life

Informal Assessment

Informal assessment can occur in the classroom setting, in conversation with the student, or by observation. Although informal assessment does not lend itself to a standardized rubric, such activities as games or storytelling can provide a holistic profile of a student. Other strategies for informal assessment include role-playing, opportunities for decision-making, writing exercises, and prioritized lists. These activities can reveal a student's thought patterns and coping strategies,

Copyright © Mometrix Media. You have been licensed one copy of this document for personal use only. Any other reproduction or redistribution is strictly prohibited. All rights reserved.
This content is provided for test preparation purposes only and does not imply an endorsement by Mometrix of any particular political, scientific, or religious point of view.

including those areas which a counselor identifies with specific treatment. Informal assessment can be particularly beneficial when working with an early or middle childhood student who may not be able to isolate and articulate difficulties. Counselors conducting informal assessment need to report their findings in a more comprehensive and less quantitative format than that of formal assessment.

Formal Assessment

Formal assessment is conducted with standardized instruments and can be beneficial in identifying specific areas and treatments for intervention. Formal assessment operates within a rubric, or set of rubrics, that incorporate behavior checklists, measurements of self-perception, value scales, and inventories of skills and interests. This type of assessment also provides the counselor with identification factors that are more targeted and specific than those of informal assessment. Formal assessment, because of its rubric-driven reporting, can sometimes provide counselors with a more objective evaluation of a student than would be gained from informal assessment. Counselors should be aware of, and trained in, an array of formal assessment methods. Results from a formal assessment may include data relating to significant behaviors or attributes that could be overlooked and therefore not addressed in an informal assessment.

RIASEC

John Holland observed that different people have different orientations and preferences to tasks and that certain tasks are associated more strongly with certain occupations. If you can ascertain the person's task preferences (or interests) and match them to a vocation, there is a better chance that person will find career satisfaction. Holland and others used traits to create vocational inventories (e.g., the self-directed search [SDS] and the Strong Interest Inventory [SII]) that could predict the type of work a person might be drawn to and succeed at. **RIASEC** (realistic, investigative, artistic, social, enterprising, conventional) is the acronym that stands for the personality types that fit into particular occupational categories—they are often called the Holland Codes. The theory is that by obtaining one's codes, one can identify careers of interest that fit into the interest of the person. After deriving a code from an inventory, students can use software programs or resources like the *Dictionary of Occupational Titles* or the *Occupational Outlook Handbook* to explore interesting careers they might not have been aware of before.

Participating in Development and Implementation of Student Service Plans

School counselors may be present from the beginning of a **service plan**, as when the parent of a new student states an already-identified need and asks for help or when a teacher sees the student struggling and consults with the counselor to find out why. The school counselor is in the unique position of being able to help at every stage of the process, from identifying a problem, arranging needs assessments and interpreting outcomes, and consulting with other professionals (such as psychologists, psychiatrists, speech pathologists, etc.) to making sure the student's academic schedule is modified to the best possible fit. The school counselor can check in regularly with the student, teacher, or other direct-service providers, track progress, and collaborate with others to provide counseling and other learning services. The school counselor stays in touch with the parents as well and may act as mediator if problems arise in service teams. Along the way, the counselor can provide the student with individual-based advocacy, support, and encouragement.

Strong Interest Inventory, MMPI, WAISC-II, and Beck Depression Inventory

The assessments listed are measuring different aspects of a person's makeup—they're used for different purposes. The Strong Interest Inventory is a career inventory, usually administered to students in high school, that gives the taker an idea of his/her inclinations in the vocational arena. The **Minnesota Multiphasic Personality Inventory (MMPI)** is usually given to people for whom there is a suspicion of personality problems that run deeper than the average neuroses: a student

Copyright © Mometrix Media. You have been licensed one copy of this document for personal use only. Any other reproduction or redistribution is strictly prohibited. All rights reserved.
This content is provided for test preparation purposes only and does not imply an endorsement by Mometrix of any particular political, scientific, or religious point of view.

who shows signs of psychopathology, such as schizophrenia, may take the MMPI before school personnel begin to investigate a possible diagnosis of serious mental illness.

The **WAISC-II** is an IQ test that many students will take at some point in their education. The results may tell those who interpret it at which level a student should be placed in academic coursework. IQ tests can also help reframe behavioral problems: a student may be acting out because the material is too difficult or out of boredom if the student's intellect is not being sufficiently challenged. The **Beck Depression Inventory** would not normally be administered to a student unless there is some concern that the student is suffering from depression.

Achievement Tests and Intelligence Tests

Intelligence tests provide a score for an individual student, and because intelligence is considered a stable quality, it rarely changes significantly across a lifetime. The student is primarily affected by IQ scores, which can determine whether he/she may be placed in an ordinary classroom, in special needs education, or in a gifted program. Because IQ is seen as fairly immutable, there is no particular attempt to increase IQ by way of additional coursework or special programs. The person affected by IQ assessment results is the test taker: no one is held accountable for a student's IQ score.

Achievement tests, also called high-stakes tests affect more than the individual test taker, although they also have an enormous effect on a student's career. The Stanford Achievement Test and the ACT determine whether a student will graduate high school, go to college, and which college will accept him/her. But achievement tests are also used to evaluate teacher performance and overall school ratings (hence the high stakes). The aggregate of students' achievement test scores can affect the funding or teacher allocation—the life or death of the entire school.

Interpretation of IQ Tests

IQ tests are formal, norm-referenced assessments that help educators understand where a student's academic intelligence falls on a continuum. IQ scores help establish students' correct placement in academic courses and can help identify whether there are unusual circumstances (developmental disability, learning-related neurological problems, or giftedness) that require different types of learning support. IQ tests are standardized, with a mean (average) score of 100 and a standard deviation of 15. The standard deviation is the average amount of error (hence, deviation) around the mean of a given population.

Because the tests are standardized, a student's derived IQ score is associated with a percentile: it can be plotted on a normal curve, using the standard deviation to determine where the score falls in comparison to the norm. It's possible to state with high confidence that a score of 130, for example, is two standard deviations above normal and places the student in the upper 95% of IQ scores. A score of 85 is an indicator of low IQ or borderline intellectual disability—far enough below normal to warrant special attention from the educational team.

Causation and Correlation

In scientific assessments, many different statistical factors may be related to an issue in question, usually indicating a **correlation.** Correlations between factors do not indicate which is an independent versus dependent variable, and often, correlations can be coincidental with no relation. There are often more than two factors to consider, which leads to other issues in identifying the cause. Statistical analysis can demonstrate only correlation strengths between two variables, but **causation** comes down to inference and logic. For instance, there is a correlation between ice cream melting when it is hot outside because hot days and ice cream melting coincide.

Copyright © Mometrix Media. You have been licensed one copy of this document for personal use only. Any other reproduction or redistribution is strictly prohibited. All rights reserved.
This content is provided for test preparation purposes only and does not imply an endorsement by Mometrix of any particular political, scientific, or religious point of view.

The correlation is very strong in this example; however, causation is not indicated by statistical overlap alone. In the same way, school counselors should be wary of assuming the causation of an effect in a student's life and instead look at the problem from multiple directions before implementing a solution.

Reliability

Test Conditions

Reliability is a measure of how often a particular score will be derived under the **same conditions**. Another word for reliability is **consistency.** The importance of conditions can't be overestimated. If you measure the height of a tree using a digital laser tape measure, assuming you use it correctly, you'll get the same height every time. If you climb the tree and measure it with a shoelace, chances are you'll get different numbers each time. If you have three glasses of wine, climb the tree, and measure it with your thumb, chances are you'll fall off before you get halfway up the tree—and if you do manage the climb, your numbers will be wildly inaccurate.

Reliability uses deviations in measurement to ask, "If we gave this test again under the same conditions, would the same test taker get the same score, and if not, how different would that score be?" A highly reliable test will give a very similar score under the same conditions.

Reliability in Assessment

The Stanford-Binet, the WAIS, and the WISC have been in use for many years, been given millions of times, and been revalidated many times over the years. Recent studies on the WAIS-IV show test-retest reliability scores of .70 to .90 on tests repeated between 2 and 12 weeks. (Test-retest reliability is reported on a scale of 0 to 1.0. A score of 1.0 would mean that the person taking the test would get the same score every single time.)

Internal consistency reliability measures whether items that purport to measure a construct actually do so. Items supposedly measuring the same thing are measured in terms of how highly they correlate with each other. In this measure of reliability, researchers aren't looking for extremely high scores (such as a Cronbach's alpha of .95+), indicating item redundancy. Low correlation between items (such as $\alpha<.30$) indicate that items are actually measuring different constructs—and have poor reliability.

Inter-scorer reliability determines how closely two scorers would grade the same essay, for example: obviously, if one scorer gives an essay 95% and another scorer gives it 30%, there is low inter-scorer reliability. The scoring system itself must also be reliable.

Validity

Validity asks, "Is this test measuring what it claims to measure?" Early IQ tests, for example, often measured whether a student was male or female, rich or poor, or black or white: wealthy, white male students invariably got higher IQ scores than other students. With rising consciousness of diversity, tests were reformulated, with items and subtests measured for construct validity. Some cultural biases will always exist (the expectation that we can measure intelligence with a written exam is one such bias), but with time, more and more test-taker diversity is included in the more valid tests.

Content validity determines whether individual items actually measure the construct. If, for example, an IQ test item actually measures preference for the color blue, and we know that liking blue isn't related to one's intelligence, that item diminishes the content validity of the test.

Copyright © Mometrix Media. You have been licensed one copy of this document for personal use only. Any other reproduction or redistribution is strictly prohibited. All rights reserved.
This content is provided for test preparation purposes only and does not imply an endorsement by Mometrix of any particular political, scientific, or religious point of view.

Criterion and concurrent validity measures whether the measure (test) is highly correlated with other measures of the same construct. For example, does a high IQ test score predict academic success (criterion), and does it correlate highly with the score of the same student on another IQ test (concurrent)?

Ethical Requirements Related to Administration of Assessments

Confidentiality is an important consideration for the **administration of assessments** of groups and of individuals. In administering a group test, students will naturally know who took the test, but in cases in which an individual student is taking an assessment, it is preferable to plan the test taking to be as private as possible, so the student doesn't feel singled out and other students don't notice. Confidentiality of scores and interpretations is a vital part of protecting students as well.

Ethical guidelines remind counselors not to overstep the scope of their competence: if one has not been trained in the administration and/or interpretation of a particular assessment, a more experienced professional should be chosen.

Choosing well-constructed assessments is an ethical responsibility as well: school counselors should investigate assessments in terms of their cultural, economic, or gender biases before assuming the assessments fairly measure students from diverse backgrounds.

Nonacademic Formal and Informal Assessments

Assessments should never be given in the absence of a reason. If a child is having trouble that seems to be related to poor academic performance or is clearly personal, assessments may be used before deciding on interventions to try to determine where the problem lies. Students who are bullying or being bullied or who are showing signs of stress, depression, anxiety, or substance abuse may be candidates for **formal and informal assessments** covering nonacademic life factors. Some formal assessments of personality, emotional, and behavioral conditions may include the Meyers-Briggs Type Indicator (MBTI), Lazarus's BASIC ID, and Cameron and Turtle-Song's SOAP notes.

Components of the BASIC ID assessment help the counselor see the client holistically through the following categories: behavior, affect, sensation, imagery, cognition, interpersonal relationships, drugs and diet. **SOAP** notes are organized to help with case conceptualization:

- **S**ubjective observation—client reports and school counselor's observations
- **O**bjective observation—client orientation, physical appearance, and behaviors in face-to-face sessions
- **A**ssessment—a general idea of the client's current thinking, feeling, and social interactions
- **P**lan—treatment plans, including possible referrals

IQ Scores of Children Considered for Special Needs Education, Regular Classrooms, or Gifted Child Programs

IQ scores below 85 are one standard deviation below the norm. Although no one would recommend basing a move to a special needs program on one IQ test score, a score below 85 would ring alarm bells and indicate a need for further investigation. A score between 85 and 100 might make a school counselor pay attention to whether the student has physical, intellectual, emotional, or social needs that aren't being met or is experiencing life stressors that are seriously affecting the ability to concentrate or retain information. The "normal" IQ range is between 100 and 115, and students with scores over 115 may be considered for inclusion in gifted programs. Students who experience behavioral problems but obtain high IQ scores may need to be moved to more

Copyright © Mometrix Media. You have been licensed one copy of this document for personal use only. Any other reproduction or redistribution is strictly prohibited. All rights reserved.
This content is provided for test preparation purposes only and does not imply an endorsement by Mometrix of any particular political, scientific, or religious point of view.

challenging coursework, or to life situations that ask more of them, to prevent boredom and burnout. But whatever a student's IQ score, school personnel should keep in mind that IQ tests don't necessarily measure emotional intelligence or other forms of intelligence beyond the traditional language and math skills. Extremely bright students may lack vital intelligences in terms of communication, social skills, or empathy that less "intelligent" students may have.

Copyright © Mometrix Media. You have been licensed one copy of this document for personal use only. Any other reproduction or redistribution is strictly prohibited. All rights reserved.
This content is provided for test preparation purposes only and does not imply an endorsement by Mometrix of any particular political, scientific, or religious point of view.

Meeting Individual, Group, and Schoolwide Needs

Guidance and Counseling

Responsibilities of Counselors to School Communities and Individual Students

It is important to remember that the primary responsibility of the counselor is to the student body and the school community as a whole. This community includes parents, teachers, the student body and even other counselors. Within this context, counselors can and should strive to address the needs of individual students who will most benefit from individual counseling, particularly as it relates to their academic development and success. The counselor's role is to assess individual students to determine if one-on-one counseling would be beneficial, and then to implement it when appropriate. If a counselor feels a student is in need of additional therapy or therapy outside of the academic context, it is recommended that the student be referred to external agencies or other appropriate services.

Criteria to Be Addressed in Individual Sessions

The school counselor should try to schedule sessions at times that are **least intrusive** to the academic day. The counselor should also be sensitive to student nuances: for instance, some students may be **more receptive** after school hours than during the middle of the day. Within each session, the counselor needs to honor the **particular needs of the student** while developing and implementing therapeutic goals. It is important to consider a student's developmental or situational hindrances. Furthermore, the counselor should develop a rubric for assessing the success of the therapy.

Counseling Adolescents

Counseling approaches and intervention strategies need to be determined and assessed within the context of developmental theory. In other words, counselors should be familiar with the different stages of development in adolescents, including the **appropriate behaviors for this particular age group**. Counselors may dismiss behaviors that would be unacceptable for an adult, but **perfectly normal for an adolescent**. Conversely, if a child is exhibiting behavior that is not typical of his or her age group, this may need to be addressed in the counseling session. Furthermore, counselors developing intervention strategies should be mindful of the range of reasonable expectations within an age group. It is important that counselors enter each session with an understanding of the age group of the student, referring to outside resources for that information if necessary.

Establishing a Rapport Between Counselor and Student

Because of the importance students place on peer relationships, they are often less receptive to recommendations or inquiries from adults. It is important for the counselor to **develop a relationship of trust** with the student. One strategy is for the counselor to listen carefully to the student's perception of a situation in order to develop and convey an attitude of empathy. Likewise, once a counselor has researched a student's background and situation or precipitating event, it is important to refrain from developing biases or expectations based on this research alone. Listening to the student's experiences and perceptions will allow the counselor to form a more realistic and comprehensive approach to resolution. As the counselor and student develop a history of tackling a

Copyright © Mometrix Media. You have been licensed one copy of this document for personal use only. Any other reproduction or redistribution is strictly prohibited. All rights reserved.
This content is provided for test preparation purposes only and does not imply an endorsement by Mometrix of any particular political, scientific, or religious point of view.

situation in tandem, the counselor will not only encounter less resistance from the student, but also will benefit from the student's collaboration.

General and Age-Specific Strategies

With all age groups, it is important for the counselor to listen attentively, and to refrain from judgmental or negative behaviors or comments. With specific age groups, there are particular activities that can facilitate the **establishment of a trust relationship** between counselor and student. For younger children, playing and creative activities can provide a rich medium for developing rapport. Students in middle childhood and adolescence also can develop a solid relationship with a counselor by playing sports or other games. Counselors should be versed in an array of **rapport-building strategies** in order to apply the best strategies for each student. Other strategies include drawing, collage-making, and writing on a board. Counselors can facilitate the therapeutic benefit of these activities by isolating and discussing particular pictures or words, always remembering to be attentive and respectful to the student.

Responding to Student Resistance

It is important to remember that the student has been referred to the counselor in most cases. Not only is the student not motivated to work with the counselor, but often is confused and suspicious of the purpose of the session. Counselors need to be sensitive to this apprehension by not immediately tackling the situation for which the student has been referred. One approach is to allow the student to begin talking to the counselor about an innocuous subject, such as objects in the room. This will sometimes help the student to feel more comfortable in the counseling environment, as well as to alleviate the feeling that he or she is the subject of a therapeutic spotlight.

Counseling a Self-Referral

In some cases, students will **refer themselves for counseling**. In this scenario, the counselor should experience less resistance from the student. However, there are nonetheless **legal and ethical issues to be considered**. It is first important to refer to government and school regulations regarding self-referral. One of the issues to be addressed is when and how to obtain parental consent. Limits of confidentiality in counseling a minor student need to be thoroughly researched and clarified before the counseling sessions, whether it is an individual or a group session. A counselor should be cognizant of all of the considerations and ramifications of working with a student who self-refers before meeting with the student, and in fact may decline the session based on findings.

Explaining Counselor's Role to Students

Counselors are responsible for **explaining their role in the session**. This explanation can and should serve to establish a relationship of trust and collaboration with the student. It is important for counselors to be sensitive to a student's age when explaining their role. In other words, for a younger student, the counselor might begin the discussion with by explaining that he or she wants to help the student feel better, whereas for an adolescent this type of explanation could easily be deemed condescending. For adolescent students, it might be advisable to first begin by asking the student of his perception of the goals and purposes of counseling, and then proceeding by clarifying the student's response. Counselors will often also be responsible for explaining the role of counseling to parents.

Copyright © Mometrix Media. You have been licensed one copy of this document for personal use only. Any other reproduction or redistribution is strictly prohibited. All rights reserved.
This content is provided for test preparation purposes only and does not imply an endorsement by Mometrix of any particular political, scientific, or religious point of view.

Topics Appropriate for Various Age Groups

As a part of a comprehensive counseling program that addresses specified needs, counselors should include topics that are generally **relevant to particular age groups**. Some of these age-specific topics are:

- For elementary students - Students in this age group are dealing with issues related to friendships, family roles, problem solving, social behaviors, success in school, expressing emotions, and self-esteem.
- For middle school students - Middle school students are particularly embroiled in issues relating to body image, interpersonal relationships, social skills, conflict management, social roles, diversity issues, self-esteem, transitioning to a new school, and academic development.
- For high school students - As students are preparing to become adults, topics that are most relevant are career exploration and planning, dating protocol, intimate relationships, self-identity, assertiveness training, stress management, and time management.

Although many of these topics overlap age groups, counselors need to be cognizant of the level of development present in the particular student group or population.

Determining Group Size and Length of Sessions

Both **group size** and **session length** are primarily determined by the age and developmental level of the participants. One of the key deciding factors is the ability of certain age groups to focus on a topic for a specific period of time. Since younger elementary children have shorter attention spans, a rule of thumb for them is to have group sessions last about 20 minutes, with about 5 members in the group. Older elementary students (roughly grades 4 through 6) can meet for periods ranging from 30 to 45 minutes, in groups of 7 or so. High school students will benefit from an expanded length of session, but still will fare better in smaller groups. The ideal group size for high school students is 6 to 8, meeting for 40 to 50 minutes. If a counselor feels that a particular group could extend the recommended time or group size, he or she should refer to research regarding both the topic and the group size.

Considerations Regarding Group Size

Group dynamics are very much influenced by the **size of the group**. There need to be enough participants to provide **feedback and support** as appropriate, but not such a large group that **individuals are ignored** or that **focus becomes dissipated**. In addition to consulting published standards regarding ideal group sizes for every age group, counselors can determine effective group sizes by considering the age or developmental level of the group. One important factor is the relative attention spans of the participants. The topic being addressed is also a factor. Sometimes the therapeutic strategy to be implemented will determine group size. Finally, counselors should consider the individual participants in the group, including their modes and likelihood of participation, when determining group size.

Scheduling Group Counseling Sessions

It is important to remember that the responsibility of the school counselor is simultaneously for the student as well as the school community. Because of that, the counselor should work with school personnel and school schedules when **developing counseling schedules**. This is particularly pivotal in high school and middle school because counseling sessions that are scheduled at the same time of day will interrupt the same class repeatedly. Collaboration with teachers and other school personnel is probably the best approach; the counselor should solicit their input about the best and worst times to schedule counseling sessions, for instance by avoiding sessions on days

Copyright © Mometrix Media. You have been licensed one copy of this document for personal use only. Any other reproduction or redistribution is strictly prohibited. All rights reserved.
This content is provided for test preparation purposes only and does not imply an endorsement by Mometrix of any particular political, scientific, or religious point of view.

when standardized tests are administered. Beyond that, it is always a good idea to **stagger group counseling sessions**, especially in the middle school or high school setting, although this may be necessary in an elementary school also, if indicated by the teachers.

Selecting Group Members

Role of Demographics

While it is not always indicated for counselors to specifically focus on **demographics when choosing group participants**, it is nonetheless a good idea to be aware of how the demographics relate to the topics being addressed. Sometimes the referral process might result in a default group of students that is primarily one gender or one ethnicity. Although there are no definitive rules about this, it is often a good idea to include a spectrum of cultures and mix of genders in a group setting. This is true when working with all age groups, but especially so when working with adolescent students. This often allows students to address personal and social skills in a mixed group, within the controlled environment of the counseling session. Younger children may be more comfortable in a group of their own gender. Of course, if the topic relates to culture- or gender-specific topics, then the group should be comprised of student falling within the specified category.

Role of Topics

Selecting group members based on topic can be approached somewhat holistically, since topics may be interrelated. However, the group members will want to experience similarities and empathy among themselves. For instance, if the topic being addressed is dealing with authority, the group may include students who stay out after curfew as well as students who are perpetually late to class. Students whose parents are divorced may relate to students who recently moved from their home town, since all of them are dealing with separation issues and disenfranchisement. Nonetheless, if students are in fact dealing with the same issues, there may be enough diversity in personal coping skills to comprise a dynamic group. In terms of age similarities, it is a good idea to have students in a group who are within the same age group or developmental level, although a small spectrum of emotional maturity can provide the interactive component that is valuable in a group setting.

Recruiting and Screening Students

The primary considerations for **selecting** and **screening students** for group counseling are the willingness and capacity of the student to participate in a therapeutic group setting. Students may be self-referred, or they may be referred by parents, teachers, and other students. While self-referral indicates the student's willingness to participate, the other types of referrals indicate the need for counselors to screen students to see if they are amenable to group counseling. All students should be screened for capability to participate in a group setting, and to determine if a group counseling format would be beneficial for them. In general, the counselor should consider the parameters of the group setting, which include both speaking and listening, respecting confidentialities and differences among its members, as well as other components of the group format. Some counselors prefer to have individual meetings with potential members before the first group meeting; others devote the first meeting to information and screening.

Soliciting Participation in Group Counseling

Finding appropriate members for a counseling group can be accomplished through a combination of advertising and referrals. Of course, counselors should have a profile of the groups that would be relevant and beneficial for a particular student body. This information can be obtained during conversations and other interactions with students and school staff. Often, this input will include the referral of specific students and the request for group sessions focusing on particular topics. Once the need for a group has been indicated, counselors can **solicit additional members** with

Copyright © Mometrix Media. You have been licensed one copy of this document for personal use only. Any other reproduction or redistribution is strictly prohibited. All rights reserved.
This content is provided for test preparation purposes only and does not imply an endorsement by Mometrix of any particular political, scientific, or religious point of view.

notices in newsletters, flyers, word of mouth, or by talking with students, groups of parents, or school personnel. The counselor should specify the topic to be addressed, the philosophy and general format of group counseling, and the proposed times for the sessions.

Screening Process

A good way to begin the **screening process** is for the counselor to give the student an overview of the group counseling format. This overview should include the purpose of the group; the roles and expectations of the members; and the role and expectations of the counselor. The counselor should provide an opportunity for the student to ask questions, and to express any concerns or anxieties he or she has about the group format. In the context of this conversation, the counselor should look for indications that the student is either likely or unlikely to be able to participate in a group setting. Some of these indications relate to the student's ability to follow the rules of the group; his or her ability to attend, participate, and contribute in the group setting; his or her emotional capability to participate; and, lastly, his or her willingness to participate.

Options for Students Initially Deemed Unsuitable for Group Counseling

Students who are unsuited to the group counseling format may be referred to individual counseling. Although some students referred to individual counseling may never participate in group counseling, others may transition from individual to group counseling. For these students, the counselor will want to make a determination of readiness based on specific criteria. He or she then should communicate to parents the recommendation and the factors that indicate the student's readiness for group counseling. The intent, format, and expectations of the group setting should be distinguished from those of individual counseling. Counselors should refer to school policy regarding additional procedures to follow when transitioning a student in this manner. Also, students referred into group counseling from individual counseling should sign a consent form indicating their understanding of, readiness for, and commitment to the group setting.

Guidelines and Expectations of Group Counseling

Once the members of a group are selected and brought together, at either the first meeting or a pre-meeting, the counselor should give an overview of the **guidelines and expectations of group counseling**. This first meeting or pre-meeting will define the individual members as a group brought together for a purpose. As a collaborative group, students can be given a presentation of the ground rules in group counseling, and can then individually sign forms of understanding and consent. These ground rules can include the importance of commitment, issues of conduct, and the importance of respect and confidentiality. It is significant that they agree to these ground rules as a group, since they will be implementing them as a group, with the counselor as facilitator. The counselor can also talk about group expectations, and allow members to voice their individual concerns and expectations.

Group Ground Rules

Ground rules in a group counseling setting serve to bond the members in a unity of conduct and purpose. When reviewing ground rules, it is helpful to solicit input from the members, allowing them to participate in the establishment of the ground rules. **Rules also contribute to a healthy and productive dynamic** in a group setting. Lastly, rules can provide and ensure a sense of safety and trust in the counseling environment. Some typical rules which address these issues include, but are not limited to:

- Give respect to the counselor and other members by listening attentively and without interruption.
- Be willing to participate and contribute by sharing feelings and experiences.

Copyright © Mometrix Media. You have been licensed one copy of this document for personal use only. Any other reproduction or redistribution is strictly prohibited. All rights reserved.
This content is provided for test preparation purposes only and does not imply an endorsement by Mometrix of any particular political, scientific, or religious point of view.

- Respect the experiences, perspectives and backgrounds of the other members.
- Maintain confidentiality. (Although confidentiality cannot be legally mandated for group members as it is for counselors, it is nonetheless effective to have members include a commitment to confidentiality in their overall consent to the ground rules.)

Multi-Faceted Role of Group Counselor

The counselor in a group setting must balance and maintain healthy and productive **group dynamics**. This includes attending to both the group as a whole and to the individual members. The counselor needs to be sensitive to the **levels of participation** within the group, ensuring **fairness** and eliciting **contributions** from all members. He or she should be available for consultation regarding any concerns, and should act as the overseer and reminder of the ground rules. Counselors should facilitate the interaction of the members toward the benefit of each of the members. This may involve working with a resistant student, or intervening when there is negative, unproductive behavior. The counselor in a group setting can encourage group dynamics, while honoring the individual needs of the members. He or she should also strive toward a more integrated and self-regulating group through encouragement and guidance.

Maintaining the Group's Focus

Counselors in a group setting need to be particularly sensitive to the possibility of the group becoming **distracted** and **losing focus on the topics and goals**. Although the counselor should be flexible in order to meet the individual needs of the participants, he or she also needs to maintain the focus and progress of the group as a whole. One of the early safeguards against distraction is clear communication to the members, parents, and school staff about the purpose and goals of the group; therapeutic format; and process of resolution in a group setting. **Defining and reviewing the goals** and parameters of the group with participants is also helpful. It is important for counselors to be well-versed in the basic tenets of group dynamics in a therapeutic setting.

Counseling Theory and Developmental Theory in Group Counseling

Since school counselors are working with students of different ages and developmental levels, they need to be sensitive to any developmental issues that are relevant to counseling. When implementing group strategies, counselors may need to refine or revise their methodology in relation to the age group, or to the developmental level of the group members. Each age group has inherent developmental crises like separation anxiety, individuation, and self-worth, and counselors need to be sensitive to these crises in their topic-based strategies. A six-year-old will have different coping strategies than a fifteen-year-old, even though the problem for both may be divorce. These age-based sensitivities should not mitigate counseling strategies, but rather should make them more effective and readily received. Some therapeutic strategies that have been successful in the school setting are cognitive therapy, reality therapy, Adlerian therapy, and SFBC.

Importance of Being Knowledgeable About the Group Topic

Although a counselor will not have personal experience with every crisis treated in group therapy, it is nonetheless important for him or her to feel a sense of **empathy and recognition**. This allows students to feel safe, understood, and not isolated in their situation. Therefore, it is important for counselors to have a basic knowledge of the topics that will be addressed in group counseling. They should be able to discuss the processes and effects of such situations as divorce, teen parenting, stress management, poor academic performance, and peer pressure. It is also valuable to develop a cache of information and resources about particular topics that can be shared with students. Counselors can also recommend activities or anecdotes that relate to the student's situation. Combined, these not only provide the empathy of knowledge, but also can serve to assist and empower students toward resolution.

Copyright © Mometrix Media. You have been licensed one copy of this document for personal use only. Any other reproduction or redistribution is strictly prohibited. All rights reserved.
This content is provided for test preparation purposes only and does not imply an endorsement by Mometrix of any particular political, scientific, or religious point of view.

Multisensory Stimulation in Group Counseling

Students exposed to **multisensory stimulation** are found to be more engaged, responsive, and attentive. This is particularly valuable in a group setting, since one of the inherent weaknesses is the ease with which members can become distracted. Multisensory stimuli involve the mind and senses of children and adolescents, targeting **multiple intelligences**. This is particularly valuable in a group, which will be comprised of unique individuals with unique coping and learning styles. These stimuli provide the group with a comprehensive, experiential mode for addressing issues. Through the use of such creative and multisensory stimuli as puppets, music, drama, and movies, counselors can generate response and participation when broaching difficult topics. An added benefit is that students will forge positive associations between the topic and the creative stimuli. Various media, such as film, or puppets for younger audiences, can present a problem in a manner that may be more palatable than a lecture.

Developing a Knowledge of and Sensitivity to Cultural Differences

It is particularly common for counselors in a school setting to work with students from **varied cultural and ethnic backgrounds**. Knowledge of the **belief systems, perspectives, and sensitivities** of an array of cultures and ethnicities is invaluable when working with students from varied backgrounds, especially in a group setting. The foundation of this knowledge lies in recognition of the far-reaching influence of culture, as well as recognition of the personal biases and perceptions that the counselor might have. Counselors should be aware of how misunderstandings and miscommunications within the group could be related to **cultural differences**, and should work with the group to resolve these misunderstandings. In this context, students in the group can also gain an appreciation for different cultures.

Planning Sessions in Advance and Flexibility Within Sessions

It is the counselor's job to **maintain focus** on the topic, goals, and strategies each group session. Therefore, it is important for the counselor to **prepare in detail for each session**. This preparation should include a list of discussion topics, planned activities, and an informal agenda. Within the grid of this agenda, counselors will often allow time and **flexibility** for longer group discussion, particular concerns that might arise in the session, or individual responses or behaviors that may require extra time and attention. However, because of the preplanning and the agenda, counselors can redirect the group toward activities, specific discussion topics, and the goals of that particular session, in order to maintain the focus and progress of the group. The activities and discussion topics in each session are understood as part of a larger agenda outlining the long-term goals of the group.

Beginning Sessions of Group Counseling

Before tackling the topics and goals of a counseling group, facilitators should first establish the tenor of the group. In the **first session** or sessions, participants can become acquainted and share a bit about themselves. The counselor's role is to assist in **establishing a safe environment**. It is important that participants feel a sense of camaraderie with the other group members. Throughout the remainder of the sessions, they will be sharing personal insights and experiences as well as addressing possibly difficult topics. Therefore, this initial introductory period is vital in developing a close and collaborative group. During these first sessions, the counselor can review the purpose of the group, ground rules for participation, and the importance of confidentiality, all of which will serve to establish a safe and controlled environment.

Copyright © Mometrix Media. You have been licensed one copy of this document for personal use only. Any other reproduction or redistribution is strictly prohibited. All rights reserved.
This content is provided for test preparation purposes only and does not imply an endorsement by Mometrix of any particular political, scientific, or religious point of view.

Middle Sessions of Group Counseling

Although particular activities will vary between groups, and especially between different age groups, there are similarities that all will share. Counselors should establish a relatively standard routine for the **middle sessions**, during which the group will be pursuing their goals most intensely. A good idea for each session is to include an initial greeting of the members, in order to **reinforce each member's importance** and contributions. Counselors can briefly review the ground rules and guidelines during the early part of the session. A **review of the previous session's events, activities, and accomplishments** is recommended. Counselors can then focus the group's attention on the current topic and a preplanned activity or discussion designed for that session. As the session draws to a close, counselors can briefly review the session's activities and insights, and establish a regular routine for ending the session.

Ending Sessions of Group Counseling

Developing a structure for the **closing sessions** of group counseling require a different focus than the beginning or middle sessions. The closing sessions **review accomplishments** as a group and anticipate individual futures. There will necessarily be a refocus and possibly some apprehension. Counselors should announce the upcoming final session at least three meetings in advance. An important component in the final session or sessions is a review of the initial goals, and the reminder of the achievement of those goals. Counselors should take this time to empower and encourage participants to remember their newly discovered skills and insights, and to apply them to future situations. Time should be allowed for participants to express feelings and for leaders or other group members to respond to those feelings.

Components

Particularly in the closing sessions, counselors should refer to a defined **listing of topics and issues to be addressed**, in order to facilitate a healthy transition. Although the particular modes and media may differ between ages and topic groups, the following are key components to consider when structuring a closing session:

- Review of the initial goals from the first meetings.
- Review of the accomplishment of those goals in subsequent meetings.
- Review of strategies, resources, and activities experienced during the sessions.
- Validation of growth and new insights of the participants throughout the sessions.
- Direction for incorporating this growth and insight in future activities and behaviors.
- An opportunity to address any unfinished business or lingering concerns.
- An opportunity for the group to respond to unfinished business or lingering concerns.
- Allowance of substantial time for personal goodbyes.
- Counselors may also want to schedule a post-meeting for evaluation purposes.

Completing Group Meeting Evaluations

In order to assess the effectiveness of the group sessions, counselors should complete an **evaluation** at the end of each meeting. The format of these evaluations will in large part determine the kind of information that will be returned. If counselors are looking for the group response to particular components of the sessions, such as the scheduling or the structure, a multiple-choice or graded-response format can be used. The results of these surveys will be more quantitative and focused. Another model is that of questions or open-ended sentences that ask participants how they felt about a session, such as "my favorite part of the session was…".These types of survey instruments can provide more qualitative information, as well as provide an ongoing profile of

Copyright © Mometrix Media. You have been licensed one copy of this document for personal use only. Any other reproduction or redistribution is strictly prohibited. All rights reserved.
This content is provided for test preparation purposes only and does not imply an endorsement by Mometrix of any particular political, scientific, or religious point of view.

participant satisfaction and involvement. Counselors may also provide pre- and post-surveys to parents and school staff, as well as post-surveys to participants several weeks after the last session.

Situations Calling for Individual Counseling Instead of Group Counseling

Individual counseling would be chosen over group counseling when the **student's problems are severe** enough that paying attention to the student takes priority over investigating or changing how the student interacts with others. When a student is in a personal crisis, if he/she has been bullied at school, if the student is working with problems that are long-standing, group work will not be helpful and may even cause harm. Students struggling with issues related to trauma or current or past abuse should not be placed in groups.

When people are fragile, individual therapy is usually the best course of action as it removes the added complications of dealing with others.

In general, if a student is highly resistant to the idea of group work, it may be better to avoid it. Groups are usually short term, and working against resistance or outright sabotage from highly resistant members may take all the resources of the group and leader, with no appreciable results.

Individual Counseling for Bullied Children

Counseling research has shown again and again that when counseling works, it is primarily due to the strength of the counseling relationship. **Establishing trust is crucial** in any counseling relationship, and with children who have experienced **bullying**, the adult world has already let them down—trust is greatly diminished, and children are traumatized. Children who have experienced bullying need the support and encouragement of an adult who cares for them while teaching them about how to set and defend their own boundaries. In group counseling, the counselor's attention and support are distributed among all the members of the group, and a child whose self-esteem has been damaged will be less likely to connect and thrive as a group member.

Bullying is part of a loop, and bullied children often need training in emotional and verbal self-defense on a **one-on-one-basis** to develop the skills and confidence to participate in a group.

Group Work with Children in Crisis

When children have experienced the same type of crisis, group work can facilitate healing—and in some cases, the need for **responsive service** to a recent disaster requires group work when there aren't enough counselors to provide individual services. Children who have experienced a natural disaster, or who have all suffered a similar loss or family situation such as divorce, can be formed into a group based on their similar experience. The fact that others have been through the same experience provides validation of feelings and the opportunity to learn how to empathize with and support each other. Group leadership must be strong enough to act as a container and prevent members from becoming overwhelmed by their own feelings and the stress of the current situation.

There are **limitations to group work** with children who have experienced trauma. Those whose boundaries have been violated in various ways may not have the ego strength or the capacity for trust to benefit from group work. Anyone who is seriously decompensating is not capable of group work. Counselors must vet potential members carefully and prepare placements in individual therapy for those too fragile for group.

Appropriate Situations for Group Work with Students

Psychoeducational groups are helpful when students need to combine practical learning with more subjective experiences in the emotional realm. Groups are helpful in teaching study skills, stress or anger management techniques, and life skills such as organization and time management.

Copyright © Mometrix Media. You have been licensed one copy of this document for personal use only. Any other reproduction or redistribution is strictly prohibited. All rights reserved.
This content is provided for test preparation purposes only and does not imply an endorsement by Mometrix of any particular political, scientific, or religious point of view.

Putting a group together based around a goal more concrete than "feeling" work can do two things at once: achieve the concrete goal (such as learning a set of study skills for college entrance examinations) and give students an experience of working in a group—a skill set that can serve them in various situations all their lives.

Groups helping students address **cognitive-behavioral challenges** like test anxiety and social skills building can maximize resources and help many students at one time. Groups are appropriate for teaching skills, and students can help each other learn. Students can bond, form friendships, and practice emotionally intelligent skills, like empathy, active listening and providing support and encouragement. Students also practice mature skills such as maintaining confidentiality, resolving conflicts in the group, and being peer mentors to each other.

Academic Advising Using a Pychoeducational Group Model

Group advising is most effective with students of a similar age or grade who have similar interests. After taking a career inventory, for example, a group of students with a particular common interest could be identified and formed around the concept of career exploration in their common areas of interest. Students might pair up to investigate and report to the group on particular careers, even going so far as to determine the best course to take after high school to enter the career. Colleges, trade schools, and universities might be identified based on their study programs, financial aid opportunities, and postgraduate employment statistics.

Students who are particularly interested in a certain occupational path could be encouraged to come together to study for placement exams, participate in field trips, create projects, or build portfolios for later applications. Using the energy of the group and its interests, the school counselor can take a role as facilitator and advocate, allowing students to work as a group and only stepping in to assist in conflict or "stuckness."

Schoolwide Assemblies

Schoolwide assemblies may be a necessary response to a variety of circumstances that affect a large number of students within the student body. These kinds of circumstances can take the form of behavioral issues, tragedy, urgent new policies, or any other reason that the school as a whole is affected. When the target subject of an assembly is a sensitive topic, such as the death of a student, drugs, violence, or some other responsive matter, the counselor should speak gently and broadly, without bringing up the impacts on a specific student. School counselors should remain ethical and produce an air of safety when discussing a topic in front of the student body. Student assemblies should also be held as a gateway or informational setting in which students are reminded about paths they can use to get help when needed. Because schoolwide assemblies are generally used to open the doors for further services, clear presentation of contact information is particularly important so that students can know how to follow up.

Peer Mediation

In **peer mediation**, students help each other resolve interpersonal problems using peaceful interventions. **Peer helping programs** teach students the skills that build **character education**; empathy, integrity, respect, and honesty are pieces of the constellation that make up good character. In peer mediation, students learn how to listen empathically, communicate respectfully, handle difficult emotions, and solve problems. Peer mediation is a group process requiring more than two people. **Conflict resolution** is the primary purpose of peer mediation, and peer mediation programs have been shown to reduce school violence. Those who participate in peer helping programs are developing deep areas of emotional learning that too often go ignored in education—making them better citizens, more responsible family members and friends, and stronger, more

Copyright © Mometrix Media. You have been licensed one copy of this document for personal use only. Any other reproduction or redistribution is strictly prohibited. All rights reserved.
This content is provided for test preparation purposes only and does not imply an endorsement by Mometrix of any particular political, scientific, or religious point of view.

caring human beings. Aside from the great good of building a peaceful, accepting school community and keeping each other safe, they are learning skills that will serve them anywhere they go in life.

Copyright © Mometrix Media. You have been licensed one copy of this document for personal use only. Any other reproduction or redistribution is strictly prohibited. All rights reserved.
This content is provided for test preparation purposes only and does not imply an endorsement by Mometrix of any particular political, scientific, or religious point of view.

Roles of the School Counselor

Transformed Role of the School Counselor

The **role of the school counselor** has broadened and integrated, so that the goals and delivery of the counseling program dovetail with those of the **school as a whole**. School counselors as educators recognize that school curriculum delivery and achievement standards are quantifiable media to address the access, attainment, and achievement goals of each individual student as well as the student body as a whole. Counselors also frame their approach with a basic premise that students who are given rigorous curricula and good support are capable of realizing their potential. Besides leading individual sessions and group workshops, counselors can participate in academic program planning. By **integrating educational and counseling goals**, counselors can provide the bridge between personal success and academic achievement. The counseling program can provide immediate assessment that describes the holistic achievement of the students.

Development of School Counseling

Until the 1940s, school guidance counseling was primarily focused on **helping students choose vocations** suited to their personality traits. In the 1940's, Carl Rogers instigated a change in the professional focus from vocational to **individual counseling**. In the 1950s, professional organizations appeared, setting standards for school counseling training and the profession. The **National Defense Education Act**, a reaction to the start of the Cold War, changed the focus back to vocation as the U.S. government provided funding to increase the number of scientists and mathematicians in the arms race. In the 1960s and 1970s, the focus again shifted to **individual support and developmental guidance**. In 1987, a journal article defining the perception of school counseling as unnecessary prompted the profession to take on a holistic focus and to create national standards for training school counselors and for the professional activities of school counselors, in effect saving itself from becoming obsolete by both increasing its professional scope and taking an active interest in promoting and advocating for the profession.

Promoting Parental Involvement

Parents are often hesitant about getting involved in school functions because they often feel that they are not important and that their opinions do not count. In some cases parents may have had a negative experience involving a principal or other school official. It is the responsibility of the counselor to **make parents feel valued and important** before discussing any type of involvement. An effective counselor knows the **value of parental involvement** and realizes that they must invite, recruit, and motivate all parents to get involved. When these efforts do not work, a counselor may have to offer incentives or rewards in order to get parents to take the first step toward involvement. Involving a parent does not mean they have to speak in public or put on a carnival; it could be as simple as donating time to repair something in the school.

Characteristics to Promote When Building a School Culture

When a counselor is striving to **build a school culture**, it is important to promote certain characteristics. School culture consists of everyone: teachers, students, parents, and other staff members. One of the important traits is attention to the values of the members. One sign of an effective culture is the behavior of the members: that is, whether or not they are positive and upbeat. Another sign is whether teachers, students, and parents are interacting in a positive and effective way. A strong culture also respects the written and unwritten policies and procedures. In order for the counselor to truly understand the school's culture, they should take the time to perform group interviews, in order to accurately understand the issues of the school.

Copyright © Mometrix Media. You have been licensed one copy of this document for personal use only. Any other reproduction or redistribution is strictly prohibited. All rights reserved.
This content is provided for test preparation purposes only and does not imply an endorsement by Mometrix of any particular political, scientific, or religious point of view.

Responding to Negative Reactions to Authority

When a counselor is faced with a **negative reaction to authority**, his or her first reaction may be to become defensive or upset. However, the appropriate way to handle this situation is to **investigate** and **examine** the reasons why others are responding this way. This may be a difficult reaction to have for many counselors. The feelings of hurt and anger are normal: however, an effective counselor knows how to put those feelings away and move on to the problem-solving stage. The challenge to authority can be a positive situation, especially if the causes are understood. The key to diagnosing the reasons for the negative reaction is to have a **discussion with the parties involved**. Every effort should be made to avoid putting anyone on the defensive, and every attempt should be made to understand the person's point of view.

Exercising Authority Successfully

There are numerous reasons why people **question and challenge authority**. However, if a counselor follows certain guidelines, then this issue can be overcome. Counselors are obviously going to have to make some very difficult decisions and give directives to others. One consideration a counselor should decide on is how and in what style the directive will be given. It is important for a counselor to remember that regardless of how professional the directive was given, if the person who received it does not feel that it is in their best interest, there is going to be an issue of resistance. A counselor should also consider the strengths and weaknesses of the person before giving a directive. Issuing an order for someone who is not motivated will result in failure. They should also explain the rationale behind the directive and remember that not everyone may understand the value in it.

Importance of Self-Nurturing

Counselors have an extremely difficult job: they must motivate, coach, lead, attend meetings, and maintain the mission and goals of the school. These job duties can be rewarding; they can also be emotionally draining. Many times, this can cause **burn-out** among counselors, which can have a negative impact on the rest of the school. In order for a counselor to perform their responsibilities effectively, they must remember that they are individuals too, and take care of themselves. It is important for counselors to find a **healthy balance** between work and personal life. Sleep, relaxation, fitness, and a healthy diet will enable a counselor to be a well-adjusted person. When a counselor has found a way to balance their responsibilities, they become a healthier individual and a better role model for staff members, students, and parents.

Barriers to Effective Communication

Every message a counselor sends out will be interpreted in different ways by every person who receives it. Many times, the message will not be successfully communicated simply because of factors outside the control of the counselor. Often, a counselor will send out a message they believe is extremely important, only to find that the recipients do not share the same opinion. Sometimes, the person receiving the message lacks the background knowledge needed to understand the message. Certain phrases or words require a base of knowledge to be understood. Understanding the group who will be receiving the message can help the counselor determine how the message should be written in order to help reduce the misunderstanding.

Enhancing School Culture

Before a counselor can **enhance a school culture**, he or she must first achieve a good understanding and full knowledge of what the organizational culture is. After this has been achieved, the counselor can move on to enhancing the culture. If the school culture is not an effective one, it will be a challenge for the counselor to change it. The counselor must envision the

Copyright © Mometrix Media. You have been licensed one copy of this document for personal use only. Any other reproduction or redistribution is strictly prohibited. All rights reserved.
This content is provided for test preparation purposes only and does not imply an endorsement by Mometrix of any particular political, scientific, or religious point of view.

future of the school: what is the goal that will make the school improve? A counselor must also make it a priority to meet the needs of the teachers and students. Enhancing the school culture will more likely be achieved if the counselor views a problem as an opportunity to find solutions rather than as a burden. It will also be enhanced if teachers are encouraged to use creative practices and are given opportunities to share their ideas and made to feel they are a vital part of the improvement of the school. The most important factor that will enhance school culture is a relentless focus on student achievement.

Scope of Practice of a School Counselor

School counselors are not expected to engage in either diagnosis or long-term therapy with students. A student demonstrating out-of-the-ordinary behavioral problems of a complex nature is beyond the expertise level and **scope of practice** of a school counselor. Speaking to the parents will help give more context to the behavior and possibly shed light on potential causes and conditions: physical, social, or emotional. It is one of the ethical duties of a school counselor to inform and partner with parents in the care of children, and it's a practical first step in understanding familial conditions that may contribute to or potentially help solve the student's problem.

Referral to a psychologist for assessment and diagnosis is a logical next step, and having the child's physical health checked by a doctor helps rule out medical conditions that might be contributing to or causing the behavioral problems. Seeing that the student's problems are beyond his or her ethical remit, the obligation is to facilitate. Primarily, the school counselor, rather than attempting diagnosis or treatment him/herself, becomes the person who **liaises** with family, teachers, and other professionals, assembling a treatment team that takes over the continuing care of the student.

Handling Conflict Between Formal and Informal Leaders

When a school has a number of different leaders, there is a strong potential for **conflict**. There could be a disagreement on a wide variety of topics, and any type of conflict could make it harder for the counselor to build a unified organizational culture. The most important habit a counselor needs to cultivate is listening to both sides in order to understand the main issue of the conflict. There should be an opportunity for both the **formal and informal leaders** to voice their opinions and feel they are contributing. A counselor can use their influence to persuade one party of the direction that is more suitable to the overall school organizational culture. There is no one correct way of handling a situation like this; however, a counselor with strong conflict resolution skills can change a difficult situation.

Adolescent Risk Behaviors and HIV and AIDS

The Center for Disease Control asserts that a tendency to have unprotected sex and multiple sex partners places adolescents at a greater risk of contracting HIV and the AIDS virus. The risk seems to be especially high for minority adolescents. Individuals are considered to be at special risk of contracting HIV if they are regular substance abusers, do not have much awareness of the risks of HIV, come from a poor and/or uneducated background, or have dropped out of school. In order to combat this problem, the CDC has developed a number of programs to continue providing education to students in both classrooms and community centers. Many of these programs specifically target minorities.

Adolescent Risk Behaviors and Sexually Transmitted Infections

Because they are more likely to engage in **risky sexual activity** with multiple partners, adolescents are more likely to contract a sexually transmitted infection. The CDC believes that **adolescents are particularly at risk** if they are frequent drug users and if they do not have access to contraceptives or to sex education. In order to meet the ongoing needs, the CDC has developed programs to

Copyright © Mometrix Media. You have been licensed one copy of this document for personal use only. Any other reproduction or redistribution is strictly prohibited. All rights reserved.
This content is provided for test preparation purposes only and does not imply an endorsement by Mometrix of any particular political, scientific, or religious point of view.

present important information to adolescents so that they can protect themselves, as well as so that they can seek treatment if they do contract an STI. Part of the CDC's mission is to increase the level of parental involvement in the lives of adolescents. The CDC has published a number of statistics indicating that when parents actively supervise their children's lives, the children are less likely to engage in dangerous sexual behavior.

Addressing Child Abuse

Counselors are required by federal mandate to report any cases of **child abuse or neglect**. This is mandated by the Keeping Children and Families Safe Act of 2003. If a counselor or other professional has reason to believe that abuse or neglect has occurred within 24 to 72 hours, she or he is obligated to call **Child Protective Services (CPS)** and report orally and in writing their suspicions within a time frame specified by the state. Note that if a report proves false, the counselor/professional is not liable unless the report was made with malicious intent. Child abuse can include physical abuse, mental injury, sexual abuse or exploitation, maltreatment of a child under 18 or the age specified by the state child protection law, and negligent treatment. Counselors should be knowledgeable of state and other mandates regarding the report of child abuse.

HIPAA and FERPA Regulations

There are three key federal acts governing the disclosure of student records. The most significant is the **Family Educational Rights and Privacy Act** (**FERPA**) of 1974, which limits the disclosure of student records. The Privacy Rule of 2001 established national rights for privacy and security regarding health information, and these rights were in concert with FERPA. The **Health Insurance Portability and Accountability Act** (**HIPAA**) of 1996 generated national standards regarding the privacy of individually identified health information, set criteria for health records, and delineated patients' rights. Any school records, including health records, that are protected under FERPA are not subject to HIPAA regulations, however, educators in special education may be required to obtain the services of outside professionals whose services are governed by HIPAA. Counselors should be knowledgeable and aware of regulations regarding the exchange of student information and when exceptions to FERPA are warranted by HIPAA or other law.

Developing Teaching Plans

A teacher cannot be effective without **properly planning every aspect of class**. Good plans give a teacher confidence, security, and a definite direction in class. Teachers that are successful planners typically follow four steps when they plan an activity. First, they have a total understanding of the activity: what it will involve, what it is designed to teach, and what potential problems it might have. Next, the teacher imagines its implementation in the classroom, and makes whatever modifications to the environment are necessary. Then, the teacher evaluates the strengths and weaknesses of his or her class, and alters the activity to suit them. Finally, an effective teacher will create a mental image of the finished activity, and imagine exactly how it will be accomplished.

Case Studies

Teachers can effectively use **case studies** to solidify conceptual knowledge that has been taught in a particular unit. In a case study, the teacher provides specific information, and students are required to analyze and evaluate the information. For example, students might be presented with a business plan and asked to describe its strengths and weaknesses. When developing case studies, a teacher should make sure that the information is comprehensible to all the members of the class and that no untaught concepts are required to perform an adequate analysis. It is also important to limit the amount of information given: too much data may confuse students and detract from the power of the exercise. Finally, teachers should ensure that there are some areas of the assignment that require creative thought, rather than simply recitation of the course material.

Copyright © Mometrix Media. You have been licensed one copy of this document for personal use only. Any other reproduction or redistribution is strictly prohibited. All rights reserved.
This content is provided for test preparation purposes only and does not imply an endorsement by Mometrix of any particular political, scientific, or religious point of view.

Syllabus

A **syllabus** is essential for effectively organizing and administrating a class. Preparing a clear and detailed syllabus before the start of the school year allows teachers to be sure that all of the essential areas will be covered, that there will be enough variety among assignments to hold the interest of the class, and that all the students will understand the program and the expectations. A proper syllabus should include a defined aim for the course, clear assessment objectives, an outline of the assessment structure (that is, how students will be examined), the content of the curriculum, and a grading scale. The grading scale should include a sufficient description of the quality of work that merits each letter grade.

General Course Structure

Although there is no one way to order the material of a course, some ways seem to make more sense than others. For instance, most teachers will want to begin the course with an overview of the general themes of the course, so that students will have an idea of the **structure of the course** and will be prepared for its various transitions. This process is enacted in miniature at the beginning of each lesson, as the teacher describes the rough elements of the material that will be covered during the class period. In most courses, there is a sequential order that must be followed; for instance, some elements of geometry cannot be taught until algebra has been learned. In other subjects, however, as for instance literature, a teacher will have more freedom to arrange course material according to improvised themes or narratives.

Differentiation

In classes that consist of students with varying abilities, it is crucial for a teacher to practice **differentiation**: that is, distinguishing between students and adjusting the class material to engage all of them. This of course is a great responsibility for a teacher: more time must be spent planning, and teachers must guard against settling for lessons that appeal strictly to the middle level of the class. Besides differentiating between students, teachers must also differentiate between classes. Some classes may have a different "character" than others, depending on the time of day when they are held and their composition. Differentiation is especially important in classes, because they are frequently available to all students, regardless of aptitude.

Tips Concerning Assignments in Class

Teachers will typically assign students a task or series of tasks to solidify and assess learning. **Class assignments** encourage students to manipulate and analyze course material. When making assignments, teachers should make sure to have a clear idea of what knowledge they are seeking to reinforce. Assignments should have varying degrees of difficulty, such that the least able students can attempt everything and the most able students will feel challenged. If research is required to complete the assignment, the teacher should have established the means for the students to perform this research. Finally, teachers should always grade every particular part of an assignment separately, so that students will have a better idea of what is expected of them, and in what areas they need to improve.

Factors Indicating Effective Use of Affective Skills

Some of the factors that can be used to measure how well-developed an individual's **affective skills** are include determining how well the individual receives emotional stimuli and how well the individual responds to those stimuli. It is also important to determine how easy it is for the individual to acknowledge the worth of a particular situation, relationship, or individual and whether the individual has an organized and well-conceived value system. An individual's ability to receive and respond to emotional stimuli can be measured by how aware the individual is of a

Copyright © Mometrix Media. You have been licensed one copy of this document for personal use only. Any other reproduction or redistribution is strictly prohibited. All rights reserved.
This content is provided for test preparation purposes only and does not imply an endorsement by Mometrix of any particular political, scientific, or religious point of view.

particular stimulus, how willing the individual is to acknowledge that particular stimulus, and how focused the individual is on that stimulus. An individual's ability to assign value to a situation and uphold a value system can be measured by how motivated the individual is, how the individual behaves, and how consistent that individual's behavior is. For example, a student that always comes to class and clearly always pays attention may have well-developed affective skills.

Working Cooperatively with Other Educators and Mental Health Professionals

School districts may employ or call upon numerous **professionals** in the endeavor to provide **mental health services** to students. These may include psychologists, school nurses, social workers, crisis intervention counselors, as well as staff educators and administrators. School counselors often form a part of this larger network of mental health professionals on the school campus, working with the same population of students. It is in the counselor's and program's best interest that school counselors develop and maintain a spirit of cooperation when working with these diverse groups of mental health professionals. It is not advisable, nor is it generally successful, to generate an attitude of superiority or a hierarchical stance when working with other professionals. Remember that all of the groups and individuals involved are striving for the same goal: the mental health of the students. By working cooperatively and inclusively, counselors can benefit from the support and expertise of those in peripheral professional positions.

Expectations When Reporting Suspected Child Abuse

It is important to remember that the counselor is obligated to **report suspicion of child abuse**. Counselors who suspect child abuse and do not report it could lose their license or certification, face disciplinary action, and/or have their employment terminated. It is also significant to remember that an individual who reports reasonable suspicion of child abuse is not required to prove the abuse, but rather just to report suspicion. The law protects the individual who **reasonably suspects child abuse**. Also notable is that parents and guardians are not granted rights to information during this process, and should not be informed regarding the report. The department of social services and/or law enforcement agencies will contact the parents as appropriate and will conduct the investigation. Counselors should be knowledgeable about laws regarding child abuse, as well as school, district and other applicable procedures.

Copyright © Mometrix Media. You have been licensed one copy of this document for personal use only. Any other reproduction or redistribution is strictly prohibited. All rights reserved.
This content is provided for test preparation purposes only and does not imply an endorsement by Mometrix of any particular political, scientific, or religious point of view.

Addressing Specific Concerns

Concerns Addressed in Counseling

For concerns such as relationship issues, anger or stress management, family dynamics, sexual topics, and academic goals, the counselor acts as a **guide and mentor** for students in their academic, personal, and professional lives. Since students may be referred by school officials, family members, or other students, the counselor should anticipate varying levels of openness by the student and/or the family. It is vitally important for counselors to be trained in the strategies for recognizing and addressing issues in a manner that will capitalize on the counseling session to the maximum benefit of the student. The first step in this process is recognition of the key issue or issues, which may take more than one session to identify. Beyond that, counselors can use various strategies focusing on the particular situation as well as the idiosyncrasies of the student.

At-Risk Students

Factors and Behaviors

It is important for counselors to be aware of the **events and influences that place students at risk**, as well as the potential ramifications of unstable behavior and mental state. Counselors should be aware of **changes in student behavior** that may signal depression or other mental or emotional fragility. It is worth mentioning that the leading cause of death for young people is suicide, and therefore that counselors are in a pivotal position to notice and respond to these symptoms. Some students may need more intensive treatment than school counseling. Some of the factors that can contribute to emotional vulnerability for at-risk students are rising levels of poverty, substance abuse of the student or parents, domestic violence, and community violence. Other kinds of behavior problems may be a result of ADHD or other behavior disorders, and may indicate the need for the student to be referred to special education resources in the school.

Including Needs of At-Risk Students When Delivering Curriculum

Counselors are generally responsible for addressing the **academic** as well as the **career** and **social development** needs of students. To that end, they should be well versed in the areas of leadership, advocacy, systemic change, and collaboration. Also, they should develop and continually refine the skills to teach these subjects to diverse groups of students, including at-risk students. Within the category of at-risk students are included those students whose behavior and performance are a result of family or socioeconomic factors, as well as students who come from a more stable background but suffer from physiological disabilities.

At-Risk

Although the behaviors of at-risk students fall within a rather large spectrum, there is an umbrella definition that can be used to identify at-risk students. Generally speaking, if a student shows **decline in any or all of the areas of physical, mental, social, spiritual or economic health, then the student is considered at risk**. In addition, community and social circumstances may contribute to a student's sense of isolation, increasing the possibility of deterioration in one or more of these areas. Students who are at risk in any or all of these areas have a diminished likelihood of becoming productive members of society. Counselors are encouraged to refer to guidelines from professional organizations or literature to identify and appropriately respond to at-risk students. Counselors can provide the support, resources, and encouragement that can significantly mitigate deteriorating factors.

Copyright © Mometrix Media. You have been licensed one copy of this document for personal use only. Any other reproduction or redistribution is strictly prohibited. All rights reserved.
This content is provided for test preparation purposes only and does not imply an endorsement by Mometrix of any particular political, scientific, or religious point of view.

Cautions When Identifying a Student as At-Risk

There are **five key areas of caution** to consider when identifying a student as at-risk:

- Students who fall within the definition of at-risk may nonetheless be very resilient, with strong coping skills, and therefore at-risk may be a temporary status for that student.
- If a student is overtly and obviously treated differently than other students because of the at-risk designation, this may discourage creativity or confidence.
- The term *at-risk* can easily become a label rather than a status, in which case there is no mechanism to identify when the student is no longer at risk.
- The term *at-risk* by itself encompasses so many situations and behaviors that the response may be also very generalized and not address the issues specific to a particular student.
- Cultural factors should always be considered, as they may be contributing to or masking an underlying issue.

Difficulty of Assessing At-Risk Youth from Culturally Diverse Backgrounds

When a student is identified as at-risk, the identification is usually based on overt behaviors or shortcomings. These may include poor academic performance or inappropriate behavior. An initial assessment may point to the need for more native language materials or conflict resolution workshops. However, for some **first- or second-generation immigrants**, these outward circumstances may be noticeable, but **not the underlying or most problematic issue**. Often, the underlying issue can be masked by overt behaviors, until the need for treatment is long past due. Students from diverse cultures may be contending with issues related to isolation, sadness for loved ones left behind, bridging the gap between cultures, and other issues directly related to poor cultural assimilation. Although there are no clear guidelines for identifying such cultural factors, counselors should be aware of the possibility of precipitating circumstances when dealing with at-risk students from other cultures.

Peer Association

Adolescent students between the ages of 14 and 17 are particularly **susceptible to peer association and influence**. Youth in this age group generally gravitate to peer groups besides their family. Often, young people join groups that are formed around a common ethnicity. Unfortunately, if some of the members of the group engage in violent or illegal activities, those who join the group often mimic this activity in order to be accepted. Consequently, students who participate in violent behavior or drug use engage in a lifestyle that leads to the decline of their physical, mental, social, spiritual, and/or economic health, which places them clearly in the at-risk category. Although counselors need to refrain from making assumptions based on associations, they nonetheless should be aware of a student's associations, particularly as they relate to at-risk behaviors and attitudes.

Current and Declining Trends

Within a large student body, there will be a small percentage of students engaging in at-risk behaviors. Counselors should be on alert for this type of behavior. At-risk youth commit various **crimes** after school, generally between the hours of 3 and 8, and especially right after school. Robberies are sometimes committed by youth, usually during the week and usually after 9 p.m. Today's students still face problems with **premarital sex and unwanted pregnancies**, which can put them at significant risk of **poor academic performance**. However, the incidence of student suicide is on the decline, as are the incidences of students riding with drunk drivers and carrying weapons to school. Although these activities and behaviors still occur, counselors should be aware of rising and declining trends in at-risk behavior in order to be aware of the signs and symptoms associated with them.

Copyright © Mometrix Media. You have been licensed one copy of this document for personal use only. Any other reproduction or redistribution is strictly prohibited. All rights reserved.
This content is provided for test preparation purposes only and does not imply an endorsement by Mometrix of any particular political, scientific, or religious point of view.

Rejection of At-Risk Students by the School System

Students who are displaying at-risk behavior often pose a challenge to educators who are striving for academic success and good classroom management. The at-risk behavior can cause a disruption on both fronts. This can be exaggerated when there are multiple at-risk students in multiple class periods. Teachers and school counselors faced with this disruptive activity will first attempt to remedy the behavior using known strategies. However, if this proves unsuccessful and the disruptive, at-risk behavior continues, teachers may become discouraged and begin to **develop an attitude of complacency** about the behavior. This can grow into complacency about teaching in general. Consequently, faced with this possibility, counselors will sometimes make the decision to **remove a student or students from the school**. Unfortunately, this solves the short-term problem by creating a longer-term issue of underserved youth becoming unproductive adults. Counselors can provide a valuable service by preventing this downhill slide in at-risk youth.

Designing Programs for All Students to Benefit the Larger Community

Since schools are the primary focal point for issues relating to adolescents, counselors and educators often work with other **community entities** in discussing and developing strategies for **addressing the needs of youth**. Some of these entities are libraries, police departments, private schools, recreation centers, and other organizations. One of the ways that counselors can work as **liaisons between students and these entities** is by dispelling the idea that the burden of at-risk behavior lies with the student. They can work with community representatives who feel that students are solely or primarily to blame for their behavior. Counselors can collaborate with educators to develop programs that are designed to address the needs of not only mainstream students, but also at-risk students. These programs can incorporate the needs and concerns of the larger community as well as the academic goals identified for the student population.

Reasons Educators Have Not Addressed Needs of At-Risk Youth

Many educators have not addressed the needs of at-risk youth for some or all of the following five reasons:

- Funding has not been allocated for programs focusing on at-risk youth. Counselors can assist appropriate entitles in reevaluating the need for programs to address the needs of these students.
- Existing systems and programs do not include strategies for at-risk students, and changing the systems can be very challenging. Counselors can work with educators to overcome this challenge.
- There is an assumption that at-risk youth will always be at risk. Counselors can implement goal-setting strategies that guide and encourage at-risk students to adopt productive behaviors.
- Social and community groups usually do not have programs that focus on at-risk students. Counselors can increase awareness for the need to do so.
- Graduate programs do not always include pedagogy focusing on at-risk youth. Counselors can collaborate with their peers by educating each other about at-risk youth.

Government Funding and Allocations for Assisting At-Risk Youth

Federal and state departments of education and mental health have developed the 1967 **Elementary and Secondary Education Act (ESEA)**, which provides for continuing public education through grade 12. There is also funding allocation for disadvantaged children, focused on the goal of drug-free schools and available after-school care. The National Defense Education Act (NDEA) of 1958 authorized schools to hire counselors who encouraged students in the areas of math and science. Counselors and other educators who are committed to assisting at-risk youth can

Copyright © Mometrix Media. You have been licensed one copy of this document for personal use only. Any other reproduction or redistribution is strictly prohibited. All rights reserved.
This content is provided for test preparation purposes only and does not imply an endorsement by Mometrix of any particular political, scientific, or religious point of view.

find government support that relates to a guaranteed education for all youth, safer schools, and improved academic performance.

Counselor's Role After a School or Community Trauma

Numerous kinds of **trauma** can affect a student population, from individual crises to those affecting the entire student body. Counselors need to be aware of the types and levels of trauma and how they impact students. It is prudent for them to be aware of the possible ramifications of trauma, how to identify these effects, and the strategies for intervention. Counselors need to be aware of the scope of trauma, and the scope of the needed intervention. **School-wide traumas** can include natural disasters, school shootings, and widespread gang activity. **Individual traumas** can include family illness, depression, domestic abuse, and even suicide. Sometimes an individual crisis can escalate into a school-wide trauma like a school shooting or suicide. Counselors should be well versed in the types of trauma and how to assess and treat victims.

Crisis

A **crisis** is defined in part by the event, and in part by the response to the event. Generally speaking, a crisis is a situation that is perceived as **overwhelming and intolerable** by the individuals facing it. Crises can affect people cognitively, psychologically, behaviorally, and even physically. Although full-scale disasters necessarily affect entire populations and inherently pose overwhelming circumstances, counselors also need to be aware of how individual students are equipped to cope with a crisis. For most crises, which fall significantly short of full-scale disaster, counselors can employ intervention strategies that help students through the present crisis and help them develop coping skills for future challenges. Early intervention will minimize the possibility of traumatic response to a crisis.

Review Video: Crisis Management and Prevention
Visit mometrix.com/academy and enter code: 351872

Crisis Intervention

Since crisis by definition is a situation that is overwhelming and intolerable, **crisis intervention** serves to provide immediate support and help victims develop coping skills. It is good to remember that one of the factors that can contribute to a crisis is that the situation or event poses a new challenge to the individuals. Some of the components of crisis intervention include:

- Defusing of emotions to allow the exploration of possible solutions.
- Interpretation of the event or situation causing the crisis.
- Organizing of the situation in terms of information, resources, etc. Proper preparation to calm the student and help him or her handle the situation.
- Integration of the event into personal experience. Assistance to the students in recognizing the life lessons to be realized.
- Recognition of the positive impact gained from a crisis, e.g. the coping skills or new awareness gained.

Crisis Response Plan

Counselors can work with school staff and counselors, both at the school and district levels, to develop a **crisis response plan**. Counselors should facilitate regular meetings with school personnel, parents, and other professionals as appropriate, to educate them on crisis intervention both at the school and at the community levels. **Crisis response teams** should coordinate campus-wide and community-wide services as part of the critical response team. Counselors can educate and prepare the team on strategies and methods for handling the crisis. The team should be versed

Copyright © Mometrix Media. You have been licensed one copy of this document for personal use only. Any other reproduction or redistribution is strictly prohibited. All rights reserved.
This content is provided for test preparation purposes only and does not imply an endorsement by Mometrix of any particular political, scientific, or religious point of view.

on methods for crisis prevention, strategies to employ during a crisis, and post-crisis needs. The team should work together, with the counselor acting as facilitator, to develop a well-organized, systemic response plan. The coordination of the team and the crisis response plan should be implemented as a matter of preparation, and not in response to an immediate crisis.

Logistical Considerations in School Crisis Intervention Plans

Crisis response plans need to address the possibility that normal logistical operations may be suspended, particularly in the case of a school-wide or community-wide crisis. Therefore, a good crisis intervention plan will address the following needs:

- **Locations** should also be established for communications, first-aid treatment, emergency personnel, storage of supplies/food, and a break room or safe room.
- **Communication needs**: Crisis response teams will need to communicate with one another. They may also need to communicate with parents, as well as with the press. Part of the communication requirement will be the oversight and monitoring of team activities.
- **Other considerations**: An overall plan, including assigned assessment personnel and assigned intervention tasks.

Identifying and Addressing Suicidal Behaviors

School counselors need to be educated on potentially **suicidal behaviors**, and need to be prepared to intervene if necessary. These behaviors can include ideation, or any other behavior that indicates a student is contemplating suicide. **All threats of suicide should be taken seriously**. Counselors should consult institutional directives and state laws regarding responsibility for notification. In some cases, parents should be notified immediately, and may even need to pick up their children from school as soon as possible. In any case, students who are at risk for suicide should be in the presence of an adult at all times during the school day. Since the possibility of suicide can be extreme and immediate, intervention may include referral to an outside agency or institution. Counselors can work with parents and consultants in order to transition to treatment facilities, and should be familiar with the community services available.

Addressing the Possibility of Suicide

Suicide is all too prevalent among young people, and has been deemed the most common cause of death for adolescents. School counselors working with youth need to be well versed on the factors and behaviors contributing to suicides. There is no guaranteed strategy to prevent suicide and, in fact, suicide may occur despite the best efforts of the student's support network. However, counselors should still be informed and prepared in the event of suicidal behavior. It should be noted that suicidal ideation may be expressed differently in different cultures, and therefore counselors should respond to every potential ideation seriously. Some of the **common circumstances** precipitating suicide are alcoholism, depression, and a sense of hopelessness or helplessness. Counselors who observe suicidal tendencies should meet with the student regularly to discuss and work on the student's problems and state of mind.

Helping Students Recover Emotionally from Suicide Ideation

Working with students who are presenting **suicidal ideation** includes reconnecting the student to his or her network of support. In the process of working with a student, a counselor can determine which activities and people in his or her life provide meaning, and can contribute to an attitude of hope and resiliency. If a counselor deems that suicide is an imminent threat, the first consideration is the **student's safety**. This may include the involvement of the parents, within the parameters of relevant privacy mandates. Counselors can also encourage the student to reach out to his or her network of support for encouragement. This network could include parents, friends, church, and

Copyright © Mometrix Media. You have been licensed one copy of this document for personal use only. Any other reproduction or redistribution is strictly prohibited. All rights reserved.
This content is provided for test preparation purposes only and does not imply an endorsement by Mometrix of any particular political, scientific, or religious point of view.

coworkers. As the student's ideation begins to subside, this network can also provide a grid upon which the student can reestablish positive connections. Counselors can remind students of their responsibility, purpose, and place in this network and in the larger community.

Warning Signs of Suicidal Ideation

Although there are innumerable manifestations that **suicidal thoughts** can take, there are seven key identifiers that counselors should take note of:

- Communication, either spoken or implied, which incorporates suicidal thoughts and possibly includes themes of escape, punishment, or self-harm.
- Well-thought-out plans for dying. If the plans are feasible, concrete, detailed, and specific, this may be a good indicator that the student is seriously contemplating suicide.
- Well-thought-out plans for self-harm or for murder. Remember, suicide is self-murder.
- A rush of completed business, closure, or a potential suicide note.
- Extreme stress, such as a traumatic loss, illness, or failure. Counselors should also be wary of the anniversaries of significant losses in a student's life.
- Mental state indicators pointing to alcoholism, depression, or any recent changes in attitude.
- A sense of overwhelming hopelessness or helplessness.

Indicators for Violent Behavior in a School Environment

Often, students who feel disenfranchised will act out by bullying or otherwise victimizing other students. This sense of separation can result from a **student feeling isolated** from peer groups, cultural groups, family, or other groups from which the student feels excluded. This sense of exclusion may precipitate the student attacking, bullying, ignoring, or otherwise harassing other students. This sense of isolation may also be a precipitator of suicide, or attacking the self. Students may intensify this attacking behavior by bringing weapons on campus, or by inciting physical violence. Recent years have seen more covert and violent victimization on school campuses. Counselors and other school personnel need to be attentive to any incidents of bullying, which can escalate into more intense behaviors. Bullying and other victimization may be more prevalent among certain groups of students, and should provide the counselor with the opportunity to address the prevailing attitudes and behaviors.

Implications of Bullying

Any act of **bullying** or other **victimization** implies a **power hierarchy**. The victim is perceived and treated as powerless against the perpetrator, and each act of victimization further endorses that hierarchy. Often, social injustices and inequalities in a community or school environment provide fertile ground for bullying and victimization, which perpetuates the inequalities. If a comprehensive program to balance inequalities is not implemented, the bullying and victimization will most likely continue. Counselors can begin to address **chronic victimization** problems by educating students and relevant adults about how to effectively break the cycle of victimization. Victimization can also take the form of gossiping or excluding certain individuals from group activities. Although some schools have rules specifically prohibiting victimization, counselors can provide a valuable service by working with the parties involved to recognize and stop the cycle of victimization.

Impact of Abuse or Neglect on At-Risk Students

Students who have been **abused, neglected**, or who have been **witness to abuse** within their own family are **inherently at risk of decline** in any or all of the areas of physical, mental, social, spiritual, or economic health. Often students with a history of neglect or abuse display chronic behavior problems including anxiety, depression, substance abuse, and/or other emotional or

Copyright © Mometrix Media. You have been licensed one copy of this document for personal use only. Any other reproduction or redistribution is strictly prohibited. All rights reserved.
This content is provided for test preparation purposes only and does not imply an endorsement by Mometrix of any particular political, scientific, or religious point of view.

mental disturbances. Furthermore, victims of childhood abuse or neglect often feel a deep-rooted sense of shame or embarrassment, which translates to chronic social and emotional isolation. They often exhibit poor academic performance and retreat from normal activities with friends and fellow students, particularly if they have been helpless bystanders to abuse perpetrated against a parent or siblings. Counselors find that there is often a clear correlation between at-risk behavior in school, and abuse or neglect in the home.

Growing Incidence and Impact of Dating Violence

The definition and parameters of **dating violence** vary between studies. However, the overall incidences of dating violence have been steadily increasing in recent years. The figures of violence occurring in a dating situation range from a few incidences to a significant portion of the student body. As indicated by the term *dating violence*, the general parameters define an individual victimizing another individual in a dating environment. This can occur with middle school, high school, or college students. Most of the victims are women. The impact of this dating violence is felt at the individual level, often throughout the students' school, family and community network. The victim often is left with feelings of helplessness, which can expand into depression, substance abuse, and risky sexual behavior. Counselors need to be aware of the possibility of dating violence in a student who is presenting at-risk behavior.

Preparing for Campus-Wide Student Violence

Counselors should first be assured that the frequency **of campus-wide student violence** has declined in recent years. Nonetheless, there is always some possibility of a student or students committing violent acts that harm the campus as a whole. Unfortunately, there are not always clearly identified indicators of potential campus-wide violence. Most experts agree that this type of wide impact violence is usually the culmination of several factors in at-risk students. The best preparation strategies for counselors include both individual interventions for at-risk students and an intervention plan for the school. On the individual level, counselors should always work with students to mitigate their violent tendencies or fantasies, regardless of whether or not they appear to pose a threat to others. On the campus-wide level, counselors can work with school officials to develop a rubric for threat assessment, as well as an intervention plan to minimize the casualties should a campus-wide event occur.

Factors Associated with Violent Tendencies in Students

One of the factors that makes it difficult to **predict violent incidents** is that many students who display violent behavior do so on an **impulse**, meaning that most violent incidents are unplanned. Generally speaking, students who feel disenfranchised, helpless, or threatened may act out by perpetrating violent acts or behaviors. Often, violence will be motivated by feelings of desperation or an irrational fear that others may be threatening harm. Males are generally more likely to commit violence than females, and the highest incidence of violence falls between the ages of 15 and 24. Lower socioeconomic status is also a common factor in violent tendencies. In addition, if a student has a history of violence, he or she will be more likely to commit violence. Lastly, students who have disorders related to conduct, ADHD, hallucination, delusions, etc., will be more likely to commit violence.

FBI Classifications for Threats of Violence

Most of the research on the violent tendencies of students has been completed by governmental and FBI profilers and analysts. This research is made available to counselors and other educators to

Copyright © Mometrix Media. You have been licensed one copy of this document for personal use only. Any other reproduction or redistribution is strictly prohibited. All rights reserved.
This content is provided for test preparation purposes only and does not imply an endorsement by Mometrix of any particular political, scientific, or religious point of view.

mitigate the possibility of future occurrences. There are four basic classifications of threats of violence identified by the FBI:

- **Vague threats** that imply violence. The threat is implied in the terminology, but not specified. Time and place are not generally specified.
- **Veiled threats** of violence. The terminology is more specific, but time and place are still not specified.
- **Conditional threats** of violence. The terminology refers to violence if certain conditions are not met. A common example of this is extortion.
- **Direct threats** of violence. These threats are clearly stated and straightforward. The terminology is in the form of a warning which specifies a target, time, and place.

Levels of Threat Seriousness

According to government publications, the likelihood or seriousness of a threat can be classified according to three sets of criteria:

- Low-level threats are generally characterized by vagueness or a lack of specificity. Students may make a general, indirect statement of threat with little or no detail and little or no specific plan of action. Minimal risk is associated with low-level threats.
- Medium-level threats are more direct and plausible but do not appear to be realistic. They may contain details about time and place, but lack evidence of comprehensive planning. A medium-level threat may include phrasing that indicates seriousness, but lack the specificity to make it happen. The risk level for a medium-level threat is higher than for a low-level threat, but generally does not indicate imminent danger.
- High-level threats are distinguished by their high levels of specificity, and by the comprehensiveness and plausibility of the plan. High-level threats should be taken very seriously, and school officials should always contact the local authorities when they are discovered.

FBI's Four-Pronged Assessment Model for Threat Assessment

The **FBI has developed a four-pronged model of threat assessment** that focuses on the specific characteristics of the student making the threats:

- Prong 1 assesses the behavior and emotional dynamics of the individual, including signs of alienation, poor anger management, poor coping skills in general, lack of trust, or marked changes in behavior.
- Prong 2 assesses the circumstances of the family and home of the student, including a lack of limits or lack of monitoring, access to weapons, lack of intimacy, and/or volatile relationships within the family, particularly between the student and parents.
- Prong 3 assesses the student's perceived marginal place in the school community, evidenced by bullying, a lack of attachment to the school, inflexibility about culture, and hierarchy among the students.
- Prong 4 assesses the student's other connections, including peers at school, use of drugs or alcohol, and other outside activities or interests.

Intervening with At-Risk Youth and Mitigating the Possibility of Violence

Counselors can provide at-risk students with opportunities to develop **healthy dynamics** and **self-validating experiences** among their peers as well as with significant adults. Threat assessment teams can be formed and trained to focus on preventative strategies. Peer mentor groups should be established so that at-risk students and students not considered at risk can interact under the guise

Copyright © Mometrix Media. You have been licensed one copy of this document for personal use only. Any other reproduction or redistribution is strictly prohibited. All rights reserved.
This content is provided for test preparation purposes only and does not imply an endorsement by Mometrix of any particular political, scientific, or religious point of view.

and facilitation of the counselor. These groups can provide an **insulated environment** for learning healthy strategies for coping with bullying, neglect, and other forms of abuse. Counselors can teach healthy interpersonal skills within these groups. Counselors can also collaborate with local authorities and community groups to provide opportunities for at-risk youth to have positive experiences with adults and outside groups. At-risk students can be encouraged to join community support groups such as Big Brother/Sisters. Counselors can also encourage family members to develop connections with available support groups and resources.

Identifying At-Risk Behavior Associated with Substance Abuse

Since the prevalence and diversity of substance abuse among youth is increasing, counselors should be at least generically educated on common legal and illegal substances and behaviors associated with substance abuse. Counselors should also be aware of the local resources available for students involved in substance abuse. Although school guidance counselors cannot be expected to be experts on substance abuse, it is nonetheless a good idea to be aware of the behaviors and other signs of possible substance abuse. However, many students will not admit or discuss substance abuse, so the counselor should be prepared for referral if necessary. In addition, counselors should be aware of how substance abuse affects academic performance and mental ability, in order to best address these issues with students for whom substance abuse appears to be a contributing factor.

Encouraging Students to Self-Report Substance Abuse

Although students may be hesitant to self-report or even to recognize substance abuse, counselors can facilitate this recognition and self-reporting through a series of questions. The following questions target alcohol abuse and are identified by the acronym CAGE:

- C – Questions about **cutting down**. Ask the student if he has thought he should cut down on alcohol/substance use.
- A – The **annoyance factor**. Ask the student if he becomes annoyed when people criticize his drinking.
- G – The **guilt factor**. Ask the student if he ever feels guilty about the amount of alcohol/substance consumed.
- E – Alcohol as the **eye opener**. Ask the student if he ever needs alcohol to get going in the morning or to calm his nerves.

Counselors should also have regular access and referral to the Physician's Desk Reference to maintain current knowledge about drugs and alcohol, including possible side effects.

Alcohol and Prescription or Other Drugs

The following questions can be used as a guide for encouraging students to **recognize and self-report substance abuse**. Counselors can ask students that may have a substance abuse problem:

- If they are taking over-the counter or prescription medications.
- The reason they take the medications.
- Any other medications/drugs they take.
- How long they have been taking these medications.
- Side effects, including severity and when they noticed the effects.
- If they drink alcohol.
- How they are affected by alcohol.
- About their drinking and substance habits – alone, with friends, etc.
- If their alcohol/substance use has affected their personal, financial, professional, or legal circumstances.

Copyright © Mometrix Media. You have been licensed one copy of this document for personal use only. Any other reproduction or redistribution is strictly prohibited. All rights reserved.
This content is provided for test preparation purposes only and does not imply an endorsement by Mometrix of any particular political, scientific, or religious point of view.

- If anyone in their network of family/friends has asked them to stop using drugs/alcohol.
- If they attempted to quit alcohol/drug usage.
- If an attempt to quit caused withdrawal symptoms.

Loss That Students May Experience

One thing that counselors should remember is that a loss is still a loss, even though it may be as severe as the loss of a parent or as seemingly trivial as failing a class. Divorce of parents can be a particularly devastating but unfortunately a commonly experienced loss for young people. In addition, friendships are very important at this age, and the loss of a friendship can be very upsetting and can be experienced as a major loss. What is significant about these different types of losses is that young people feel loss just as intensely as adults, and that each loss needs to be grieved and processed. Students need to move through the grief, and on to acceptance. By understanding that a sense of loss can be experienced regardless of the precipitating event, and by knowing about the grief process, counselors can provide the support and the guidance to move students through the loss and on to acceptance.

Stages of Grief Process

The **grief process** encompasses the following **five major stages**:

- Shock and denial usually define the first stage of the grief process. Counselors can help students identify their fears.
- The second stage is usually anger, which involves indignation and questioning of why this loss was perpetrated on them. The student may argue that he or she did not deserve this loss.
- Guilt is generally the third stage, evolving to a sense that the student's actions or inaction may have caused the event leading to the loss, and that therefore they did deserve the loss.
- The fourth stage is hopelessness and depression. This tends to be the longest stage, and may include feelings of sadness. As this stage becomes less intense, this is usually a signal that the student is almost ready to move on to acceptance.
- Acceptance is the fifth stage, in which the student adjusts to his or her new life circumstances.

Assisting Students Through the Grief Process

Throughout the **grief process**, counselors can assure and remind students that their feelings are normal, and that eventually life will improve for them. This is not intended as a denial of their feelings, but rather as an assurance that grief is a process, and not a permanent state. Counselors can work with students in the grief process, remembering that there are four major tasks to be accomplished during grief:

- **Accept** the reality of the loss, both emotionally and intellectually.
- **Experience** the pain, both internally and externally.
- **Acclimate** to life after the loss, accepting help from others as appropriate.
- **Assimilate** the loss and reinvest energies elsewhere.

Counselors should be watchful for the stages and tasks involved with the grief process and be prepared to refer to the student to outside or specialized resources if the situation becomes overwhelming or too complicated for the counselor to be of assistance.

Copyright © Mometrix Media. You have been licensed one copy of this document for personal use only. Any other reproduction or redistribution is strictly prohibited. All rights reserved.
This content is provided for test preparation purposes only and does not imply an endorsement by Mometrix of any particular political, scientific, or religious point of view.

DROPPING OUT OF HIGH SCHOOL

PRECIPITATING FACTORS AND PREVENTATIVE MEASURES

Counselors should be particularly alert and responsive to the possibility of **students dropping out**, especially if students present any or all of the following:

- High rate of absenteeism
- Low or dropping grades
- Low participation in extracurricular activities
- Limited parental support
- Evidence of alcohol or drug problems

The following are recommended **intervention strategies** for students at risk of dropping out:

- Tutoring services – either peer tutoring or other trained assistance
- Career and skill training for success after high school
- Expressing high but reasonable expectations for students
- Additional general/foundation classes for students with disabilities

Continued support and **resources** are recommended for at-risk students who stay in school, including:

- Relevant curriculum
- Significant support and assistance from teachers and others as appropriate
- Useful and accessible textbooks and other classroom materials

KEY AREAS TO BE ADDRESSED AND INTERVENTION STRATEGIES FOR AT-RISK STUDENTS

During all interventions with at-risk students, counselors should address interpersonal skill-building and self-reflection. It is important for counselors to encourage students to develop strong relationships with peers and school staff/counselors, in order to increase their sense of community and belonging. Throughout the intervention, counselors should always assure students that they can discuss personal issues in both individual and group sessions. Often, at-risk students are struggling with numerous issues in several areas of their lives. There are four key areas that are possibly involved when students are at risk of dropping out:

- **Personal/Affective** – counselors can offer retreats or other groups to encourage interpersonal participation
- **Academic** – counselors can arrange for tutoring and/or other individualized methods of instruction
- **Family Outreach** – encompassing increased feedback to parents
- **School Structure** – possibilities include class size reduction or alternative school options
- **Work/Career** – vocational training

COLLABORATING WITH COMMUNITY RESOURCES TO DEVELOP A NETWORK OF SUPPORT

Many schools will have ongoing relationships with **community groups** as a part of a general philosophy of community outreach. However, for at-risk students to receive any direct benefit from these groups or relationships, counselors may have to initiate and coordinate auxiliary relationships for addressing the specific needs of at-risk students. Understanding that at-risk

Copyright © Mometrix Media. You have been licensed one copy of this document for personal use only. Any other reproduction or redistribution is strictly prohibited. All rights reserved.
This content is provided for test preparation purposes only and does not imply an endorsement by Mometrix of any particular political, scientific, or religious point of view.

students are often overwhelmed by a variety of life challenges, counselors can collaborate with a number of **community resources**, including:

- Businesses
- Families
- Recreational Centers
- Police Departments
- Universities

Counselors should cultivate these relationships, possibly in tandem with existing school relationships. With the counselor's facilitation and coordination, these resource groups can cooperatively address many of the needs posed by at-risk students. This comprehensive coordination of resources can provide a significant hedge against students dropping out.

Facilitating Change in Intervention Policies to Better Accommodate Cultural Diversity

Counselors who work with **at-risk youth from diverse cultures** are in a good position to reduce the gap between intervention strategies designed for the dominant culture and those that address the needs of minorities. Counselors need to communicate to school officials that under the umbrella of at-risk students may be ethnic groups whose problems are defined or exacerbated by their marginalized status. Counselors can consider the **cultural differences of at-risk students** and how they will interpret different activities when creating preventative and intervention programs. If necessary and when appropriate, counselors can act as liaisons on behalf of students from diverse cultures, making recommendations for program changes to better accommodate cultural diversity. Counselors can make significant and important changes in the school system, which will benefit present and future students.

Modeling and Advocating Empowerment for At-Risk Students

Recognizing that at-risk youth are generally overwhelmed and under-supported, counselors can be particularly effective by providing students with numerous opportunities to develop empowerment and self-confidence. When setting goals, it is important to set **achievable, short-term goals** to best ensure success by the students. Each success should lead to further and **larger successes**, and counselors can provide **scaffolding goals and challenges**. Counselors can also encourage listening and cooperation among family members through their own willingness to take a back seat and emphasize the importance of collaboration and teamwork, facilitating when appropriate. In terms of advocacy, counselors may be aware of policies or procedures within the school system that inherently pose an obstacle or inequity for at-risk students, and may need to intervene on behalf of the students. This is another way that counselors can model empowerment.

Authentically Documenting Intervention Outcomes

In the absence of available success/failure rates for many intervention strategies, the onus is often on the counselor to document the outcomes of the strategies used. In order to authentically and effectively produce this outcome assessment, it is at first important to document student responses during and/or after an intervention. In keeping with the assessment model, counselors should produce documentation that either quantifies or clearly identifies specific outcomes. Counselors should also be mindful of their role as advocates for the students by realistically reporting successes and failures, so that program improvements can be made if necessary. By doing so, they can also provide a model for reflection and willingness to change. Counselors who provide authentic documentation and are willing to revise strategies are excellent candidates for added

Copyright © Mometrix Media. You have been licensed one copy of this document for personal use only. Any other reproduction or redistribution is strictly prohibited. All rights reserved.
This content is provided for test preparation purposes only and does not imply an endorsement by Mometrix of any particular political, scientific, or religious point of view.

funding or other resources, and can provide comprehensive parameters for the role of school guidance counselor.

Various Roles When Working with Disabled Students

As defined by the ASCA, the school counselor should address the following **functions in his or her role as facilitator and advocate** for student needs:

- Lead and facilitate activities of the comprehensive school counseling program.
- Collaborate with other student support personnel to deliver appropriate services.
- Provide services to both disabled and other students.
- Provide individual and group counseling.
- Work with staff and parents to develop an understanding of students' special needs.
- Refer students as appropriate to auxiliary resources in the school system or in the community, to address needs not met in the context of the counseling program.
- Advocate for the rights of disabled students in the school and the community.
- Assist school staff with issues related to students transitioning between grade levels.
- Serve on interdisciplinary groups that assess students who may have undiagnosed special needs.

Multiple Disabilities, Specific Learning Disability, Orthopedic Impairment, and Other Health Impairment

The term "**multiple disabilities**" refers to a combination of impairments, such as intellectual disabilities with either blindness or orthopedic impairments, whereby the student's educational needs cannot be accommodated in the traditional classroom. Excluded from this group is deaf-blindness.

Specific learning disability refers to a disorder whereby a deficiency in one or more of the basic psychological processes inherent in using or understanding spoken or written language causes a person to have difficulty communicating linguistically or performing mathematical calculations.

Orthopedic impairment refers to physical impairments that adversely affect a student's academic performance. Included in this category are loss of a limb, clubfoot, cerebral palsy, and disease-related conditions like poliomyelitis and bone tuberculosis.

Other health impairment describes the presence of such chronic or acute health problems as diabetes, epilepsy, ADD, heart conditions, or sickle-cell anemia, that adversely affect the student's educational performance.

Intervention Strategies for Eating Disorders

Eating disorders in youth commonly manifest as either bulimia nervosa (BN) or anorexia nervosa (AN), or both. Because both of these disorders result in extremely poor nutrition, and bulimia nervosa can result in esophageal injury, students who are suffering eating disorders are at risk for poor health, poor intellectual and social development, and in some cases death. Counselors can implement intervention strategies through a complete medical assessment and multifaceted therapeutic assessment. In particular, the combination of behavioral therapy and cognitive therapy can be very effective in treating eating disorders. **Cognitive therapy** can address issues of control and self-esteem, while **behavioral therapy** can promote healthy eating habits and discourage destructive behaviors like purging. **Group therapy** may also be quite helpful and in some cases, family therapy may be indicated. **Medical assessment** may also be indicated, to ascertain if the student is in immediate physical danger from an eating disorder.

Copyright © Mometrix Media. You have been licensed one copy of this document for personal use only. Any other reproduction or redistribution is strictly prohibited. All rights reserved.
This content is provided for test preparation purposes only and does not imply an endorsement by Mometrix of any particular political, scientific, or religious point of view.

Intervention Strategies for Tic Disorders

Tic disorders are characaterized by recurrent, non-rhythmic sequences of movements and involuntary sounds from certain muscle groups. These disorders can include Tourette's tic, transient tic, and not-otherwise-specified (NOS) disorders. Counselors should initially garner enough information to recognize the condition and should direct the parents to a doctor who can diagnose the disorder and educate the family on the condition. Therapy can include identifying any underlying stressors as well as assessing family interaction and understanding regarding the disease. Various therapeutic strategies can be effectively implemented for tic disorders. Cognitive-behavioral therapies can address stress management. Self-monitoring, relaxation training, and habit-reversal training are effective strategies to consider, once initial data about the tic have been collected. Habit-reversal training is more commonly indicated, requiring the student to relax the affected muscles and introduce a competing response. If students present with frequent or explosive outbursts, counselors should collaborate with a physician to determine if medication is indicated.

Intervention Strategies for Mood Disorders

Mood disorders are generally defined as those in which students externalize feelings of depression, sadness, guilt, or other negative emotion, possibly including thoughts of suicide. Students with mood disorders may present with somatic complaints. Counselors should be wary of misidentifying a mood disorder when a student may just be experiencing temporary sadness. On the other hand, counselors should be cognizant of the signs of mood disorder, especially symptoms that may signal the risk of suicide. Effective therapeutic strategies for mood disorder include cognitive and behavioral interventions, as well as psycho-educational programs that focus on improving social skills and promoting rewarding activities. Some students suffering from mood disorders have improved with antidepressants. However, studies regarding the efficacy of medicinal treatment for depression are inconclusive, and therefore the use of antidepressants should not be immediately considered, if at all.

Intervention Strategies for Substance-Related Disorders

One of the **initial intervention steps for substance abuse** is to identify the pattern of abuse and the substances involved. Parents may conduct drug tests at home, although students may also self-report. An important factor to remember is that students with substance abuse problems may have family members with substance abuse problems, since the correlation is very strong. In addition to individual counseling and education, counselors can conduct school and community workshops that address the benefits of early detection, the risk factors involved, and the treatment options available. Based on the type of substance abuse, duration, and intensity, various treatment models are available, ranging from outpatient therapy to intensive inpatient treatment. The spectrum of treatment options encompasses very restrictive models as well as more participatory models. Treatments include detoxification, contracting, self-help groups, behavior therapy, family therapy, social skills training, as well as nutritional and recreational counseling.

Intervention Strategies for Generalized Anxiety Disorder

Generalized anxiety disorder (GAD) is defined as a pervasive anxiety that is characterized by excessive, uncontrollable, and often irrational worry about everyday things, which is disproportionate to the actual source of worry. Physical, somatic symptoms may include shortness of breath and/or muscle tension in other parts of the body, both of which can be difficult to control. Although GAD is not limited to adolescents, it does present problems particular to students, in that the physical symptoms and the irrational worry can overshadow attention to academics, and therefore negatively affect performance. Students who are chronically anxious are unable to focus

Copyright © Mometrix Media. You have been licensed one copy of this document for personal use only. Any other reproduction or redistribution is strictly prohibited. All rights reserved.
This content is provided for test preparation purposes only and does not imply an endorsement by Mometrix of any particular political, scientific, or religious point of view.

on their lessons. Counselors can use cognitive-behavioral strategies to mitigate the intensity of the anxiety and the accompanying physical symptoms. Students can be taught coping strategies such as identification, modification of anxious self-talk, education about emotions, modeling, relaxation techniques, and related self-regulating models.

Drug Addiction

In recent years, medical professionals have shifted from viewing **drug addiction** as a sign of immorality to seeing it as a legitimate physiological disorder, which can be treated by medicine and psychological therapy. Scientists believe that prolonged use of drugs can cause chemical changes in the brain that create addiction, and can endure for the entirety of the person's life. The most common traits of **chemical dependency** are loss of control over dosage and frequency of use, and continued use despite harmful consequences. Unfortunately, one of the other common characteristics of drug addiction is the refusal to admit that it exists. Many doctors believe that only by removing the stigma of drug addiction will it be possible to treat all those who need help.

Copyright © Mometrix Media. You have been licensed one copy of this document for personal use only. Any other reproduction or redistribution is strictly prohibited. All rights reserved.
This content is provided for test preparation purposes only and does not imply an endorsement by Mometrix of any particular political, scientific, or religious point of view.

The School Counseling Program and Professional Knowledge

Research-Based Practice

Effective Operation of Data-Driven Counseling Programs

Counselors may find that many counseling programs or other student services models are **data driven**, meaning that statistics are routinely collected and used as the basis for institutional decisions. Counselors may discover that either the data being generated is incomplete, or that it is being organized and presented in a manner that does not reveal pertinent information about particular student issues. Data may describe the entire student body without focusing on groups of students in need. Counselors can apply system analysis to the data system with the goal of isolating the student needs that can be addressed by the counseling program. When the right students are placed at the center of the system, data regarding school, family, and community becomes more relevant. School counselors can also view the entire system, including the subsystems and the interconnectedness of those systems.

Benefits of Holistic Counseling in Systemic, Data-Driven Programs

It is understood that the benefits of a data-driven counseling program include **quantifiable accountability** and assessment of professional review organizations. The ASCA describes these programs as clearly defined and sequential. They can also offer a **holistic, comprehensive assessment** of individual students. Counselors can combine the systemic overview and the needs of individual students by creating a data collection system that promotes holistic development in students. This includes nurturing individual qualities in students, and cultivating the particular goals and skills identified in the data. Using the data-driven system for the implementation of the program, counselors can partner with school members to develop a comprehensive program that identifies the needs of individual students and the student body as a whole. This type of program will help the students by giving them the confidence and leadership to pursue their dreams.

Promotion of Social Justice in School Systems

A campus that endorses and supports **social justice** does not differentiate on the basis of culture, race, economic status, special needs, sexual orientation or gender, religious background, appearance, or primary language. Counselors can encourage this kind of campus through their work with individual students, and by working with the particularities of the data system. All members of the community will expand their commitment to social justice and **educational equity** when the systemic data-driven approach is initiated at the school, which will increase the probability of all students having equal opportunities within the school counseling program. The counseling program in particular is a prime area in which to model equal access to resources by advocating for all students with no attention to personal characteristics that define each student. By promoting social justice, campuses provide a model for the surrounding community.

School Mission Statement

Counselors should refer to the **school's mission statement** when developing or revising programs or data systems. A mission statement represents the **basic tenets, philosophies,** and **goals** of the school as a whole, which should be represented appropriately in its programs and practices. The mission statement can assist counselors in the development of programs or outreach efforts, so that the overall direction and mission of the school can be incorporated into the rationale for the

Copyright © Mometrix Media. You have been licensed one copy of this document for personal use only. Any other reproduction or redistribution is strictly prohibited. All rights reserved.
This content is provided for test preparation purposes only and does not imply an endorsement by Mometrix of any particular political, scientific, or religious point of view.

proposals. Counselors may also be in a position to collaborate with school officials in developing or revising a mission statement, possibly to better serve a diverse population and/or the surrounding community. The statement should embody a collective result for all students, and should provide a clear and concise focus that will frame future program development and evaluation.

Systemic Approach

Assessment

When developing **assessment methods** for a systemic approach, counselors may first want to refer to existing data from school and district databases as well as **adequate yearly progress** (AYP) reports for a baseline representation of academic achievement or other pertinent information. Qualitative assessment from focus groups, interviews, and observations can provide a profile of key areas to be addressed. Counselors can then glean a basic understanding of what influences the access to resources and the academic achievement of students. Counselors may then want to choose the best format for assessment, incorporating best methods for garnering information, most comprehensive participation, and best feedback. They will want to look at those specific areas that will provide the clearest and most comprehensive picture of assessment of the program. Once the data is synthesized into a rubric, or other assessment vehicle, counselors can identify the students' needs more clearly.

Goals

Counselors developing a **systemic approach** to counseling and assessment should first refer to the **goals** identified by the school, district, state and federal levels, so that the quantitative data can be tailored in accordance with recognized goals for which the school is accountable. Some of the identified goals are as follows:

- National goals: reduction of attainment and achievement gaps, attendance improvement, and likelihood of a drug-free school environment
- State goals: national goals, some of which are identified above, as well as state-specific goals such as improving the rates of literacy and post-secondary matriculation
- District goals: at the district level, there may be additional goals that address areas of particular concern to the region.
- Local goals: further focus on the needs of students and how those goals can be realized in students' lives

Program Integration

The effective data-driven approach to improving student achievement is a collaborative endeavor shared by educators, counselors, and other school personnel. Recognizing that each program strives for equal access, attainment, and achievement for the students, counselors can work with educators and other school staff toward a comprehensive data assessment system, and ongoing oversight and revision as needed. A holistic **systemic approach** utilizes inherent connections between programs. Education and counseling programs are connected by a related structure that allows for the alignment of content, delivery, and the reporting of results. The systemic data-driven counseling program is further connected to the school mission, inherently aligning it with the program goals, development, and evaluation of educational goals. All school-based programs are aligned with federal and state goals, and any counseling goals are aligned with ASCA standards that address goals and strategies to best target student needs. Through these combined efforts, students are helped toward their academic and career goals.

Copyright © Mometrix Media. You have been licensed one copy of this document for personal use only. Any other reproduction or redistribution is strictly prohibited. All rights reserved.
This content is provided for test preparation purposes only and does not imply an endorsement by Mometrix of any particular political, scientific, or religious point of view.

Programs and Participants

Schools that are regulated and data driven nonetheless recognize that targeting the whole student can include not only classroom delivery, but also extracurricular activities. Since the school is also a social system, it includes a hierarchy of activities and relationships that incorporate the entire school community. **Standards-based educational programs** can generate protocols and competencies for classroom delivery, tutoring programs, extracurricular clubs, peer programs, mentoring programs, school sports, service learning projects, honor societies, and arts-music groups. The **comprehensive education program** can also include the contributions of parents, business collaborators, and pertinent outreach programs. The presence or absence of this kind of holistic inclusion can define a school culture in a way that either supports or hinders students' achievement. When developing a counseling program, counselors should endeavor to support and enhance existing educational program approaches, to the maximum benefit of students.

Reporting Outcome Assessment to School Community

As a member of the school community, counselors should report **outcome assessment** in a way that will be most accessible to the other members of that community. One of the ways that this can be achieved is by categorizing outcome results in alignment with the groupings established by the school. By presenting data that aligns with educational outcomes, the connection between the counseling and educational programs will be more clearly understood. Counselors may also want to provide access to outcome assessment to the larger school community. Results can be disaggregated to profile outcomes for grade levels, individuals, or subgroups on the school campus. Some counselors may also provide online access to outcome results for students, families, or community, in a report card or other user-friendly format. By providing reasonable access to easily understood data, counselors can further cultivate the integration of both educational and counseling goals.

Role of Assessment Documentation in Addressing Equity in School Policies and Practices

Well-documented assessment provides accountability for the success of the program in addressing student needs. **Assessment reporting** and **documentation** can also isolate and identify student groups that are not being served by current programs and policies. By disaggregating data, school counselors can reveal portions of the student demographic – such as those identified by race, ethnicity, socioeconomic status, and other defining categories – who are not being met. Counselors may also want to conduct **longitudinal studies** that will reveal the success or failure of various strategies within these subgroups. This kind of focused, delineated data can clearly point to underserved students, and can help prescribe revisions in policy or program development. The contemporary school counselor can serve as a leader in the creation and refinement of school programs that equally address the needs of all students. Documented assessment can provide tangible evidence to garner school support for policy changes.

Implementation of Data-Driven Programs at Different School System Levels

Implementation of a data-driven program is delivered differently at each of the following levels within the school community:

- Individual levels focus on particular students, including crisis situations and student-specific situations, and can provide insight into issues experienced by the entire student body.
- Grade levels focus on age-specific experiences and may be best implemented by long-term planning.
- Classroom levels align the counseling program with the academic curriculum.

Copyright © Mometrix Media. You have been licensed one copy of this document for personal use only. Any other reproduction or redistribution is strictly prohibited. All rights reserved.
This content is provided for test preparation purposes only and does not imply an endorsement by Mometrix of any particular political, scientific, or religious point of view.

- School-wide levels call for coordination of interventions, in the interest of benefiting the entire school.
- Family levels involve parents and/or guardians as equal partners in the promotion of student achievement.
- Community levels involve members of the surrounding area to form partnerships toward the promotion of student achievement.

Value of Data-Driven Systemic School Counseling Programs

Counselors and other interested parties can view firsthand the **value that data-driven accountability** can add to the contributions of counselors toward student achievement. Data-based assessment that is designed around standardized categories can also assist state and national data management in **evaluating their goals** for equity in academic achievement. The information gleaned can help counselors identify which programs were successful, and which programs could be improved. Data revealed in well-designed systemic programs can isolate particular academic areas, student issues, or student populations that are not being well served. Counselors can implement strategies for **program improvement**, incorporating its assessment in the data system. As counselors are regularly able to evaluate and revise the process of setting goals and assessing their achievement, they can adjust the school counseling program to effectively and comprehensively serve the needs of the students, the school, and the community.

School Counselor's Responsibility in Developing Data-Driven Counseling Programs

Counselors who do not adopt the data-driven model of program development place themselves out of the school and district accountability sphere. They may place the **program at risk** by not aligning it with the accountability paradigm. Counselors who are ethically responsible should reap the benefits of a data-driven system of planning and accountability. Counselors can embrace the systemic approach by utilizing the expertise of school counselors and district counseling resources. They can then serve as mentors for emerging school counselors. Counselors should take the time to research available information about data-driven programs and how they can best benefit the students and the counseling program. This includes learning how to analyze the data, apply it to existing strategies and programs, and revise intervention strategies accordingly. Although data-driven counseling does not replace individual counseling, it can provide valuable empirical oversight to assist the counselor in maintaining an effective and relevant program.

Utilizing a Data-Driven Program

Counselors can apply the following steps to realize a program that embodies social justice with a mission of access and equity:

- Analyze data to identify need: for example, graduation rates may identify inequity between demographic groups
- Develop goals: for example, graduation for all students
- Align goals with school mission: for example, sequential-year plans for graduation involve all stakeholders
- Integrate interventions: for example, utilize existing educational programs toward the goal of graduation for all students
- Implement interventions at different levels: for example, incorporate interrelated and interdependent interventions at various levels.
- Collect data results: all levels of program intervention should be collected

Copyright © Mometrix Media. You have been licensed one copy of this document for personal use only. Any other reproduction or redistribution is strictly prohibited. All rights reserved.
This content is provided for test preparation purposes only and does not imply an endorsement by Mometrix of any particular political, scientific, or religious point of view.

- Analyze data and present it for evaluation: include goals met, goals not met, and potential strategies in response
- Revise programs if needed: make changes to program strategies in accordance with new data

Components of School Counseling Accountability

A proactive approach to school counseling accountability includes **clearly articulated parameters** for responsibilities and duties, well-defined **evaluation** and **assessment vehicles**, and **reporting the results** of the evaluation to stakeholders. The following components contribute to a dynamic accountability model:

- Identify and collaborate with stakeholder groups. Take a proactive, collaborative stance.
- Collect data and assess the needs of students, educators, and community.
- Set goals and establish outcomes as revealed by data.
- Implement effective interventions that address the goals and objectives of the program.
- Design and implement effective outcome assessment for the interventions.
- Utilize the results to improve the counseling program.
- Share the results with students, parents, educators, school counselors, school boards, school counselors and supervisors, and community leaders.

Serving as Ambassadors and Proponents of Data-Driven Counseling Programs

Data-driven accountability for a school counseling program can provide counselors with ordered data and methodical strategies for strengthening appreciation for the program by the school community. Counselors can provide the following accountability information:

- Program evaluations or audits when asked about the comprehensive, standard-based program in place.
- Needs assessment results when asked about the specific needs of the student population based on the results of evaluations.
- Service assessment results when asked to provide examples of implementations that address student needs.
- Results or outcomes of studies when asked about the results of interventions.
- Performance evaluations when asked about counselor performance.

The school counselor must perform the tasks of needs assessment, program evaluation, test program management and interpretation of assessment results in order for the counseling program to be accountable to school boards, parents, or other members of the community who may be concerned about the value of the program.

Accountability Studies

Advantages

Accountability studies can enhance counselors' overall knowledge and awareness about the effectiveness of strategies or programs, so that they can provide **valuable input** during the decision-making process involved in new programs or practices. Based on the results of these studies, counselors may become aware of professional development or staffing needs. The quantitative data from the studies can provide the tangible rationale for these requests. Counselors who are well versed on the assessment results of their program are better able to network with other counseling professionals to share program results and learn about new intervention strategies. Accountability studies can be a valuable **public relations vehicle** for informing educators and the larger community about the accomplishments of the school counseling program

Copyright © Mometrix Media. You have been licensed one copy of this document for personal use only. Any other reproduction or redistribution is strictly prohibited. All rights reserved.
This content is provided for test preparation purposes only and does not imply an endorsement by Mometrix of any particular political, scientific, or religious point of view.

and the focus of the school system for its students. Counselors who engage in accountability studies demonstrate a personal and professional commitment to ongoing standards of quality and success.

Disadvantages

Although **accountability studies** can provide valuable information for the school counselor, as well as the school community as a whole, there are inherent disadvantages associated with these studies. An obvious disadvantage is that the studies take time away from individual or group counseling, in order for the counselor to implement and assess the accountability model of evaluation. Although this time could be well justified by the overall benefits to the program and to the student body, these benefits can only be realized if the counselor is trained in utilizing the data and spends the time on research and evaluation to achieve any useful results. Counselors may have misgivings about utilizing accountability studies because they may produce **results that are counterintuitive** to implementation strategies that have proved successful in individual and/or group counseling. Some counselors may also be hesitant to perform accountability studies because of a perception of being micro-managed by the stakeholders requesting the data.

SCPAC

Purpose and Parameters

The **school counseling program advisory committee (SCPAC)** is generally comprised of counselors, parents, educators, and other members of the community, all of whom have a stake and influence in the school's decision-making. The school principal should always be included, particularly since he or she will need to be included in the discussion about proposed program improvements or recommendations, and will be instrumental in approving funding for these proposals. The SCPAC can serve as a sounding board during decision making and can assist the counselor in introducing needed program changes or requesting resources. The SCPAC can serve as a liaison committee with the larger community, and can include parent-teacher organizations by invitation or at least by communicating with them regarding relevant impending decisions. By including community input through the liaison SCPAC committee, counselors demonstrate their willingness to consider outside perspectives and additional sources for funding.

Role

Assuming that the **SCPAC** is active, ongoing and not undergoing significant changes, it is customary for the group to meet once each semester to discuss the needs and available resources of the counseling program, and to provide recommendations and endorsement for **proposed improvements**. The group can analyze assessment results, propose program modifications, and consider recommendations from staff members. Program proposals are generally based on the results of assessments. The group can identify potential funding sources, but the school principal should always be included in any funding discussions. The group can serve as a valuable resource for demonstrating support among the school community for program enhancement, and potentially for influencing the principal in funding and approval decisions. Counselors should consider the benefits and the potential impact of the SCPAC and should focus their attention and time on the group as needed.

Needs Assessment

Needs assessments serve to analyze and identify the needs of the school, the student body, and the community. An effective needs assessment will identify the **particular needs of specific subgroups**, and whether or not the needs of all groups and subgroups are being met. A **comprehensive needs assessment** will reveal areas to be addressed in the student body and its respective demographic subgroups, as well as in the school community, including parents, staff, counselors, local business, community organizations, and community members. Counselors can

Copyright © Mometrix Media. You have been licensed one copy of this document for personal use only. Any other reproduction or redistribution is strictly prohibited. All rights reserved.
This content is provided for test preparation purposes only and does not imply an endorsement by Mometrix of any particular political, scientific, or religious point of view.

create effective, comprehensive counseling programs that will enable students to realize improvements in their personal and academic performance. Needs assessments can also assist counselors in better understanding the various needs of different subgroups and addressing the significant issues of the school community.

Program Evaluation

The **purpose of process evaluation**, or program audit, is to determine if the program is appropriately implemented in all areas, and if that implementation is properly documented. The evaluation reviews whether there is implementation and sufficient documentation of all relevant facets of a comprehensive school counseling program. By providing an analysis of each component of the program, the audit identifies areas of strength and weakness within the program, and indicates how these areas compare with district or state mission statements. The following terms are used to evaluate areas of the program:

- None: not in place
- In progress: started but not completed
- Completed: possibly not implemented
- Implemented: fully in place
- Not applicable: areas where the criteria do not apply

Service Assessment

Event-Topic Counts

Counselors may be required to **provide service assessment reports** to guidance supervisors, superintendents, and school boards. Although guidance supervisors may request general service assessments, school boards and superintendents may ask for more specific event-topic counts. These counts refer to how a counselor spends his or her school time. Counselors are asked to document each time a student is contacted, receives any type of counseling service, or interacts with the counselor in any capacity. The reporting of these counts may be in the form of a log or a simple count, and requires the counselor to maintain a weekly or monthly recording of how many students receive general counseling or individual sessions to treat depression, behaviors, anxiety, social skills, anger management, family changes, or conflict resolution. Counselors and school boards can appreciate the contributions of the counselor evidenced by quantified event-time counts.

Time Logs

The purpose of **time logs** is generally determined by the school, the district, or some other oversight entity. Time logs can provide valuable **compliance documentation** to counselors and school boards for funding purposes. Certain states and school counseling programs require the use of time logs in order to quantify the type of work being done in the school community and surrounding areas. Some school programs may require the counselor to spend a certain percentage of their time in meetings with students individually, in groups, or for guidance purposes. Counselors should set up the time log format in a manner that will best document the time spent in each capacity, and be categorized in a manner that will be most useful to the entity requesting the time log. The amount of time spent on any counseling-related activity should be documented and categorized as accurately as possible. Counselors may want to maintain daily time logs to effectively capture data regarding time spent.

Outcome Assessment

In contrast to a service assessment that quantifies time spent, a well-defined **outcome assessment** can provide a profile of the effectiveness of particular aspects of the program. Counselors should

Copyright © Mometrix Media. You have been licensed one copy of this document for personal use only. Any other reproduction or redistribution is strictly prohibited. All rights reserved.
This content is provided for test preparation purposes only and does not imply an endorsement by Mometrix of any particular political, scientific, or religious point of view.

recognize that it is not intended as an evaluation of his or her performance, but rather as a useful assessment of the program itself. Counselors should focus on the two key features of outcome assessment:

- It is not a professional evaluation of the counselor, a limit to his or her ability to perform the job, a requirement for standardized tests or curricula, or a prescribed process with no capacity for expansion.
- The assessment is:
- A vehicle for garnering information on program-related questions.
- The responsibility of an accountable counselor.
- An ongoing and evolving process.
- A cooperative outreach to other SCPAC members and stakeholders.
- A path toward better education for all students.

Assessment Terms

The following are assessment-related terms and their definitions:

- ***Evaluation*** implies a measurement of worth, indicating that the effectiveness will be judged.
- ***Evidence*** refers to all data that can be used to judge or determine effectiveness. It is either quantitatively or qualitatively derived.
- ***Formative evaluation*** describes specific feedback received during a program implementation.
- ***Summative evaluation*** refers to anecdotal feedback received during the evaluation process.
- ***Stakeholder*** refers to any person or persons who are involved in or benefit from the school counseling program.
- ***Baseline*** refers to data gathered at the onset of evaluation, to define a starting point.
- ***Pretest*** describes an administered measure given before an intervention.
- ***Posttest*** describes an administered measure given after the intervention has been completed.
- ***Value-added assessment*** refers to the timing and final result of the intervention.

Review Video: Formative and Summative Assessments
Visit mometrix.com/academy and enter code: 804991

Planning for Outcome Assessment in Research Design

When **designing research** or implementing new intervention strategies, counselors should consider outcome assessment in the initial stages of planning. Otherwise, they are reliant upon prescribed case studies, non-experimental design paradigms, or static-group comparison studies to analyze the effectiveness of the intervention. By planning for outcome assessment, counselors can **tailor the assessment to the intervention**. The optimal format for research design is random assignment of participants to treatment conditions. This will allow the counselor to implement true experimental designs. Otherwise, with little or no control over assignments, counselors must rely on the results of a quasi-experimental or non-experimental design. The completion of pretests and posttests is also optimal, although not all counselors require the dependent variable.

Copyright © Mometrix Media. You have been licensed one copy of this document for personal use only. Any other reproduction or redistribution is strictly prohibited. All rights reserved.
This content is provided for test preparation purposes only and does not imply an endorsement by Mometrix of any particular political, scientific, or religious point of view.

Implementing an Original Outcome Assessment

There may be a time when a counselor chooses to develop an **original outcome measure** that directly addresses the application, or is more appropriate for the group. When posing questions to the group for responses to be used in the assessment, the **following considerations** should be incorporated:

- Use simple language and question the group members only on events or circumstances with which they are familiar.
- Each question should be specific, and any unclear terms should be specifically defined in the appropriate context.
- Counselors should always avoid yes-no questions.
- Counselors should always avoid double negatives since these can confuse the response group.
- Questions should be posed individually, and not in combination with another question.
- Topic-specific wording should be consistent with the wording used in the discipline.
- Counselors should be sensitive to cultural differences.
- Counselors should learn to handle difficult response groups effectively.
- Second-hand opinions should only be accepted if first-hand information is unavailable.
- Background information can be provided to remind the group members of a specific event or reaction.

Data Collection Methods

Counselors can **collect data** through the **following methods:**

- Interviewing counselors, educators, or members of stakeholder groups in a structured, semi-structured, or unstructured manner.
- Observing students informally and formally.
- Distributing written questions, rating scales, and surveys containing open- and closed-ended questions requesting factual responses or anecdotal perceptions. This method may prove problematic for participants to complete in its entirety.
- Reviewing program records or schedules usually kept in a database format for easy retrieval and archival use.
- Quantitatively comparing the results of standardized tests with educator-generated tests to measure student performance.
- Analyzing performance indicators such as grade-point average, classroom grade, attendance, and daily behavior.
- Studying products and portfolios of student performance in the classroom.

Choosing an Appropriate Assessment Method

The following considerations should be incorporated when **choosing an assessment method**:

- How the test developer defines the construct that will be used, e.g. aptitude, achievement, etc. The counselor should not utilize the assessment in a context other than the original one, since the results could be misrepresentative. The technical manual should also be studied, in order to value the utility of the test as well as the reliability and validity of the scores.
- How other organizations reviewed the test. Professional literature is available that will provide reviews from other counselors and similar organizations.

Copyright © Mometrix Media. You have been licensed one copy of this document for personal use only. Any other reproduction or redistribution is strictly prohibited. All rights reserved.
This content is provided for test preparation purposes only and does not imply an endorsement by Mometrix of any particular political, scientific, or religious point of view.

- The key factors that should be considered. Counselors considering a quantitative or qualitative assessment should analyze if the baseline and original population are appropriate for the student and whether the instrument can indicate a direction for intervention.

NEED FOR CURRENT RESEARCH AND EVALUATING RELIABILITY OF SOURCES

School counseling is a relatively young field; it has been around only since the 1920s. Since its establishment, school counseling has changed in focus and added much to its foundation, but there is much left to be learned. It is important that school counselors be familiar with **current research** so they can understand the most effective counseling trends.

Because research drives practice, it is important to use only research that is reliable. The source of a study should be peer-reviewed, which assures the reader that several professionals have reviewed the study for **ethical quality**, potential **biases**, and **methodology** to ensure the results are valid and reliable.

Considering the **literature review** that founded a study may also be helpful because it can point the reader to other related and reliable sources. A school counselor should read research skeptically and not only read the abstract of a study but review the data to see if the study was large enough to signify trends. Small studies may be informative but are more prone to population and sampling biases.

ANOVA

Analysis of Variance (ANOVA) is statistical calculation that determines whether the new teaching strategy has enough of an effect on a dependent condition (e.g., children's math scores) to make using the strategy worthwhile. Researchers compare two groups of test scores. One group did not experience any new teaching: the other participated in the new math program. The more people in a study, the more you can account for individual differences that might get in the way of seeing if the teaching strategy is what is determining the change in test scores. ANOVA equations look at the difference between the non-taught students' scores and the taught students' scores and evens out the differences that are not accounted for by the teaching method. Finally, the F-test shows whether or not the test scores were statistically significant. If F is more than 1, it is considered significant, and the amount over 1 (e.g., an F could be 17) gives an indication of how strongly the new teaching method is associated with the rise in test scores. A high F score indicates that there is a strong, positive relationship between the new

USE OF RESEARCH TO PROMOTE UNDERSTANDING OF NEED FOR SCHOOL COUNSELING TO COMMUNITIES

Counselors can use **research to inform the public**; for example, in newsletters to parents, a counselor might write a research-based article that describes the signs of cyberbullying.

Research studies can be used to create highly effective in-school programs informed by up-to-date findings. Well-established, recently re-validated assessments can be identified from professional journals before being offered to students.

Conducting thorough assessments of school counseling programs and presenting the findings to the greater community can help raise awareness of the usefulness of school counseling.

Action research is a trend in research in which educational professionals can bring research principles into their own practice to actively evaluate their own practice and provide information to

Copyright © Mometrix Media. You have been licensed one copy of this document for personal use only. Any other reproduction or redistribution is strictly prohibited. All rights reserved.
This content is provided for test preparation purposes only and does not imply an endorsement by Mometrix of any particular political, scientific, or religious point of view.

expand the research base. Action research is used to identify weaknesses in one's own practice, become informed, and take recursive action in response.

Current Research Databases

School counselors can use **databases** such as ERIC, PsycLIT, or PsycINFO to locate thousands of **peer-reviewed articles** published in a vast number of journals. For one seeking widespread information on a particular topic, databases provide the option of accessing scores of studies across hundreds of journals and decades of research.

Maintaining subscriptions to important peer-reviewed journals such as the *Professional School Counseling Journal* or *Journal of School Counseling* helps counselors stay abreast of current research and discussion in the field. Journals covering gender and cultural diversity aid in keeping important sociocultural issues in the forefront of the counselor's awareness.

Attending seminars and continuous education classes not only aids in the professional development of the counselor but also brings her or him into contact with current issues and discussions in the field.

Joining local groups of colleagues expands awareness of regional issues, creates opportunities to work together to implement relevant local change, and provides a forum of professional support.

Copyright © Mometrix Media. You have been licensed one copy of this document for personal use only. Any other reproduction or redistribution is strictly prohibited. All rights reserved.
This content is provided for test preparation purposes only and does not imply an endorsement by Mometrix of any particular political, scientific, or religious point of view.

Counseling and School Guidance Program Design

Designing and Implementing Interventions

The procedure for **intervention** entails **setting goals**, **designing intervention strategies** toward achieving those goals, and **evaluating the success of the intervention**. One of the first considerations in the intervention process is the counselor's consideration of a student's developmental stage, as well as the social and environmental settings and context. A counselor will want to make the decision to apply either formal or informal assessment methods, which in turn will affect evaluation procedures. Other factors to consider are informally assessing the level of parent and teacher support available for an intervention, as well as gauging the time constraints. Counselors should carefully consider all aspects of a student situation when determining intervention strategies. Another thing to be considered is whether resolving a situation may be beyond the scope of the school counseling setting, at which point the student should be referred to an outside resource.

Incorporating Collaboration and Flexibility in Setting Goals

Although it is important for each session, with each student, to be guided by clearly defined therapeutic goals, it is also important to recognize that reaching those goals is often a result of **collaboration** with the student, and may require some **flexibility** on the part of the counselor. The counseling relationship is inherently a dynamic one, which is most successful when there is a partnership between the counselor and the student. Setting and realizing goals in counseling should include the following considerations:

- What is particular about this student or this situation that needs to be incorporated into the strategy for intervention?
- What are the student's goals for this situation?

Answering these questions will enable the counselor to develop and refine goals, timelines, best approaches to each phase of the goals, and possibly even adjustments to the physical counseling environment. All of these and other interactive, collaborative considerations will contribute to the success and efficacy of the counseling session and relationship.

Criteria for Determining Appropriate Intervention

Initiating an intervention for a student or situation is a complex strategic decision that should take account of a number of factors. It is important to remember that a number of strategies are applicable in most situations, so counselors are wise to isolate those strategies that are most effective in an academic setting. It is also important to remember that a particular strategy that is appropriate and effective for one student and one situation might not be suitable for another student with the same situation. Counselors should **implement interventions** that will serve to develop and maintain a dynamic counseling relationship; that will work in tandem with a student's evolving development; that have reasonable goals for the allotted time frame; that are flexible in relation to individual student circumstances;to the student's overt behavior; and that are respectful of diversity and culture.

Choosing Interventions in an Academic Setting

The general considerations for an **intervention in an academic setting** are the age, development, cultural background, and social skills of the student. Cultural and social considerations are particularly pivotal because they can provide the parameters for establishing recognition and context for some interventions. It might be useful to consult the families of students when determining the cultural and social relevance of a particular therapeutic method. Categories of

Copyright © Mometrix Media. You have been licensed one copy of this document for personal use only. Any other reproduction or redistribution is strictly prohibited. All rights reserved.
This content is provided for test preparation purposes only and does not imply an endorsement by Mometrix of any particular political, scientific, or religious point of view.

therapy generally fall into broad areas of multimodal counseling, family counseling, direct and indirect play therapy, and expressive art therapy. Common therapy strategies for school-age children include drama, storytelling, music, art, puppetry, use of tactile materials like clay and sand, and an array of play therapies. Other formal methods include reality therapy, Gestalt techniques, cognitive-behavioral counseling, and Adlerian counseling. Knowledge of the spectrum of available therapies is particularly valuable for counselors seeking appropriate interventions for students in an academic setting.

Determining Appropriate Interventions According to Behavior and Symptoms

Once a counselor has narrowed down the **choice of appropriate therapies for a particular situation**, it is then a good idea to further narrow the options to those that would be appropriate for a particular student, with **particular overt behaviors** or **symptoms**. For instance, a student with ADHD might benefit most from a therapy that focuses on impulse control and self-monitoring, while a student who displays difficulty completing assignments might be better served by a kind of reality therapy that allows him or her to apply abstract thinking to consideration of the impact of their actions and to develop alternative behaviors. Another significant example is working with a student suffering from depression, who may need to first work on thought patterns through cognitive therapy, before or in tandem with other therapies targeting the situation. It is always appropriate to consider the cultural background, age, and developmental level of the student when choosing therapies.

Intervention Implementation

A **successful intervention** is best preceded by the establishment of a strong relationship between counselor and student. From there, the counselor can recommend an intervention to the student, who in turn will feel empowered by the effect of collaboration. This approach also provides students with validation, encouragement, and the endorsement of their own desires for resolution. Once the intervention is in place, it may be appropriate for counselors to discuss the progress and goals of the therapy with parents, teachers and others included in the student's support network. Likewise, if the intervention therapy is not progressing as anticipated, it may be appropriate to work with teachers to develop behavioral strategies in the classroom to complement the therapy. This communication and collaboration with teachers and/or parents should be within the context of the counseling sessions, and should honor the counselor's responsibilities to the school and the community.

Including the Student in Evaluation Procedures

Communicating with the student about the success of interventions, and the progress toward therapeutic goals, should take account of the counseling relationship. Indeed, the **student's response to evaluation practices** helps decide the success of the intervention. Without student response, counselors run the risk of losing the student's trust. A counselor can determine if a particular student, in a particular environment, would be best served by an informal or a formal evaluation of progress. In a collaborative informal evaluation, both student and counselor are present and the counselor can observe and monitor student response. Formal evaluations take into account reports from parents and teachers, as well as the student's documentation of his or her success in a particular area. With either formal or informal evaluation of progress, the counselor should make it a practice to take into consideration the relationship that has been established with the student.

Cautions and Safeguards Regarding Evaluation Procedures

While counselor-generated evaluations are to some extent inherently subjective, there are several recommended safeguards to ensure a **reasonable level of objectivity**. In terms of the relationship

Copyright © Mometrix Media. You have been licensed one copy of this document for personal use only. Any other reproduction or redistribution is strictly prohibited. All rights reserved.
This content is provided for test preparation purposes only and does not imply an endorsement by Mometrix of any particular political, scientific, or religious point of view.

to the student, the counselor should maintain a professional emotional distance, while still demonstrating sensitivity to student needs and feelings. The counselor should guard against becoming too emotionally attached to a student, since this could obscure the counselor's ability to evaluate empirically the level of success of the therapy or intervention. It is also important that the counselor and/or counseling team develop evaluation techniques and a rubric that will appropriately assess the achievement of therapeutic goals. A single-case study experimental design may be advisable. Another common suggestion is for the counselor to implement both formal and informal evaluation techniques to allow for more objective assessment.

Sensitivities Involved in Ending the Counseling Relationship

The academic counseling relationship is perhaps more susceptible to difficulties in closure than the professional relationship, for the mere fact that the student and counselor may have met several days a week, or even several times a day. For this reason, the **termination of the relationship** needs to be approached carefully and methodically. Although there is no definitive research regarding this process, there are some generally agreed-upon practices. Termination can be an abrupt or a gradual process, but it is nonetheless recommended that the counselor use his or her discretion in choosing a time to prepare the student for the last session. It is a good idea for the counselor to take this time to reinforce with the student the success of the counseling relationship, including the progress and improvements made by the student. Counselors should be attentive to student feelings and responses, and should recommend outside resources as appropriate.

Brief-Counseling Method

Parameters and Purpose

The brief-counseling method, sometimes referred to as **solution-focused brief counseling (SFBC)**, is often indicated in schools that have regimented time constraints for counseling. The parameters of these brief-counseling sessions are designed to mimic the parameters of longer individual sessions, but modeled for the indicated time period. The SFBC model also incorporates the unique aspects of the school counseling session. The model includes an opportunity for the student to concretely describe his or her particular situation, present any previous attempted resolutions, and then develop and implement an intervention. The SFBC model is most effective when the counselors utilize the time to endorse student strengths, successes, and resources. This model is often found to be effective for students of diverse backgrounds and cultures.

Basic Premises and Strategies

Some of the key premises that underlie the SFBC model are:

- Focus should be directed toward solutions, and not toward the problems.
- Within each problem is an identifiable exception that should be isolated and addressed when formulating a solution.
- Large changes often begin with small changes.
- Within each student are the resources needed to solve his or her problem.
- The basic strategies of SFBC are:
- If the counselor determines that no problematic issue exists, he or she should be cautious not to create one.
- Counselors should develop tasks similar to those with which the student has found success.
- Counselors should be open to the necessity of changing strategies, if it is found that a particular strategy is unsuccessful with a particular student or situation.

These premises and strategies have been carefully researched and formulated by a consortium of counselors well versed in the SFBC model.

Copyright © Mometrix Media. You have been licensed one copy of this document for personal use only. Any other reproduction or redistribution is strictly prohibited. All rights reserved.
This content is provided for test preparation purposes only and does not imply an endorsement by Mometrix of any particular political, scientific, or religious point of view.

Core Concepts

The strategies indicated for SFBC are based on the following set of core concepts:

- If the counselor develops and presents the goals in a positive context, then cooperation, collaboration, and positive response from the student are more likely.
- In the SFBC model, a pragmatic approach is much more indicated than a theoretical one; in other words, this model focuses on what works rather than what the problem is.
- Counselors should be careful to formulate intervention strategies that can be reasonably attained within the allotted time frame.
- Because of the nature and parameters of the SFBC model, counselors should encourage students to focus on present and future circumstances, and to avoid past experiences as much as possible.
- Counselors should focus intervention strategies on students' behaviors and actions, rather than on reflective insights.

All of these strategies contribute to the efficacy and success of the SFBC model of counseling session.

Interactive Format in the First Session

One of the goals of the **first session** of the SFBC model is for the counselor to present the student with a series of questions designed to **elicit a response**. These responses will form the foundation for developing an intervention. A recommended format for introducing these questions is for the counselor to first present the basic goals and premises of SFBC. Second, he or she will inform the student that questions will be asked, and that the questions could prove to be difficult or challenging. This precursor strategy often sets the stage for the student to be poised with a response to a challenge. The student's response will often provide the counselor with a starting point for intervention. This posturing will contribute to the efficacy of questioning in the first session of the SFBC.

Empowering and Encouraging Students to Create Positive Goals

Creating positive goals requires the capacity to envision oneself realizing those goals. Some of the strategies that counselors can use to facilitate this process include:

- Asking the student how he or she would feel and react if his or her situation were suddenly resolved.
- Asking the student to identify instances where the current situation was not problematic, or when there were exceptions to the situation. This can be a very powerful step, in that it may recall a recent instance of resolution that the student can recognize and respond to.
- Asking the student what actions or behaviors led to some resolution, or mitigation, of the situation. The counselor should encourage positive actions and results.
- Asking the student to rate their feelings about their behavior or the situation on a scale of 1 to 10.
- Anticipating possible obstacles, and working to guide the students around and/or past those obstacles.

Benefits of Group Counseling in Addition to Individual Counseling

As a rule, adolescents tend to learn better and respond more when interacting with peers. Therefore, **group counseling that augments individual counseling** can be beneficial. In group counseling, students have the opportunity to both give and receive support for positive behaviors. Likewise, group counseling provides immediate feedback for negative behaviors and thought

Copyright © Mometrix Media. You have been licensed one copy of this document for personal use only. Any other reproduction or redistribution is strictly prohibited. All rights reserved.
This content is provided for test preparation purposes only and does not imply an endorsement by Mometrix of any particular political, scientific, or religious point of view.

patterns, allowing the student to reflect on his or her choices. The format of a group counseling session can also serve as a microcosm of larger society, providing a venue for students to experiment with behaviors in a controlled environment, and to experience the feedback of peers with whom they have developed a trust relationship. Group counseling, in tandem with the more remedial individual counseling, provides a comprehensive therapeutic environment for the student. Counselors who utilize both formats reap the benefits of opportunities for preventative therapy, as well as a richer school counseling program.

Types of Group Counseling

There are many **models of group therapy**, including **psycho-educational groups, crisis-centered groups, problem-centered groups**, and **growth-centered groups**. Each of these groups carries its own considerations as a model for various situations. The psycho-educational group is generally helpful in promoting a student's awareness of common issues in life. Crisis-centered groups are often short-term and responsive to a major trauma on a community-scale. Problem-centered groups and growth-centered groups are preventative in nature. Growth-centered groups are designed to help students grow in areas of deficiency, such as self-esteem, whereas problem-centered groups are designed to reduce risk of major problems occurring in the future or developing over time. The problems in question include substance abuse or stress-related issues in students' lives.

Psycho-Educational Groups

Differences Between Psycho-Educational and Counseling Groups

To appreciate the distinctions between **psycho-educational** and **counseling groups**, it is a good idea to first identify the similarities. Either group can address life management issues such as loss, stress issues, academic success, etc. Either group can be categorized into developmental, remedial, or school environments. Where they differ is in the focus within the groups and group sessions. Counseling groups tend to address matters of managing crisis, targeting issues of process more than specific content issues. Psycho-educational groups, on the other hand, apply a more concentrated focus on particular content. Counseling groups tend to be less structured than psycho-educational groups. The effect and impact on students in the two groups is often perceived as distinctively different, although counselors tend to view them as similar in format and purpose.

Parameters and Benefits

Psycho-educational groups serve to address and develop **personal growth factors within an academic or educational setting**. The academic setting provides a framework for targeting common adolescent issues like emotional development, self-image, identity definition, and interpersonal skills. The student in the psycho-educational group develops socially and emotionally while addressing academic skills. The counselor in the psycho-educational setting can provide students with increasingly difficult developmental tasks, resulting in optimum benefit for the student. An important added benefit of this model is that it provides students with an array of resources, contributing to an increased feeling of self-worth and self-confidence. An effective psycho-educational counseling group can contribute positively to the futures of the students involved, by both mitigating future problem occurrences, as well as by providing a cache of resources that will be useful in career planning.

Choosing Topics or Themes

The initial consideration for **choosing topics for psycho-educational groups** should be the age and developmental level of the students involved. While adolescent and pre-adolescent groups will respond better to a focus on social and interpersonal skills, groups of younger students thrive in a friendship or playgroup, or a group focused on problem solving. These topics or themes can provide

Copyright © Mometrix Media. You have been licensed one copy of this document for personal use only. Any other reproduction or redistribution is strictly prohibited. All rights reserved.
This content is provided for test preparation purposes only and does not imply an endorsement by Mometrix of any particular political, scientific, or religious point of view.

a framework for students to address peripheral issues. It might be advantageous to refer to the school's agenda for academic and social skill development, in order to compile topics for psycho-educational groups. Some typical topics, particularly for adolescents, are stress management, romantic relationships, time management, and career planning. It is also a good idea to ask the school if there are any survey instruments they have used to identify topics of interest among their students.

Components in Creating a Group

The first step in creating a psycho-educational group is to define the following:

- Purpose of the group
- Anticipated membership
- Focus of the group
- Interventions and expected outcomes

Then, the counselor should clearly identify both long-term objectives and measured short-term steps toward those objectives, applicable to each session. The counselor should develop content and exercises that use an experiential framework which will incorporate and address the following:

- The demographics and targeted needs of the group
- Educational content that fits within the students' academic agendas
  * Opportunities for students to learn from experience
- A format that allows students to make connections between tasks and skills
- Exercises that generate group discussion and response

Finally, evaluation of the success of the group should include evaluation of each session and the process involved in achieving the long-term objectives.

Counseling Groups

Focus and Student Population

Counseling groups are generally formed to address **personal issues that hinder or prohibit academic success**. The groups can target behavioral problems such as outbursts of temper, class disruption, social maladjustment, etc.; or they can target specific life-altering events such as the death of a loved one or a pregnancy. The groups are formed to work solely on the personal issues, aside from any resulting academic problems. Students referred to counseling groups have demonstrated an inability or diminished ability, particularly in the case of a personal crisis, to manage and positively respond to their academic responsibilities. Within the counseling groups, facilitators can provide an environment for students to benefit from peer support, particualrly by removing the sense of isolation. Benefits include a stronger sense of self-worth and the adoption of healthy strategies to handle emotions.

Parameters and Format

The counseling group provides a **safe venue** for students to express and process overwhelming emotions. The **overall tone of the group** should be one of caring, compassion, and empathy. Many of its members will have experienced, or will be experiencing, similar events and emotions. The **format of the group** should be one of support, trust, and understanding. Members of the group should feel a sense of camaraderie with the other members. Acting as facilitator, group counselors can encourage peers within the group to provide support and suggestions for emotional healing to the other members, contributing to the general benefit of the entire group. Counselors should also

Copyright © Mometrix Media. You have been licensed one copy of this document for personal use only. Any other reproduction or redistribution is strictly prohibited. All rights reserved.
This content is provided for test preparation purposes only and does not imply an endorsement by Mometrix of any particular political, scientific, or religious point of view.

be cognizant of each student's need to address both actions and thought patterns in the process of working through their issues or trauma with the group.

Crisis-Centered Groups

A **crisis-centered group** is formed in direct response to a **traumatic precipitating event**. The event could involve a few individuals, or could be school-wide, such as a shooting or bus accident. The overarching purpose of a crisis-centered group is that of providing a controlled venue where students can express their feelings. In the case of an issue involving a few students, such as a disruptive conflict between students, an additional goal of the crisis-centered group is to facilitate resolution of the conflict. In this case, the group will form for the purpose of resolution, and will meet at least until the matter is resolved. In the case of a large population trauma, the group will form to assist the students in coping. In both of these instances, additional meetings could be held to work on personal development issues for the student members.

Problem-Centered Groups

Problem-centered groups are often an outgrowth of crisis-centered groups, formed after the crisis has passed or been resolved. These groups are formed to address issues that either precipitated the crisis or could cause problems in the future. The students in these groups come together to focus on specific issues that may be hindering their academic progress or their general well-being. Some of the issues that are addressed in problem-centered groups are stress management, conflict resolution strategies, academic or career goals, and substance abuse. The effectiveness of the group depends on the openness of its members to resolution. Participation in problem-centered groups is usually an option chosen by the students involved. The members of these groups, which are usually smaller than crisis-centered groups, benefit from the support and input from other members in resolving an issue that may feel overwhelming when faced alone.

Growth-Centered Groups

Similar to problem-centered groups, **growth-centered groups** often form as an outgrowth of a previous group. For instance, if a crisis-centered group is formed to address situation by discussing anger management, the growth-centered group will instead address each individual student's issues and concerns, which may be peripheral or essential to the group topic. Under the umbrella topic of a common issue like anger management, students may be dealing with low self-esteem, stress as a result of poor time management, conflicting value paradigms, etc. The tone of the group is supportive and empathetic, allowing students to develop healthy responses to their situation. The group as a whole works on positive behavior dynamics. Growth-centered groups allow counselors to identify and address students on an individual basis.

Forming Groups in School Settings

Once a counselor perceives a need to form a group, based on input from teachers, parents, and/or students, the following parameters need to be explored and established:

- Topic and purpose of the group
- Group meeting schedules and the time allotted for sessions
- Proposed members of the group and total group size
- Established process and rubric for recruiting and screening potential members

The focus and purpose of these groups should be primarily for the benefit of the students, within the context of the therapeutic paradigm. Counselors should discuss the group's formation with teachers and other school personnel as appropriate before launching the group. Issues of confidentiality should be clearly and firmly established and communicated to students, parents, and

Copyright © Mometrix Media. You have been licensed one copy of this document for personal use only. Any other reproduction or redistribution is strictly prohibited. All rights reserved.
This content is provided for test preparation purposes only and does not imply an endorsement by Mometrix of any particular political, scientific, or religious point of view.

school personnel. Although the groups are generally established for the benefit and well-being of the students, the provisions of confidentiality and other counseling ethics continue to apply.

Dovetailing of School Counseling Curriculum to Standard Academic Curriculum

While the **school counseling curriculum** is developed within the same parameters as the standard academic curriculum, there are distinguishing characteristics and processes. One of the differences is that the standard academic curriculum is generally developed to address grade- or age-based curricular goals, whereas counseling curriculum also incorporates behavioral strategies and expectations. Counselors can further augment curriculum with professional expertise and knowledge gleaned from professional journals or other resources. In terms of process, standard academic curriculum is often a collaborative product of committees that include parents, school staff, and administration. School counseling curriculum is generally developed by counselors and teachers. However, many schools have liaison committees available to assist school counselors in developing curriculum. Nonetheless, all school staff should be aware of the goals and strategies employed in school counseling curriculum, and counselors should align academic curricular goals with the school counseling curriculum.

Standards for Developing School Counseling Curriculum

There are both state standards and national models (from associations such as the ASCA) for the development of school counseling curriculum. These models address **expectations for grade and education levels**, as well as school guidance models targeting different regions and grade levels. A number of states have developed counseling programs that are derived from national recommendations, incorporating current literature and the success rates for particular models or strategies. When developing school counseling curriculum, counselors should follow these **national and state models** while continuing to consider recommendations from the school community. The **local school community** is often the best source for strategies to improve the academic, personal, and career development of the students. Collaboration with a school advisory group can also facilitate development of a counseling curriculum that best meets students' needs and the goals of the school community at large.

Designing Programs for All Students That Will Also Benefit the Community

Since schools are the **primary focal point for issues** relating to adolescents, counselors and educators often work with other community entities in discussing and developing strategies for addressing the needs of youth. Some of these entities include libraries, police departments, private schools, recreation centers, and other community-based programs as well as national- and state-based organizations. One of the ways that **counselors can work as liaison** between students and these entities is by dispelling the idea that the onus of at-risk behavior lies with the student. They can work with community representatives who feel that students are solely or primarily to blame for their behavior. Counselors can collaborate with educators to develop programs that are designed to address the needs of not only mainstream students, but also at-risk students. These programs can incorporate the needs and concerns of the larger community as well as academic goals identified for the student population.

Family Systems Theory

Family systems theory focuses on the particular context of the child's family. Whereas individual approaches may focus on modifying a particular behavior, or considering the personality traits of a student, systems theory attends to the **interactions of the child with parents, siblings, extended family members, and family history**. Theorist and practitioners like Murray Bowen and Virginia

Copyright © Mometrix Media. You have been licensed one copy of this document for personal use only. Any other reproduction or redistribution is strictly prohibited. All rights reserved.
This content is provided for test preparation purposes only and does not imply an endorsement by Mometrix of any particular political, scientific, or religious point of view.

Satir recognized that individuals are under constant pressure in the family system to act in ways that maintain stability of the system—sometimes at great cost to the well-being of the individual.

Virginia Satir, who started working with families in 1951, was arguably the first family systems therapist in the United States. Satir identified the omnipresent characteristic of family homeostasis but also insisted on the lifelong potential of change for the better. Children are helped by addressing family interactions, and the entire family becomes healthier.

Satir also attended to the negative effects of low self-esteem on marital partners and how unhappy marriages create dysfunctional families. One dysfunctional process, triangulation (also researched by Murray Bowen), puts a child between the warring adults, perhaps as scapegoat, confidante, or go-between but always to the child's detriment.

School Counseling Advisory Group

A school counseling advisory group can provide guidance counselors with the **comprehensive expectations of the school community** as well as a track record of current and previous school counseling models. Generally, these advisory groups are comprised of school staff, school counselors, parents, and community members. The overall focus of most counseling programs, and therefore their advisory groups, is often the development of curriculum that **addresses common and relevant issues** like sexual harassment, bullying, and social relationships. Counselors can refer to past discussions and studies to glean information about strategies that did or did not work, as well as areas that may have required particular attention. Advisory groups can inform counselors about pedagogical or counseling approaches that work best in their school environment. It is advisable for counselors to maintain ongoing communication with advisory groups and other school community members in order to keep apprised of current needs or problem areas.

Considerations When Generating Student Outcome Expectations

Expected student outcomes should reflect the combined input of **state and national standards**, **current literature**, and **formal and informal needs assessments** conducted at the school or district level. Advisory groups, when undertaking the task of generating student outcome goals, should first amass the relevant information and resources. This will form the basis for future discussions and collaboration within the group and with the school counselors. Student outcomes should represent what students should know or be able to do upon graduation from high school. The National Standards for School Counseling Programs delineates 9 standards that incorporate academic, personal, social, and career development areas. Student outcome expectations should be broken down into smaller sequential goals. Counselors working with the district and school community can develop strategies and a rubric for addressing these sequenced student outcome goals.

Developing Instruction and Assessment

Designing K-12 Grade-Based Curricula

Although counselors teaching at various grade levels are generally responsible for developing and delivering curricula appropriate to the level, it is recommendable to develop that curricula as an integral part of a comprehensive K-12 curriculum. For example, counselors who teach at the elementary level, while **delivering curricula appropriate for that grade level**, also should be cognizant of the **larger curricular goals** as well as the next phase of students' studies. It is important that students receive curricula that builds on previous learning foundations. Student learning within each classroom should not be an isolated experience, nor should it be unnecessarily redundant. Although some schools and districts operate within a paradigm that allows for quasi-

Copyright © Mometrix Media. You have been licensed one copy of this document for personal use only. Any other reproduction or redistribution is strictly prohibited. All rights reserved.
This content is provided for test preparation purposes only and does not imply an endorsement by Mometrix of any particular political, scientific, or religious point of view.

isolated curriculum development within broad age groups, it is nonetheless usually recommended that all curriculum development be designed within a larger K-12 context.

Facilitating Student Expansion of Knowledge

Counselors can and should encourage the furtherance of student knowledge, either through synthesis between disciplines, or through sequential learning within a particular discipline. Counselors and teachers can communicate and collaborate, both within a grade level and between grade levels, to develop lesson plans that encourage students to **form correlations between counseling curricula and academic curricula**. This can also extend to correlation between disciplines, such as between history and narrative or between math and music. Teaching in the classroom can include the Socratic approach, encouraging student curiosity about the connections between disciplines. Counselors can also work with students to strive for the next level of sequential learning within a particular discipline, by making those connections explicit within the lesson plans. Sequential learning strategies contribute to future student success as they move to higher grade and school levels.

Lesson Plan Components

Generally, regardless of the grade level or the discipline, most **successful lesson plans** will include three basic components. The first of these components is the **introduction**. In this part of the lesson, students are introduced to the general topic or the particular focus area of the lesson. Secondly, the lesson plan should include **activities that will serve to develop the lesson**. These activities can be performed by the counselor, a teacher, or can be participatory activities by the students. The third section of the lesson not only **concludes the lesson**, but also evolves into an **application portion**, whereby students are able to project the lesson into their daily lives. This portion of the lesson often also includes student discussion. The total effect of this kind of sequenced lesson plan is increased student engagement and a greater likelihood that students will remember and assimilate the lesson.

Lesson Introduction

Introducing a lesson topic serves several purposes in classroom teaching. Initially, it focuses students' attention on the topic to be addressed. In this sense, delivery of the introduction should be clear and compelling, **soliciting student interest and engagement**. It can also be valuable to let students know the planned learning goals or areas to be covered. Students can begin to develop a mental blueprint as the lesson progresses, and will be more receptive to each step of the lesson development, like a concert attendee following a program. It also helps to make connections with previous lessons or knowledge foundations, encouraging class participation. Lesson plans that are well introduced are more likely to result in comprehensive student understanding.

Including Previous Knowledge in Lesson Plans

Incorporating previous knowledge in a lesson plan imbues students with the self-confidence and orientation to the lesson to be more engaged. It also helps to establish a **participatory trust** between counselor-teacher and students. Students are more likely to feel that they already possess useful information, and the counselor is there to facilitate the expansion of their knowledge base. A useful strategy for incorporating previous knowledge in a lesson plan is to ask questions, to which students can positively respond. Building on this, counselors can introduce next sequences or facets of knowledge, possibly by asking relevant questions and volunteering the answers. Another valuable strategy is to reiterate previous knowledge, with which students are already familiar, and then to lead the class to the next phase of knowledge or skill development. Students whose previous knowledge is acknowledged are likely to be more receptive and participate more fully.

Copyright © Mometrix Media. You have been licensed one copy of this document for personal use only. Any other reproduction or redistribution is strictly prohibited. All rights reserved.
This content is provided for test preparation purposes only and does not imply an endorsement by Mometrix of any particular political, scientific, or religious point of view.

Developmental Activities in Lesson Plans

Counselors can also **incorporate previous knowledge** in the developmental activity portion of a lesson plan. Planned activities can address students' existing knowledge about a topic, giving them opportunities to express that knowledge, and then can lead the students to a new level of of understanding. It is important that counselors develop a **clear outline for planned activities**, cognizant of the strategies being utilized to reach the objectives. Additionally, a **rubric** should be established in order to clearly assess the effectiveness of activity strategies. A distinguishing characteristic of developmental activities is that they provide a vehicle for expression through multiple intelligences, further contributing to the collective benefit of the class. Counselors should be sensitive to individual strengths and needs, and should tailor activities accordingly. Developmental activities can provide another vehicle for student confidence and participation.

Eliciting Responses Through Different Intelligences

Counselors can augment the traditional verbal/text-based classroom lesson plan with activities that engage students' artistic, spatial, logical, kinesthetic, and other learning modes. Counselors can **present lesson topics through various media**, including music and pictures. They can also ask students to respond experientially by drawing, writing a poem, playing drums, or possibly composing and performing a song or dance. **Multiple media responses** are particularly valuable when working with students on qualitative issues like problem-solving or personal crises. Counselors employing multiple-media and multiple-intelligence approaches to curriculum delivery provide students greater opportunity for engagement and expression. This increases the efficacy of the lesson, and is a more inclusive strategy for students with diverse learning styles. Counselors should be sensitive to the particular student group in the classroom, and the individual learning styles represented.

Effectiveness of Passive and Active Learning Styles

The **traditional lecture-based curriculum delivery style** is effective in terms of transmitting information, but only requires the student to participate in a very **limited, passive manner**. Students who simply hear the information are limited to a particular learning style and more subject to distraction. Complementing the lecture with videos or handouts can increase students' receptivity by adding visual stimuli. A more effective augmentation would be to include opportunities for students to actively participate and learn. Some examples of **active learning** include verbal question response, writing on the board, note taking, and other activities that require students to be engaged. Also, if students are asked to reiterate information through writing or other activities, they necessarily are focused on the lesson. Active learning strategies significantly increase the amount of data that students acquire.

Conclusion to a Developmental Lesson or Activity

Although the **conclusion** is generally fewer than five minutes, there are several objectives to be accomplished in its various components. The conclusion is a time to reiterate what has been learned, and to give students the opportunity to **assimilate new knowledge**. Counselors can begin by repeating the knowledge that students brought into the classroom, and the increased knowledge that was obtained during the session. Students should be asked to give a **recap or response to the lesson**, to indicate that they have understood. Student response increases their receptivity, and gives the counselor an indication of how much the students have understood. This time can also be used to cite examples and applications for the lesson, further increasing students' assimilation of the lesson. Student participation and response is pivotal to this part of the lesson.

Copyright © Mometrix Media. You have been licensed one copy of this document for personal use only. Any other reproduction or redistribution is strictly prohibited. All rights reserved.
This content is provided for test preparation purposes only and does not imply an endorsement by Mometrix of any particular political, scientific, or religious point of view.

Importance of Assessing Learning Objectives

Counselors can **informally assess the effectiveness of a lesson** and the general level of student receptivity by listening to student responses during the lesson and at the conclusion. However, a more **formal assessment** can be advantageous for a few reasons. If a counselor develops a written rubric before presenting a lesson, this rubric can provide a real-time backdrop for counselors to both assess and guide the lessons toward its conclusion. Having a kind of inventory for lesson objectives can provide an outline for the discussion that can be at least informally shared with students, allowing them to realize their progress. In addition, a written rubric can provide the kind of quantitative, formal assessment vehicle that is very valuable in **building credibility** with the school community. With clear assessment information, counselors can experience increased collaboration and support from school staff, counselors, and parents.

Designing an Assessment Rubric

Designing an **assessment rubric** for school counseling classroom strategies begins with defining the learning objectives. Also included should be the demographics of the group, expected learning outcomes, and clear criteria for measurement. Once this rubric is clearly delineated, counselors can **target learning objectives** with specific planned activities. They can **assess the success of the activity** by comparing student responses with the rubric criteria. It is important that the components of the rubric be clearly defined before the commencement of the lesson, in order for the counselor to design and deliver activities that will elicit appropriate responses. All of this can be conducted during the normal course of a classroom lesson, with its introduction, activity, and conclusion. A clearly written rubric designed well before the lesson will ensure a successful, non-disruptive assessment.

Role of Assessment in Designing Lesson Strategies

Lesson plan assessment results can provide a **metric for the success of the lesson** as well as the **relevance of the learning objectives**. If student responses have met the criteria set forth in the rubric, counselors can be fairly assured that the lesson or activity was relevant and targeted the expected objective. However, if student behaviors or responses do not meet the rubric criteria, there are several possible explanations that should be considered, individually or in concert. An initial consideration is that of the lesson or activity, to review its **applicability to the group and to the objectives**. Another consideration is the objectives themselves. Counselors should determine whether the objectives were reasonable for the student group. The value of a rubric with clearly defined components is realized if some of the criteria are met, but others are not. Counselors can then adjust the lesson or activity according to the results of the assessment.

Copyright © Mometrix Media. You have been licensed one copy of this document for personal use only. Any other reproduction or redistribution is strictly prohibited. All rights reserved.
This content is provided for test preparation purposes only and does not imply an endorsement by Mometrix of any particular political, scientific, or religious point of view.

Ethics and Legal Issues

Legal and Ethical Obligations of School Counselors

Counselors are obligated both explicitly and implicitly to treat each of their clients **ethically and within legal boundaries**. Counselors need to be aware of all federal, state, district and other institutional laws and mandates regarding school counseling. Counselors also should recognize the ethical obligation to be cognizant of current research and resources pertaining to issues that students will be dealing with in the counseling sessions. Although it is understandable that no one can know resources for all the possible situations facing students, it is nonetheless ethically required of counselors to endeavor to add to their knowledge as is reasonable, to best serve the students. Counselors who are beginning their careers may spend more time researching specific issues, but will become more knowledgeable about issues affecting students. Professional associations provide guidelines and sources for counselors regarding this aspect.

Review Video: Ethical and Professional Standards
Visit mometrix.com/academy and enter code: 391843

State and Federal Confidentiality Regulations

Federal statutes generally address the right of a parent to access records of a minor student. Both state and federal mandates dictate that parents have the right of access to privileged information, although some state laws mitigate that right in the case of abuse or neglect. It is important for counselors to be cognizant of both federal and state statutes regarding the protection of information relating to minor students. Since federal law generally protects the right of parents to view their minor child's school records, counselors should probably keep counseling records separate from school records, in accordance with school and/or district rules. Awareness of both federal and state laws regarding confidentiality can impact not only a counselor's treatment of information, but also his or her approach to the counseling relationship, including informing both students and parents of these rulings.

Overarching Rule and Importance of Confidentiality in Counseling

The general **rule of confidentiality**, as denoted by the American School Counseling Association, specifies that counselors be mandated to protect the confidentiality of the student unless there is indication of intent to harm self or others. It is important to both the student and the integrity of the counseling relationship that this confidentiality principal be explained in a manner that is aligned with the student's age group and ability to perceive the explanation. This confidentiality ethic needs to be explained to parents also. The benefits of clearly explaining issues of confidentiality include the student's trust to divulge sensitive information, as well as the parents' understanding of the ethical obligation of the counselor to protect the student's confidentiality. It is also important that the student understands the counselor's obligation to breach confidentiality if he or she fears the student will harm him/herself or others.

Review Video: Ethics and Confidentiality in Counseling
Visit mometrix.com/academy and enter code: 250384

Approaching the Issue of Confidentiality with Students

It is important that the student not only understands the tenets of **confidentiality**, but also feels comfortable with the counselor's obligations and respect of confidentiality issues. Younger students may participate in a counseling situation with their parents present, but it should be clearly explained to both parents and students that information divulged in a session without the parents

Copyright © Mometrix Media. You have been licensed one copy of this document for personal use only. Any other reproduction or redistribution is strictly prohibited. All rights reserved.
This content is provided for test preparation purposes only and does not imply an endorsement by Mometrix of any particular political, scientific, or religious point of view.

will be protected. Although young students need to understand that this confidentiality can be breached in the presence of threat to self or others, it is more an assurance to parents to indicate that this aspect of confidentiality is in place. On the other hand, adolescent students are particularly sensitive to protection of their confidentiality, and it is important that they be aware of the criteria for breaching that confidentiality. To best respect the rapport established with an adolescent, a counselor could approach these criteria using humor or exaggerated examples.

ACA

The **American Counseling Association (ACA)** is a professional organization that promotes the development of counselors, advances the counseling profession, and promotes social justice within the profession. Their scope is all professional counselors. The ACA seeks to apply the profession and practice of counseling to the purpose of promoting and respecting cultural diversity, while enhancing the overall quality of life in society. The ACA includes 18 divisions, which focus on particular areas or work settings within the counseling profession, four geographic regions and 56 affiliate branches. It actually is comprised of a partnership of associations. The ACA influences many aspects of professional counseling, including credentialing of counselors, accreditation of counselor education programs, public policy and legislation, and professional resources and services. The ACA, operating in part through committees, holds functions and develops specific programs for the advancement of the profession.

Standing Committees, Task Forces, and Outreach

The following are the 15 standing committees of the ACA:

- Audit
- Awards
- Branch Development
- Bylaws
- Compensation
- Conference Program Selection
- Ethics
- Financial Affairs
- Graduate Student
- Human Rights
- International
- Nominations and Election
- Professional Standards
- Public Policy and Legislation
- Publications
- Research and Knowledge

Ad hoc task forces are created annually to address current concerns and business issues. Most task forces are brought together 1 year, but can stay together longer if needed. In that case, members must be re-appointed. The ACA offers training workshops, professional development conferences, and learning institutes. ACA publications address current research and are often used as textbooks in counseling courses.

ASCA, NBCC, and CACREP

A subgroup of the ACA, the **American School Counselor Association (ASCA)**, addresses those issues in professional counseling that pertain to students, with a focus on academic, personal-social,

Copyright © Mometrix Media. You have been licensed one copy of this document for personal use only. Any other reproduction or redistribution is strictly prohibited. All rights reserved.
This content is provided for test preparation purposes only and does not imply an endorsement by Mometrix of any particular political, scientific, or religious point of view.

and career development issues. School counselors are particularly pivotal in the lives of students, in that long-term life success patterns are often closely tied to academic success and a positive school experience. The ASCA provides additional information to school counselors through professional development, research and advocacy.

The **NBCC, the National Board for Certified Counselors**, is the only national credentialing organization for counselors. The Board also has established several specialty-area certifications requiring passage of the **National Counselor Exam (NCE)**.

A corporate partner of the ACA, the **CACREP, the Council for Accreditation of Counseling and Related Educational Programs**, establishes state-of-the-art standards for counselor education programs that address curriculum, program objectives, program evaluation, faculty and staff criteria and other requirements.

Ethical Standards in School Counseling

Ethical standards are developed by most professional organizations, and are designed to direct the behavior of its members. The ethical standards for school counselors are frequently updated to reflect changes in the school system, usually at the federal level. These updated standards are revised in order to be relevant and appropriate for the school counseling profession. Ethical standards generally address the following three purposes:

- To educate members about sound ethical conduct
- To provide a mechanism for accountability
- To provide a mechanism for improvement of professional practices

The ACA's Code of Ethics is based on the following five moral principles:

- Autonomy: the ability to make independent decisions
- Justice: treatment that is fair and appropriate
- Beneficence: services and actions that are in the students' best interests
- Fidelity: commitment to the student regarding honor, loyalty and faithfulness
- Nonmaleficence: avoidance of actions or services that would cause harm to others

Laws Related to School Counseling

Although **laws** are based on generally accepted norms, customs, values and beliefs, they are more binding and carry more severe penalties than ethical standards. Laws are codified into written governing documents. Laws are more prescriptive and require that counselors comply or be penalized. Both laws and ethical standards are designed to ensure that professionals follow appropriate behavior patterns and act in the best interests of the student(s). Laws and ethical standards should adhere to the same patterns and expectations, but if on occasion a law conflicts with an ethical standard, the counselor is encouraged to comply with the law. Counselors must advise the student if they encounter a situation where the laws and ethical standards are in conflict, and inform the student that they will follow the legal course of action, provided there is no harm to the student as a result.

Discrepancies in Ethics Codes

There is some responsibility on the part of the school counselor to critically apply codes of ethics in his or her professional life. It is worth noting that there are minor differences in the codes of ethics published by different professional organizations, for instance between those published by the ACA for counselors in general, and by the ASCA for school counselors in particular. Counselors should be

Copyright © Mometrix Media. You have been licensed one copy of this document for personal use only. Any other reproduction or redistribution is strictly prohibited. All rights reserved.
This content is provided for test preparation purposes only and does not imply an endorsement by Mometrix of any particular political, scientific, or religious point of view.

cognizant of the codes and any relevant disparities, and be prepared to apply the appropriate code based on both the counseling setting and capacity in which the counselor is operating. There are also, on occasion, ethical codes regarding a particular situation or relationship that seem to conflict with laws governing the same relationship or situation. Counselors are, within reason, obligated to adhere to the applicable law. However, counselors are encouraged to participate in the dynamics of setting ethical standards by initiating changes to mandates as appropriate.

ACA Code of Ethics

Codes of ethics for the counseling profession generally apply to and are designed for actions and behavior that are best for the student, the situation, and the profession. These codes are reviewed and revised as appropriate. The most current revision in August 2005 addresses the following key areas:

- The Association asks for clarity regarding all ethical responsibilities for current members.
- The Association and its Codes support the mission of the membership.
- The Association endeavors to establish principles by which ethical behavior is identified, and the practices of its members are delineated.
- The Association assists its members in generating a course of action that will utilize counseling services and promote the overall values of the counseling profession.
- The Association establishes the manner in which ethical complaints should be processed, and inquiries against its members should be initiated.

ASCA Code of Ethics for School Counselors

Since the **ASCA** falls under the organizational umbrella of the ACA, its **Code of Ethics** parallels that of the ACA in general scope of benefit to the student, the situation, and the profession. The ASCA Code is delineated more specifically through its eight major sections:

- Duties to Students
- Duties to Parents
- Duties to Colleagues and Professional Associates
- Duties to the School and Region
- Duties to Self
- Duties to the Profession
- Adherence to Standards
- Resource Materials

Counselors should treat each student with respect and consider the student's best interest. They should involve the parents when possible, and exhibit professional and ethical behavior. They should also maintain their expertise through continued learning and development. School counselors should be well versed in both the ACA Code of Ethics and the ASCA Code of Ethics. They should endeavor to incorporate the tenets of both in their professional lives, and carefully research both in the event of an ethical dilemma.

Determining if an Ethical Problem Exists

There are prescribed **steps to take in the process of identifying & addressing an ethical problem**. Both the ACA and the ASCA delineate these steps. The ACA model specifies:

- Recognize the issue.
- Consult direction from the ACA Code of Ethics.
- Identify the type of issue and its components.

Copyright © Mometrix Media. You have been licensed one copy of this document for personal use only. Any other reproduction or redistribution is strictly prohibited. All rights reserved.
This content is provided for test preparation purposes only and does not imply an endorsement by Mometrix of any particular political, scientific, or religious point of view.

- Consider possible courses of action.
- Compare the potential consequences of each course, and choose the most appropriate action.
- Assess the results of the course of action.
- Implement the course of action.

The ASCA model specifies:

- Identify the issue both realistically and philosophically.
- Consult direction from the law, the ACA Code of Ethics, and the ASCA Code of Ethics.
- Factor the developmental & chronological age of the student.
- Assess the student rights, parental rights, and circumstances.
- Adhere to ethical and moral principles.
- Compare the potential courses of action and consequences.
- Assess the results of the selected action.
- Consult.
- Implement the action.

LEGAL MANDATES FOR PROFESSIONAL COUNSELING BEHAVIOR

There are numerous **laws and levels of law governing the behaviors, expectations and limitations of school counselors**. Counselors are obligated to follow the laws of their state, and those of the federal government. However, these laws may be further tempered by statutory laws, common laws and/or appellate decisions. Although counselors are not expected to be legal experts, they should nonetheless be cognizant of the federal and state laws governing their scope of responsibility. As needed, they should critically analyze relevant interpretations of the law, such as in common law. They should also refer to peripheral mandates and appellate decisions if a particular situation warrants the time and clarification of researching it to this extent. If counselors are researching appellate decisions, they should have a working knowledge of the appeal process in their particular state, and any relevant appeal procedures in other states, should the situation call for reference to precedent.

STATUTORY LAW GOVERNING SCHOOL COUNSELING

Generally speaking, federal law serves to enact the Constitution. Under this umbrella, state laws generally address education, health, and other comparable programs through mandates. These state mandates, the body of which is referred to as **statutory law**, are created through legislation passed by state legislatures and the U.S. Congress. State mandates generally are more specific and more prescribed than federal laws, although they cannot be more restrictive than federal law. State legislatures create state laws that implement federal legislation, as well as laws specific to the state. The federal government has also passed several laws, within the parameters of the Constitution, that affect professional school counselors and others in comparable fields. Because statutory law generally addresses issues related to health and education, school counselors should be well versed in relevant state law, but should also be aware of federal laws that can affect their profession.

TITLE IX

Title IX was put in place in 1972. Its intent is to prevent the **sexual discrimination** that for most of the history of this country, blocked girls from educational opportunities open to boys. Title IX made it a law that any educational institution receiving federal funding is required to provide equal opportunities in education. One effect on school counseling would be the expectation that counselors encourage girls to participate in clubs and courses—areas that have been either openly (by school policy) or covertly (by harassment and intimidation) denied to them, such as advanced

Copyright © Mometrix Media. You have been licensed one copy of this document for personal use only. Any other reproduction or redistribution is strictly prohibited. All rights reserved.
This content is provided for test preparation purposes only and does not imply an endorsement by Mometrix of any particular political, scientific, or religious point of view.

math, science, wood or metal shop, or chess clubs. Title IX also affected athletics, which had traditionally been a nearly all-male domain, with very few resources and little support accorded to female athletes. Title IX also supports male students who may want to enter fields considered nontraditional for males in this society, such as nursing, child care, or early education. Title IX also protects individuals from sex-based harassment or discrimination in federally funded public institutions such as museums, vocational rehabilitation organizations, and libraries.

Title IX of the Education Amendments of 1972

Scheduling required girls' physical education at the same time as Advanced Placement (AP) Physics would prevent girls from being able to attend the AP class, effectively excluding them based on their sex. **Title IX of the Education Amendments of 1972** is the law that prevents schools receiving federal funding from denying students access to educational activities based on their sex. Schools that receive federal funding have to make sure that educational opportunities such as classes and academic clubs are not blocked to students because of their sex, and in a case where scheduling a single-sex class interferes with the potential for taking an advanced science class, even if the scheduling conflict is accidental, adhering to it violates Title IX.

Title II

Title II (also called the **Every Student Succeeds Act [ESSA]**) is the federal funding program, signed in 2015 by President Barack Obama, that provides for increased professional development of teachers and administrators or school leaders (including counselors). It improved on the earlier **No Child Left Behind Act**, by changing the requirement that funds be used only for teachers of core academic subjects. ESSA funding covers a wider range of professionals and provides ongoing professional development in the form of grants.

Title II recognizes that there is more to school than teachers and students: support staff and other professionals are also responsible for the well-being and education of students. Making sure that teachers and other school staff receive up-to-date training ultimately benefits students and the greater community by strengthening the school as a whole organism.

Incorporation of State Laws in Rulings and Guidelines of Education Governance Agencies

In the broadest sense, governance is the interpretation and implementation of **codified laws**. Tailored to the school counseling profession, the state legislatures as a rule create legislation that addresses the field of education, from which **state and local agencies interpret and implement rules and guidelines**. The state boards of education generally enact regulations at the school district level that either address areas not specifically addressed in state legislation, or interpret it more specifically to that arena. These regulations or guidelines are not legally binding like legislation, but are representative of how agencies view certain circumstances. This interpretation is subject to the oversight of the state attorney general, particularly if a regulation is challenged. Local school systems may also develop guidelines and policies, tailoring state regulations to the local environment. Individual schools may further refine these policies, addressing the professional behavior of school counselors.

Incorporating Knowledge of Law in Professional Decisions

For school counselors to act **professionally and ethically**, a basic **knowledge of the laws** governing their profession is expected. Beyond that, counselors should avail themselves of information regarding updates or interpretations of relevant law, and other pertinent data. Sources for this information can include on-site supervisors, ACA newsletters, professional journals, commercially available newsletters, the internet, etc. Counselors should recognize that the law and

Copyright © Mometrix Media. You have been licensed one copy of this document for personal use only. Any other reproduction or redistribution is strictly prohibited. All rights reserved.
This content is provided for test preparation purposes only and does not imply an endorsement by Mometrix of any particular political, scientific, or religious point of view.

its interpretation are not static, and knowledge of the law needs to be maintained on an ongoing basis. Counselors also have the responsibility to implement and interpret the law reasonably. If state mandates appear to be in conflict with other regulations or ethical standards, counselors should apply common sense and critical thinking to the interpretation or application of the ruling. If this should occur, any decisions or actions should be documented carefully, and counselors should bring the conflict to the attention of appropriate parties as soon as possible.

Providing Current, Optimum Competence to Clients

In addition to keeping abreast of laws and guidelines, counselors should include the following practices in order to **provide current, optimum competence** to their clients:

- Pursue opportunities for professional development. Most national and state credentials even require counselors to complete continuing education training in order to stay current on theories, trends, and new data in the field.
- Remain current within the counselor's area of responsibility by reading, consulting, networking, and otherwise bringing new research, trends, and information as added resources for serving the clients.
- Represent credentials accurately. Only earned and applicable credentials should be listed.
- Provide only those services for which the counselor is trained and qualified. Counselors should have training in a particular technique before they practice it and should not try to work with students who have conditions beyond the counselor's realm of knowledge.

Response to Subpoenas

Counselors may be served with subpoenas, relating to **allegations of child abuse, neglect, custody disputes**, etc. Counselors should recognize that subpoenas are legal documents, but should respond within the context of his or her obligation to the student and the school guidelines. Counselors should not violate a student's confidentiality beyond that mandated in the school guidelines. The subpoena should always be discussed with the student or the student's attorney, and in some cases the school attorney, before any information is provided to a legal entity. Once the appropriate council approves compliance with the subpoena, school counselors should then discuss how the release of information will affect all parties, and should obtain a signed informed-consent form in order to release necessary records. If, on the other hand, the attorneys do not approve the release of information, they should file a motion to quash, which will release the counselor from the obligation to respond. All actions should be clear and documented.

Legal and Ethical Parameters of Confidentiality

Counselors are both **legally and professionally** committed to respect and protect students' confidentiality. The primary professional consideration relates to the establishment of trust with the student. Confidentiality essentially belongs to the student. It is his or her right and choice to disclose information. Counselors who respect this contribute to the cultivation of trust that is vital to the counselor-client relationship. However, if students are under 18, this legal right extends to the students' parents. In the case of counselors working with students under the age of 18, they can request that parents respect the student's confidentiality, but parents of minors are allowed to be present during the session(s). Nonetheless, whether a student is a minor or over 18, counselors can communicate with the students regarding their rights and responsibilities relating to confidentiality, such as whether it is optional that parents be informed.

Including Parents in Counseling Sessions with Minors

The ideal situation regarding a minor student is if a student readily accepts and invites his or her parents to participate in the session(s). However, if this is not the case, there are steps counselors

Copyright © Mometrix Media. You have been licensed one copy of this document for personal use only. Any other reproduction or redistribution is strictly prohibited. All rights reserved.
This content is provided for test preparation purposes only and does not imply an endorsement by Mometrix of any particular political, scientific, or religious point of view.

can take to ease the disclosure. Counselors should discuss confidentiality with students at the initial session, and let them know the **legal parameters**. Students may be hesitant to let parents know about their problems, for fear of the parents' reactions. Also, when broaching the subject of disclosure, counselors should be sensitive to the possibility of family secrets, sensitive information, cultural issues and other factors that could be problematic when including parents in counseling session. Counselors can work students to get them comfortable with the idea of including their parents, and can discuss reasonable boundaries before the parents are invited to participate. However, if minor students refuse to include their parents or to give permission to disclose information, counselors may be obligated to inform the parents without the student's permission.

Circumstances for Which Confidentiality May Be Breached

There are certain circumstances, as outlined in the **ACA Code of Ethics**, whereby a counselor may break, and in some cases is obligated to break, student confidentiality. Generally, counselors may **break confidentiality** if a student is in danger of harming himself or herself or others, if there is indication of abuse, or if there is any other life-threatening situation. There are other circumstances for which confidentiality may be breached:

- Counselors may disclose confidential documents with subordinates in the regular course of business.
- Members of treatment teams, consultation groups, families, and third-party players may break confidentiality through regular verbal interaction.
- Parents may be legally informed of the counseling discussions held with their minor children.
- Parents or family members may be justifiably informed if they could contract a life-threatening disease through association with the student.
- Court-ordered disclosure by way of a subpoena may require the counselor to share information, although that information can be restricted to what is necessary.

ASCA Ethical Standards for School Counselors

The following statements are taken from standards comprising the first section of the American School Counselor Association **(ASCA) Ethical Standards for School Counselors**, Section A, Responsibility to Students. As each profession creates and standardizes ethical standards, the standards reflect the unique aspects of that profession. Although there are ethical standards for counselors, counseling psychologists, and teachers, the ethical standards for school counselors are constructed to account for counselors' particular responsibilities, their place in the school system and community, and their positions in regard to being trusted with the young to confidentiality and to acting on behalf of students while considering the impact of their roles and actions on parents, teachers, administrators, and other stakeholders.

In supporting student development, the school counselor has the following obligations:

- Acknowledge the vital role of parents and family.
- Provide brief therapy to students in need and obtain referrals to outside therapists when longer-term therapy is needed.
- Not provide DSM diagnoses, but keep students' diagnoses in mind when working with them.
- Understand laws regarding students, and keep parents and students informed of their legal rights.

Copyright © Mometrix Media. You have been licensed one copy of this document for personal use only. Any other reproduction or redistribution is strictly prohibited. All rights reserved.
This content is provided for test preparation purposes only and does not imply an endorsement by Mometrix of any particular political, scientific, or religious point of view.

Minor Consent Laws

Minor consent laws are mandated at the state level and define the circumstances under which counselors may protect the confidentiality of a minor student. These laws fall under the federal regulation that prohibits the breaking of confidentiality for patient recovery, regardless of the patient's minor status. Generally, minor consent laws allow confidentiality regarding issues such as substance abuse, mental health, and reproductive health areas, without releasing information to parents or guardians. There is some controversy regarding the interpretation of these laws, but a common implementation is a school-based student assistant program (SAP) comprised of teams that include a counselor, a counselor or a nurse, a teacher and possibly substance abuse assessors from local agencies. School staff can refer students to the SAP team who will collaboratively determine the best action for the student. Counselors should be well informed about the state mandates and local interpretations of the minor consent law.

Prioritizing Requests Without Engaging in Tasks Outside the Role of School Counselor

School counselors may have to educate others about the limits of the role and hold fast to professional tasks when administrators ask them to work outside their areas of responsibility. Being assigned other responsibilities may create dual relationships, which complicate the counselor role and are warned against in the **American School Counselors Association (ASCA) Ethical Standards for School Counselors**. School counselors may help by locating resources in the greater community, such as peer groups or mental health facilities for students whose needs exceed school-based, time-limited therapeutic interventions. The school counselor's ongoing challenge is to balance the students' needs with the ethical standards that delimit the range of school counselors' responsibilities.

Occasionally, as when a student is in danger or potentially endangering others, a school counselor will be faced with "betraying" a student's confidence to save lives. School counselors need to know and to consider the ethical standards in regard to their decisions, even relatively small decisions, at work. Being liked by all students is far less important than acting with integrity, even when the right decision is unpleasant.

Professional Development of School Guidance Counselors

School counselors should be members of professional organizations and attend lectures, seminars, and state and national conferences sponsored by those and related organizations. School counselors should read journal articles and stay abreast of current research, which may inform their own school programming efforts. School counselors should also stay current with their legal and ethical responsibilities by attending trainings. Seeking consultation and supervision from more experienced school counselors helps build skills as well as providing much-needed emotional support for a career that balances so many activities—counseling and teaching, evaluating and reporting, working with individuals and groups, facilitating, mentoring, leading, consulting, and collaborating. Self-care is a vital part of a school counselor's mandate: if the counselor is suffering, trying to work without addressing personal problems is too difficult to sustain for long without negative effects showing up in one's work life.

Maintaining Own Mental Health

Research shows that our mental and physical health are inextricably linked. Counselors need to care for their bodies as well as their minds. Regular exercise and an intelligent diet are basic to good health. Using mindfulness and other stress reduction techniques helps bring a fresh attitude to work as well as increasing harmony in personal relationships. Creating healthy boundaries at work may mean finding a substitute at times, taking adequate time off and limiting communications with

Copyright © Mometrix Media. You have been licensed one copy of this document for personal use only. Any other reproduction or redistribution is strictly prohibited. All rights reserved.
This content is provided for test preparation purposes only and does not imply an endorsement by Mometrix of any particular political, scientific, or religious point of view.

parents, students, and administrators outside of school hours. Engaging a supervisor or participating in a group with other counselors can provide support and generate new ideas.

When a counselor experiences problems in his/her personal life (such as divorce, illness, or death in the family), self-care such as seeking help and support in crises is especially important.

Burnout

Burnout is characterized by lack of interest in the job, ironically, often while spending too much time on the job. When people burn out at work, their effectiveness drops: they make mistakes, get sloppy, or even lose the desire to do the right thing. In school counseling, students can too easily become the victims of counselor burnout. Counselors have a great deal of responsibility—as those who guide students in taking tests that will affect their college placements and future careers; as mentors, role models, and protectors; and as emotional supports and educators of academic and life skills. There's too much riding on a school counselor to have that person melt down over stress and overwork. And because the work is emotionally demanding, time-consuming, and often seriously underfunded, school counselors are at tremendous risk of burnout. To work ethically on behalf of students, the counselor has a responsibility of self-care that can't be avoided or put off.

Copyright © Mometrix Media. You have been licensed one copy of this document for personal use only. Any other reproduction or redistribution is strictly prohibited. All rights reserved.
This content is provided for test preparation purposes only and does not imply an endorsement by Mometrix of any particular political, scientific, or religious point of view.

Consultation, Collaboration, and Coordination

Collaboration with Teachers and School Personnel

An effective counseling group relies on the support, endorsement, and **collaboration of parents, teachers, and school counselors**. It is important that these individuals and administrative groups understand and support the importance and goals of the counseling group. Counselors can help sensitize parents and school personnel to the importance of counseling groups. One of the common concerns is that counseling groups require students to spend time that could otherwise be spent in the classroom. It is important to stress to parents and school personnel that the time students spend in the classroom is generally more effective if students are allowed to address personal, time management, and other issues in counseling sessions. Once counselors have established this understanding with parents and school personnel, they can unite in a partnership for the students' benefit.

Introducing School Personnel and Parent Groups to Need for Counseling Groups

It is important for individuals **advocating the creation of counseling groups** to emphasize first the comprehensive nature of a counseling program within the school setting, pointing out that an effective counseling program works collaboratively with parents and school groups. It should also be stressed that counseling groups address personal issues that can hinder academic performance. A counseling program should include vehicles for input from school personnel and parents. It might be advisable to hold meetings in tandem with PTA or other parent groups, providing a forum for open communication about the need for and implementation of a counseling program. It is recommended that these presentations be held early in the academic year, to allow for discussion and consensus. It is also important for these meetings to be facilitated by professional counselors who can appropriately address questions and concerns.

Vehicles and Media for Communicating Development of Counseling Programs

Regular communication with parents and school personnel provides continued interface regarding future and existing counseling groups. Some of the channels for keeping this communication open include:
Regular, informative meetings with school counselors discussing current counseling groups, future plans, and any peripheral activities

- Distribution of surveys assessing specific needs for groups, or for topics to be addressed
- Sharing information about groups needed as well as groups being formed, as appropriate, with parents and school personnel
- Being available on a regular basis to hear from school personnel regarding student issues or concerns that may precipitate the need for a counseling group
- Speaking with students in their classrooms about the availability of counseling groups, and providing a clear and confidential process by which they can bring concerns forward
- Developing and communicating clear procedures for group formation, group participation, and parental and school permission

Communicative Methods for Determining Topics to Address in Counseling Groups

The **choice of topics for counseling groups** should be representative of the needs of the school community and/or student body. Many topics will arise out of regular meetings between counselors and the school staff, or from meetings with parents. Others may be revealed in the

Copyright © Mometrix Media. You have been licensed one copy of this document for personal use only. Any other reproduction or redistribution is strictly prohibited. All rights reserved.
This content is provided for test preparation purposes only and does not imply an endorsement by Mometrix of any particular political, scientific, or religious point of view.

surveys that are distributed to parents, students, and school staff. Students can also be a source of potential topics, particularly if they are provided with a clear and confidential protocol for bringing these concerns forward. Counselors can be proactive in the process of choosing topics: they can ask groups to suggest topics, or they can choose from a series of topics that might be of interest. Once the counselor has established him/herself as a responsive conduit for topic suggestions, there should be a body of recommendations available from which to determine best topics to be addressed in counseling groups.

Topic Determination Arising from School Records, Research, or Other Documentation

School records are another resource for assessing the need for counseling groups and for generating topics. These records contain profiles that may **reveal patterns** of low retention, poor attendance, low test scores, or other identifiable areas of need. Counselors can also research the commonalities of specific age groups to determine which topics would be appropriate and well received. These topics can range from healthy social behavior to career planning. Some of these general areas can be addressed through a specific focus on life experiences, such as beginning a college prep program in high school. It is important that development of groups and group topics be well researched not only to discover common topics for a particular age group, but to determine the applicability of these topics to the particular student body, as documented by school records and the input of school personnel.

Follow-Up Meetings

Importance

Even when counselors have met with students for a number of sessions and feel that learning objectives have been met, it is nonetheless a good idea to schedule **follow-up meetings** with the students. It is important to realize that students may have effectively mastered particular objectives within the insulated environment of the facilitated classroom sessions, but that they may be inclined to revert to prior behaviors once they are in their familiar milieu. Follow-up sessions can serve as reminders to students of their progress in the classroom, as well as of strategies that were successful for them. They can also give students an additional opportunity to assimilate the lessons and imprint them in their everyday lives. Counselors can use some discretion in determining the best timing for scheduling follow-up meetings, but they generally occur within days or weeks of the final session in the sequence.

Benefits

Follow-up meetings with students who have completed a sequence of counseling lessons are beneficial to the counselor, as well as to the students and the overall success of the program. Counselors who meet with students shortly after the final session in a sequence can continue to assess the effectiveness of the strategies employed. As with intra-lesson assessment, follow-up assessment may identify particular areas that need to be targeted more or in a different way in future sessions. Additionally, and more importantly, follow-up sessions can provide counselors with the opportunity to reinforce the lessons and strategies employed in the sequence of sessions. This benefits the students and the program exponentially, in that it decreases the chances of repeated negative behaviors, and mitigates the need for redundant sessions targeting objectives that had been previously met. All of this contributes to the overall effectiveness of the program.

Collaborating with Parents and School Staff

Because the average student to counselor ratio can range from 100:1 to 300:1, the accessibility of counselors is sometimes well below optimum. The moderate needs of many students can be eclipsed by attention paid to the more severe needs of a few. Therefore, it is advisable for

Copyright © Mometrix Media. You have been licensed one copy of this document for personal use only. Any other reproduction or redistribution is strictly prohibited. All rights reserved.
This content is provided for test preparation purposes only and does not imply an endorsement by Mometrix of any particular political, scientific, or religious point of view.

counselors to consult with parents and school personnel in the design of effective prevention and intervention programs. Parents and school personnel experience day-to-day contact with students, and are able to observe them in the classroom and home environments. The combined student contact that parents, teachers, and school counselors have can provide valuable feedback to counselors for designing programs and intervention strategies that will benefit the most students most effectively, augmented by individual sessions as indicated. Counselors who meet with the larger school community are able to maximize the efficacy of the school counseling program.

TRIADIC-DEPENDENT CONSULTATION MODEL

The **triadic-dependent consultation model** is essentially a partnership formed between the counselor, parents, and/or school staff to provide indirect services to a student. It is a problem-solving solution for some students and situations in which strategies implemented at home or in the classroom can augment strategies implemented in the counseling sessions. In this model, the counselor works directly with the student, but augments that work by consulting with parents, schoolteachers, and school counselors. Those third parties are identified as the consultees, and the counselor as consultant can provide information and advice toward the goal of improving relations with the student. The triadic-dependent consultation model does not exist for the benefit of the student, but rather so that the parents and/or school personnel can develop strategies to improve the student's academic or personal situation.

CONDUCTING A CONSULTATION

In the **triadic-dependent consultation model**, counselors initially meet with family and/or school personnel to discuss the student's problems and goals, within confidentiality guidelines. In these meetings, counselors can obtain additional information about the student that will help in the individual sessions. Since many student problems can affect and/or be exacerbated by their social and family network, this model can address the interrelations of various dynamics in the student's life. Counselors may also want to include other members of the student's network, such as peers or other family members, as appropriate, in the process of developing a more comprehensive profile of the student. After assessing the student more comprehensively, counselors can then recommend particular prevention or intervention strategies to the family and/or school personnel. Counselors may recommend interventions focusing on changes for the student, consultee, and/or the school system.

BEHAVIORAL CONSULTATION

Counselors can apply the principles of behaviorism to a triadic-dependent consultation format very successfully. Using these principles, counselors can meet with parents and school personnel to identify and define the student's problems as well as any peripheral circumstances that could be contributing. Once the counselor has developed a comprehensive profile of the student's problems in the context of surrounding circumstances, he or she can the create strategies for changing the student's behavior, and possibly the consultee's behavior or actions. Counselors can also work to modify the social context of the interrelationship between the student and the consultee. Possible therapeutic strategies include behavioral contracting, positive reinforcement, and response cost. The behavioral consultation model can be represented by the following four areas of focus:

- Initial assessment: Identify problems and contributing circumstances.
- Analysis: Develop a comprehensive profile of student needs.
- Implementation: Develop and implement behavior modification strategies.
- Evaluation: Evaluate the efficacy of strategies and revise as appropriate.

Copyright © Mometrix Media. You have been licensed one copy of this document for personal use only. Any other reproduction or redistribution is strictly prohibited. All rights reserved.
This content is provided for test preparation purposes only and does not imply an endorsement by Mometrix of any particular political, scientific, or religious point of view.

Parameters for Counselors Meeting with Consultees

Counselors meeting with parents and school personnel should strive to make the environment and the dynamics comfortable yet professional. This is particularly important when meeting with parents. Initially, counselors can restate the purpose of the consultation, identify the student, and define the issues of concern. Initial interaction can serve to ease any anxieties and to establish a professional, comfortable dynamic. The student's behavior should be the focus of the meeting, and counselors should redirect the conversation within those boundaries if needed. Nonetheless, consultees should be given the opportunity to give input, as with any therapeutic group. Counselors should probe for any relevant conditions that would affect the treatment planning, and should glean any additional information about the student from classroom observations. Counselors may also want to provide reference materials to the consultees to offer a better understanding of the issues and behaviors involved. All consultant/consultee interactions should be in writing, and follow-up actions should be scheduled during the initial consultation.

Collaborative-Dependent Consultation Model

The **collaborative-dependent consultation model** is also a partnership, but one in which the counselor/consultant may play more of a role as participant rather than as facilitator. The counselor is expected to contribute to problem-solving expertise, but is not the sole expert. The consultee in this model may have a more in-depth knowledge of the student or the system on which the consultation is focused. In this model, the consultant and the consultee can be educated on both the problem-solving process for the student and the response of the student. Both consultant and consultee may have working knowledge of normal and abnormal student development. The consultee may be able to contribute knowledge about the efficacy of previous interventions, and/or the impact of peripheral factors. In the collaborative/dependent consultation model, the partners collaborate to develop an intervention plan, with the counselor defining the problem and completing any evaluation and follow-up services while the consultee is implementing the intervention plan.

Application for Organizational Systems

When the **collaborative-dependent model is applied to an organizational system**, the focus can be on the student, the consultee, or the initiation of change within the system. Family dynamics, or a family system, can also be included in this paradigm. In the system application of the collaborative-dependent model, the counselor participates as process consultant to address problem-solving within the context of the system. He or she can contribute his or her expertise on the assessment and interventions that are related to system change. This application should address the following six variables:

- Communication patterns within the group
- Roles and functions of the various group members
- Processes and procedures involved in group decision-making or problem-solving
- Normal group performance and expected growth
- Leadership and authority within the group
- Intra-group cooperation and competition

Collaborative-Interdependent Consultation Model

The **collaborative-interdependent consultation model** is one that is more complex and comprehensive, and is most appropriate for addressing the multiplicity of issues related to at-risk youth. In this model, the partnership may be comprised of family, counselor, students, school personnel, and community members, and all may act as equal partners. This model is a

Copyright © Mometrix Media. You have been licensed one copy of this document for personal use only. Any other reproduction or redistribution is strictly prohibited. All rights reserved.
This content is provided for test preparation purposes only and does not imply an endorsement by Mometrix of any particular political, scientific, or religious point of view.

collaborative, dynamic one in which the combined input and efforts of the members enable the group as a whole to develop and implement a comprehensive plan. The counselor is not expected to be the sole expert or the central source of information. The onus does not lie on the counselor to develop and implement a plan. The collaboratively developed plan may include change for an individual student, additional knowledge and skills for the team, and/or a change to the system.

Possible Difficulties

There can be inherent difficulties in the **collaborative-interdependent model**, relating to the fact that its members are included in the partnership because of their knowledge or perspective of the issue at hand, and not necessarily because they are good collaborators. The collaborative-interdependent partnership can be comprised of parents, school counselors, community members, and others, each of whom may have a different strategy to address the student issues. This can be particularly problematic if the members are each implementing a portion of the solution strategy, and not working together to do so. The ability to work effectively presupposes the ability to work collaboratively. Collaboration should be present at all levels of interaction: identifying the problem, determining the necessary goals, creating strategies, implementing procedures, and evaluating outcomes.

Distinguishing Features of Collaborative Style of Consultation

The **collaborative style of consultation** is distinguished by five key features:

- Voluntary participation of members toward resolution of a problem, as opposed to hierarchical direction from a counselor.
- Shared input for decision-making: This is opposed to a model in which the outcome is decided before the group convenes, or in which presuppositions color the outcome.
- Shared responsibility for decision-making: This implies both the expectation and the privilege of addressing the issue at hand. All parties participate in identifying the problem, developing objectives, implementing strategies, and evaluating outcomes.
- Shared investment and ownership of the problem and solution for all parties, potentially including family, school, and community: All parties recognize what needs to be accomplished and contribute their particular expertise.
- Shared resources: This implies less ownership, so that the group decides how the resources will be utilized.

Counselor's Role in Facilitating Collaborative Consultation

The role of the counselor in the **collaborative consultation** format is that of both **facilitator** and **role model** for the consultation. The distinguishing advantage of the collaborative format is that of shared and interactive input regarding the student. Each person's perspective, expertise, and knowledge of the student and the situation is valuable and contributes to a whole that is often greater than its parts. Counselors can model this format by encouraging input from all the members, and can facilitate the group by maintaining the guidelines that allow for interactive sharing. The counselor's role in the collaborative model is not that of leader, but more of guide and facilitator. Some of the key points to address in collaborative consultation include:

- Open consideration of other perspectives
- Willingness to revise one's perspective
- Integration of others' ideas in intervention
- Flexibility of counselor to de-emphasize his or her role as leader
- Guiding the group in a manner that encourages collaboration

Copyright © Mometrix Media. You have been licensed one copy of this document for personal use only. Any other reproduction or redistribution is strictly prohibited. All rights reserved.
This content is provided for test preparation purposes only and does not imply an endorsement by Mometrix of any particular political, scientific, or religious point of view.

Importance of Developing Strategies Within the Context of the Larger School System

Particularly in a school counseling environment, any kind of intervention or therapy must be conceived and delivered within the context of the larger school system and community. The primary purpose behind this is **efficacy of treatment**. Counselors who are working with at-risk students or students who are facing personal problems will benefit the student and the counseling program by collaborating with school personnel. This may include a collaborative consultation, or may just be a matter of using the available resources. Counselors may also want to serve as liaisons in suggesting student-oriented changes to the school system. Counselors can also adopt a holistic approach to therapy, within the context of the school community. It is important to remember that students have classmates, take course work within a prescribed curriculum, and operate within the mandates of the school system. Therefore, when working with students, counselors should be cognizant of a student's daily routines and environment.

Counselor's Role Within the Context of the Larger School System

It is important for school counselors to remember that they are just one member of the school personnel community. Their role is to provide individual or group therapy to student members of the community who are at risk for self-destructive behaviors, which usually include academic failure. It is the intervention focusing on the dangers of academic failure that serves as the linchpin of the collective goals of the entire school community, including the school counselor. For school counselors to be most valuable to their student clients, it is important for them to remember that serving their students is also serving the greater good of the school community. This greater good includes the safety of the student body, and the academic goals of the school and the district. Those academic goals can be reflected in test scores, retention, and other quantifiable data.

Becoming an Integral Part of the School Community

When becoming a part of a school community, a school counselor can take proactive steps toward **developing a collaborative relationship** with other members of the community. These steps include:

- Recognize that the school staff is in a fiduciary role, implementing the academic goals of the school and the district.
- Be open to the evolution of your role within the school community, as opposed to imposing preconceived ideas about your role on the school staff.
- Become familiar with the rules and expectations of the school community.
- Recognize that any operational entity will have both explicit and implicit hierarchies, and become aware of those levels of authority and power.
- Cultivate alliances and friendships through shared agendas and recognition of individual strengths.
- Develop effective and collaborative vehicles of communication with members of the school and the larger community.
- Maintain objectivity when working with any educator or family member.
- Refrain from provocatively challenging the authority of an educator or community member.

Copyright © Mometrix Media. You have been licensed one copy of this document for personal use only. Any other reproduction or redistribution is strictly prohibited. All rights reserved.
This content is provided for test preparation purposes only and does not imply an endorsement by Mometrix of any particular political, scientific, or religious point of view.

Areas in Which Understanding of Policies and Procedures of the School System is Important

Each school system will have particular nuances and interpretations with respect to **issues of confidentiality and parental rights**. Counselors should be aware of these policies/procedures when working with students in order to know:

- When and how to notify parents of student participation in counseling.
- How to respond to a suspicion of child abuse.
- Issues of confidentiality in the therapeutic environment, e.g., when and how to report severely at-risk behavior, and when and how to recognize and report students who may be at risk of harming others.
- When and how to open up the counseling strategies to include collaborative consultation.
- When to involve teachers and other school staff in intervention strategies.

Understanding the policies and procedures includes not only reading them but also understanding how these policies are implemented in a particular school environment. Maintaining open communication and cultivating relationships with school staff will be beneficial to the counselor in developing an understanding of school policies and procedures.

Spectrum of Policy Interpretation Among Different School Personnel

Although most **school policies and procedures** are clearly delineated in written form, their interpretation can be less clear-cut, and can even vary between teachers and classrooms. One policy area that can easily vary between educators is that of allowing students to participate in counseling during time normally set aside for classroom instruction. Some teachers may support student counseling, and may be willing to let students leave their classrooms to do so. Others may also be in support of students receiving counseling, but may feel that it should not be done at the expense of classroom time, but rather before or after school. Teachers may also have differing opinions about collaboration with school counselors, particularly about the implementation of behavior modification strategies in the classroom. Counselors should be sensitive to these differences in opinion, and the spectrum of teachers' responses to the need for and implementation of a counseling program.

Deferring to the Explicit Authority of the Principal

The principal of a school administrates the allocation of both monetary and personnel resources. For a school counselor to successfully plan and implement a counseling program at a school, the **support and endorsement of the principal** is pivotal. In deference to the principal's responsibilities, counselors should keep him or her apprised of the scope of the current counseling program, as well as revisions or plans for future revisions to the program. Not only is this respectful of the principal's agenda; it is also a good way to retain the support and endorsement of the administration. It is also recommended that counselors meet with principals on a regular basis, at the principal's convenience. Counselors should allow sufficient time to apprise the principal of updates and for discussion as appropriate. Principals may also make suggestions and recommendations for the counseling program, which should be taken into account by the counselor.

Recognizing Individuals with Either Explicit or Implicit Influence in the School System

When a counselor recognizes that he or she is just one member of a school community, he or she should also recognize that a community contains both **formal and informal power structures**. Although it is necessary for a counselor to keep open communication with the principal, that line of

Copyright © Mometrix Media. You have been licensed one copy of this document for personal use only. Any other reproduction or redistribution is strictly prohibited. All rights reserved.
This content is provided for test preparation purposes only and does not imply an endorsement by Mometrix of any particular political, scientific, or religious point of view.

communication may depend on the counselor's interactions with the principal's secretary or other assistant counselor. School counselors should also be cognizant of the network of communication and influence that exists within the school system, as it does within most communities. Counselors can cultivate relationships with teachers, parents, other counselors, etc., in order to gain an understanding of underlying concerns and agendas within the larger school agenda. These relationships can also provide a vehicle for counselors to inform the school community of their concerns and plans for an appropriate counseling program to address those concerns. A healthy environment for a school counseling program includes shared agendas and collaboration.

Cultivating Relationships with Influential Individuals in the School Community

Impact

When counselors are able to communicate and collaborate with influential and interested members of the school community regarding the counseling program, there are positive far-reaching effects. By recognizing and incorporating the interplay of agendas and concerns in a school community, counselors are able to **gain the respect, endorsement, and contributions** of those individuals. When counselors can recognize and utilize the strengths and contributions of individuals working in the school community, the counseling program is able to thrive and grow within the context of the school system. The added benefit is that when the program is working within this context, peripheral individuals and programs will associate the counseling program with the larger agendas of the school community and will more readily accept and endorse the program. As these working relationships evolve, the counselor can develop rich alliances and friendships within the school community to the benefit of all the members.

Concerns

As with any group dynamic, the interplay of agendas and concerns within a school community may be organic and healthy, may be dysfunctional and conflicting, or may be somewhere in between. Although it is not necessarily the counselor's role to analyze the dynamics at play in the school setting, he or she nonetheless needs to be aware of conflicts between individuals and agendas, particularly if individuals or groups are in opposition to the principal's goals and overall agenda. Counselors should exercise some caution when forming alliances to the benefit of the counseling program that may be in opposition to other groups or the overall agenda of the school principal. It would be better to cultivate relationships with a measure of caution, until a counselor understands the overall interplay of agendas within the school community. Counselors can also strive to facilitate cooperation and collaboration between the parties involved.

Working with Members of Subsystems in the School Community

The larger school community is comprised of many **subsystems**, including but not limited to parents, service staff, librarians, and community groups. Even within the teaching staff, there are subsystems comprised of education specialists, resource teachers, etc. Although not necessarily in conflict with each other, these groups may operate quasi-autonomously and be unaware of their effects on the larger school community. This is best illustrated within the experiences of the students, who interact with and depend on many of these subsystems. Counselors working with students with complex needs may have to involve several subsystems in order to provide effective treatment. It might be beneficial for counselors to form acquaintances with members of the larger school community, in order to better understand the complexities of subsystems in the school and facilitate communication between these entities.

Emotional Objectivity When Introducing or Implementing Counseling Programs

When counselors join a school community, they may **encounter resistance to their contributions** from certain members of that community. Although the school community as a whole may endorse

Copyright © Mometrix Media. You have been licensed one copy of this document for personal use only. Any other reproduction or redistribution is strictly prohibited. All rights reserved.
This content is provided for test preparation purposes only and does not imply an endorsement by Mometrix of any particular political, scientific, or religious point of view.

and support the counseling program and its inclusion in the larger efforts of the school, the resistance of a few may manifest in covert or overt actions that undermine or impede the counseling program. Counselors need to maintain objectivity when facing these kinds of challenges, which should be recognized as symptoms of systemic change. Recognizing this objectively, the counselor can then approach the challenges professionally. Relying on their knowledge of systems change analysis, counselors can isolate and identify the resistance, and openly approach the individuals or entities involved to find a mutual resolution. It is important to remember that, without this objectivity, counselors can become mired in conflict and programs can be rendered ineffectual.

Initial Stages of Problem Solving on a School Campus

Once a consultant is in the school system, he or she is in a position to **initiate problem solving**. Regardless of the problem, or the complexity of the problem, the initial stage of problem solving is generally that of identifying the problem to be addressed. This involves collecting the information necessary to comprehensively assess the issue at hand. If the difficulty relates to a student, the information collecting may involve parents, teachers, and/or the student. The problem-solving process can also require other educators or family members to form a collaborative problem-solving team. Problems to be addressed might also be more macrocosmic, involving several students with violent behavior, or possibly system-wide issues affecting the entire school. Once the problem has been comprehensively isolated, counselors should determine the most appropriate consultation model for working toward resolution.

Importance of Process in Problem-Solving Groups

School teams brought together to resolve an issue are often task-oriented, and generally are not focused on process. Without some attention paid to process, the collaborative effect of the team can be diffused and the efficacy of the group diminished. The counselor as consultant can contribute to the group discussion with not only knowledge about a particular issue, but also specific expertise in group dynamics. As **facilitator**, he or she can encourage the group process necessary to complete the problem-solving task. As with any professional interaction, counselors should remember they are a part of a larger whole and maintain an openness to the strengths of the group and the individual members. If approached well, a successful collaborative process will significantly contribute to the overall success of the task team, as well as establish the counselor as a valuable member of the school community.

Facilitating a Collaborative Group Dynamic

After the counselor as consultant has been assigned a role in the group, he or she may have the opportunity to **facilitate collaboration**. When working with a problem-solving team, counselors can initiate specific practices and procedures toward a collaborative group dynamic. These practices include:

- Noting and encouraging behaviors among the group that contribute to collaboration and cooperation.
- Noting and discouraging competitive remarks and behaviors.
- Working with the group to establish a collaborative group norm.
- Creating an open communication policy that allows the input of all participants to the problem-solving process.
- Recognizing and respecting the expertise and contributions of all members of the group.

Copyright © Mometrix Media. You have been licensed one copy of this document for personal use only. Any other reproduction or redistribution is strictly prohibited. All rights reserved.
This content is provided for test preparation purposes only and does not imply an endorsement by Mometrix of any particular political, scientific, or religious point of view.

- These practices can lay the foundation for a collaborative group process. Facilitating a collaborative group dynamic may also occasionally include soliciting the support and endorsement of a school counselor by explaining the value of the collaborative process in a problem-solving group.

Framing the Objectives of Problem Resolution in Group Setting

The counselor as facilitator can work with members of the group to set goals and create a viable action plan. It is important that the parameters of this action plan fall within the capabilities and contributions of the group members. Individuals in the group should be able to recognize and embrace their role in facilitating change in the students. Specific steps in the **process of developing an action plan** include:

- Identifying the goal and the action plan for achieving it.
- Determining an appropriate and reasonable measurement of outcome.
- Empowering group members to act as change agents.
- Identifying the individual and group strengths appropriate to the action plan.
- Encouraging flexibility of roles and expanded boundaries as appropriate.
- Encouraging collaboration within the group and with other entities as appropriate.
- Developing a plan to implement and retain the changes.

Identification of Goals and Outcomes

It is important to remember the initial process of problem solving is comprehensive problem identification. This identification should define the scope of the problem, specifically whether it is isolated to a particular student and/or the student's family dynamic, more generalized within a group of students, or dispersed throughout the school system as a whole. Once the problem is identified, the problem-solving team should clearly **identify goals** for the student or the particular group, as well as **anticipated outcomes**. Academic goals for students should fall within the academic parameters and mission of the school. Inherent in the process is the need to develop viable outcome assessment measures, which will be made easier by clearly-stated objectives. When the group can articulate the objectives, as well as the measurements of outcome, they can formulate goals that are reasonable and achievable.

Framing Issues in an Inclusive Manner

When a student's behavior or problem becomes such that intervention is necessary, blame is often laid at the feet of various parties. Parents may blame the school for their child's problems, and schools may hold parents accountable for student behavior. As consultants, counselors can stress that the student's situation should be viewed as a **catalyst for change** that will involve the student, the school, and the family. Viewed in this way, intervention becomes a **collaborative goal** rather than an exercise in finding evidence to support blame. Counselors can encourage participants to feel committed to resolution, and to each embrace his or her respective role in its achievement. The strengths of the teachers and family members should be affirmed and used to bring about the desired objectives. Counselors should remind participants that change is a process that will take time and the commitment of those involved in the student's life.

Approaching an Identified Need for Systemic Change

When student intervention necessitates a group effort, it usually correlates with a multiplicity and complexity of issues. Consequently, resolution is usually complex, and may involve many entities. Sometimes, any change anticipated in the student relies at least in part on changes in family dynamics and/or school systems. Counselors should remember that student behaviors indicate a need for change, and should refrain from blatantly identifying any system or individual as a cause

Copyright © Mometrix Media. You have been licensed one copy of this document for personal use only. Any other reproduction or redistribution is strictly prohibited. All rights reserved.
This content is provided for test preparation purposes only and does not imply an endorsement by Mometrix of any particular political, scientific, or religious point of view.

for the problems. Rather, counselors should use diplomacy in suggesting changes in family or school dynamics, particularly if the respective parties are operating under the assumption that the student's behavioral problems are not connected to other influences in his or her life. This is a situation in which the trust and alliances gained from members of the school community are particularly valuable. Counselors can work separately with teachers or family members to encourage change as applicable.

Encouraging More Flexible Roles and Broadened Boundaries in Problem-Solving Teams

The **optimal consulting group** is one in which the whole is greater than the sum of its parts. Practically speaking, each of the participants comes to the task with particular expertise, a specific set of skills, and a paradigm or perspective regarding the problem and the anticipated resolution. Each member sees himself or herself in a predetermined role. Educators generally approach student problems from an academic perspective; psychologists will tend to be most concerned about the student's mental health. However, in a group setting, with good facilitation, the participants can be encouraged to step beyond their prescribed roles and expectations toward a comprehensive intervention strategy that will bring their collective expertise to a cohesive front. In this setting, counselors may ask a teacher to co-lead the group, or a psychologist to facilitate a discussion about academic goals. This shared crossing over can be most beneficial in a consulting group.

How Consultants Can Plan and Strategize for Protecting Change

Counselors understand that any kind of **behavioral change is an ongoing process and will often include backsliding or digression**. When facilitating a consulting group, counselors can first remind the group that any intervention strategy needs to include plans for protecting the anticipated change. Knowing this initially will enhance the long-term success of an intervention strategy. Consultants can assist the group in developing a post-plan for this purpose. This post-plan should include a delineation of the responsibilities and benchmarks to be used in evaluating progress. It may also include mechanisms that will allow for ongoing communication among the members, as well as support resources. In a school setting, student progress is generally associated with academic achievement, which can provide a clear marker for determining strategy success. Behavioral changes can also be monitored by noting clearly identifiable actions.

Evaluating Success of Implementation

When an action plan has been developed and implemented, the **evaluation process** should begin. The action plan should include strategies for evaluation and outcome measurement. It may be appropriate for each member of the consultant group to participate in the evaluation process by monitoring such successes as academic progress and changed behaviors. The evaluation should focus on **whether any change has occurred**, and to what degree that change can be **measured**. Participants can develop vehicles for collecting as well as presenting the relevant data. Counselors should provide oversight for this phase of the action plan. They should be attentive to the degree of change, and should determine if it is sufficient to be considered successful. They should also be attentive to any changes that constitute digression or negative change. If this is the case, they might want to assess possible factors, and meet with the group to develop alternate strategies.

Bringing the Ad Hoc Consultation Group to Closure

If the consultant is not a regular member of the school community, **closure** may be more definitive than if the counselor as consultant is a part of the school staff. In that situation, counselors can maintain communication with the participants and provide confirmation of successful completion. The counselor can also conduct **debriefings** with the participants to **reflect on the process, the**

Copyright © Mometrix Media. You have been licensed one copy of this document for personal use only. Any other reproduction or redistribution is strictly prohibited. All rights reserved.
This content is provided for test preparation purposes only and does not imply an endorsement by Mometrix of any particular political, scientific, or religious point of view.

degree of success, and the value of collaboration. Counselors can also maintain communication with school counselors and peripheral professionals as a follow-up to a successful intervention. If, on the other hand, the counselor as consultant is a regular member of the school staff, it is important to be attentive to sensitivities that the student might have regarding regular proximity to the participants of the consulting group, including the counselor. In that event, formal follow-up might be less appropriate than if the consultant is regularly away from campus.

Cross-Cultural Consultation

When working with consultees from diverse cultural backgrounds, counselors should refer to their knowledge of **cross-cultural counseling** in order to facilitate the group with confidence and skill. Multicultural participants in a consulting group will inherently present special considerations regarding diversity of culture:

- Impact of culture: how diverse cultural paradigms affect the consultation process
- Recognition of culture: understanding the richness of contributions from diversity of culture

A counselor should also strive to do the following:

- Be sensitive to cultural differences when developing rapport within the group.
- Be aware of cultural factors within the group as well as between the group and the student.
- Develop appropriate interventions with these cultural considerations in mind, if indicated.
- Respond objectively to diverse circumstances.
- Identify and emphasize similarities between the represented cultures, as appropriate.
- Address balance of power issues.
- Endorse the success of the student and consultees.

Applying Collaborative Consultation to a Broader Community

It may be the case that a student is already interacting with other professionals or professional groups outside of the school community. Often this is the case when students present a complexity of issues. In order to approach the student holistically, counselors may want to include these individuals in a consulting group, or as part of the school-based consulting group. Through **collaborative consultation**, the individual members should endeavor to adopt an integrated approach that will result in **shared input and shared responsibility**. It is generally recommended that each member's interaction with the student should be suspended or altered in deference to the participant's involvement in the collaborative consultation model. Counselors as consultants should become familiar with the expertise and scope of each professional/group, and should try to involve the parents in the consultation. Overall, the collaborative consultation model can prove much more effective than if counselors were to meet individually with respective professionals or professional groups.

Including Parents in a Collaborative Consultation Model

Counselors as consultants are in a position to recognize when a student issue could be best addressed by generating dialogue between parents and members of the school community. The initial process should involve bringing the parents together with educators or other school members as appropriate, to discuss and come to an agreed understanding regarding the needs of the student. Through collaboration, parents and school members can recognize that each of their efforts as individual entities would likely not be as effective as the collaborative efforts of the group members, including the parents. Counselors can facilitate the process by helping members to understand each other's roles and prospective contributions. Counselors can guide the group

Copyright © Mometrix Media. You have been licensed one copy of this document for personal use only. Any other reproduction or redistribution is strictly prohibited. All rights reserved.
This content is provided for test preparation purposes only and does not imply an endorsement by Mometrix of any particular political, scientific, or religious point of view.

discussions by allowing each of the participants, which may just be a teacher and a parent, to understand their mutual goal of academic success for the student, and to encourage trust in the collaborative process.

Increasing Parental Involvement in Student Academic Achievement

Increased **parental involvement and awareness** strongly correlates with **increased academic success** in students. There is also a significant benefit to students who are able to dovetail their school experience with their home experience, such that their parents become more involved in their academic requirements. When parents are able to supplement classroom instruction with additional teaching at home, their children generally perform better and are more engaged at school. Counselors and other members of the school staff can cultivate parental involvement through a number of vehicles. Open-house events and parent-teacher conferences are common modes for increasing parental involvement. Other recommendations are parent resource centers, phone calls, or even visits to the home when appropriate. If the school community as a whole recognizes the value of parental involvement and endeavors to forge a partnership with parents on a regular basis, overall student achievement can be expected to improve.

There are numerous arenas in which counselors can **encourage parental involvement** in students' academic achievement. Augmenting those events in which parents are invited to visit the campus, counselors can build on this involvement by including parents in planning and decision-making programs as appropriate. Another suggestion is to research the talents and skills of parents, and develop a volunteer pool. Educators and counselors will need to give specific directions for participation, and can diversify the selection of areas in which parents can contribute their time and expertise. Counselors can also acknowledge parental involvement through written newsletters or at school events. Counselors should emphasize the goal they share with parents: namely, the academic success of their students. Counselors can **distribute additional academic resources to parents**. The school should be portrayed as welcoming to families. Counselors may want to coordinate transportation and baby-sitting for parent visits.

Effective Communication with Parents

Counselors can set a welcoming tone each year, by proactively welcoming parents and encouraging their participation in the academic lives of their children. The following are some effective ways to set this tone:

- Send a welcome letter at the beginning of the year that includes a calendar of events and invites parents to participate.
- Provide a resource brochure or informational handout with general school policies and the an explanation of the counselor's role in the students' lives.
- Distribute informational resources describing the counseling programs, community resources, and pertinent contact information.
- Regularly send event and meeting calendars, which should include contact information for support resources and counselors.
- Generate a school newsletter that will give parents and the surrounding community information about school resources and any other material of interest.
- Schedule new-family meetings right before school starts.

Copyright © Mometrix Media. You have been licensed one copy of this document for personal use only. Any other reproduction or redistribution is strictly prohibited. All rights reserved.
This content is provided for test preparation purposes only and does not imply an endorsement by Mometrix of any particular political, scientific, or religious point of view.

Technology and Counseling

ASCA's Ethical Guidelines in Relation to Counselors' Use of Technology

The technology a school counselor chooses to use must be both **applicable** to the student's needs and **ethical** in its implementation. The American School Counselor Association's (ASCA's) guidelines promote safe and confidential practices, emotional and social consideration, and equitable practices.

ASCA Ethical Guidelines (2016):

- Demonstrate appropriate selection and use of technology and software applications to enhance students' academic, career, and social/emotional development. Attention is given to the ethical and legal considerations of technological applications, including confidentiality concerns, security issues, potential limitations and benefits and communication practices in electronic media.
- Take appropriate and reasonable measures for maintaining confidentiality of student information and educational records stored or transmitted through the use of computers, social media, facsimile machines, telephones, voicemail, answering machines, and other electronic technology.
- Promote the safe and responsible use of technology in collaboration with educators and families.
- Promote the benefits and clarify the limitations of appropriate technological applications.
- Use established and approved means of communication with students, maintaining appropriate boundaries. School counselors help educate students about appropriate communication and boundaries.
- Advocate for equal access to technology for all students.

Potential Limitations in Virtual/Distance (Remote) School Counseling

Limitations in working with students remotely include the following:

- Emergency situations when the client needs someone in person and the counselor is not available—Counselors should assist clients to identify one or more trusted people living near the student: in an emergency, the student has backup support.
- Potential loss of confidentiality—Someone could enter the room (either the student's or the counselor's) room during a session. An email or voicemail could be accessed by someone who is not the counselor or client. Arranging student privacy in the session is important. Using a special, secure, school email server is one way to keep records of emails confidential while also assuring there's a reliable archive.
- There is always potential for misunderstanding, especially with the written word, as there are no nonverbal cues to interpret. Ideally, a backup plan for texting and emails would be to check in by phone or video call.

Use of Technology to Provide Services to Students Being Schooled in Remote Locations

Counselors can talk with students informally or schedule formal counseling sessions via phone, Skype, Facetime, WhatsApp, or other calling apps. Online learning programs give students access to emotional and cognitive skills development as well providing information on nearly anything—health, relaxation, college preparation tutorials, or stress reduction practices, for example—by way of videos. Online courses, e-books, or audiobooks can be purchased, and there are multitudes of free resources on YouTube.

Copyright © Mometrix Media. You have been licensed one copy of this document for personal use only. Any other reproduction or redistribution is strictly prohibited. All rights reserved.
This content is provided for test preparation purposes only and does not imply an endorsement by Mometrix of any particular political, scientific, or religious point of view.

Curating and sending links to students not only provides them with important information in an accessible format—it also sends the message that the counselor is working on behalf of the student, caring, even at a distance.

Limitations in technological client care may increase risk when a student is in crisis. Ideally, when someone is in real trouble, there's an actual person available to help. In crises such as potential or attempted suicide, the counselor may contact a local crises unit, call an ambulance, or arrange and pay for an Uber ride to a clinic or away from a dangerous situation.

Technology can't completely replace a face-to-face relationship, but it can make counseling possible in places or situations in which it would otherwise be impossible.

TECHNICAL REQUIREMENTS OF COUNSELORS

The ACES list encompasses the **technological requirements** involved in nearly every aspect of the school counselor's job from providing one-on-one services to mass communication and doing research to interpreting the research of others. Counselors need to be able to use software to build web pages, write letters, create spreadsheets and presentations, send emails, access databases, collect data, advance their own professional development, and help students use career, academic, and counseling-related resources.

Along with the nuts and bolts of knowing how to operate and maintain a computer, its software and associated printers, and other hardware, counselors also have to understand the potential pitfalls of technology use in terms of ethics and legalities. Like most professions, school counseling requires computer literacy, and counselors have the added mandate of showing students how to find the resources they need online. Familiarity with the Internet is also an important part of understanding, preventing, and stopping cyberbullying.

Copyright © Mometrix Media. You have been licensed one copy of this document for personal use only. Any other reproduction or redistribution is strictly prohibited. All rights reserved.
This content is provided for test preparation purposes only and does not imply an endorsement by Mometrix of any particular political, scientific, or religious point of view.

OSAT Practice Test

Want to take this practice test in an online interactive format?
Check out the bonus page, which includes interactive practice questions and much more: **mometrix.com/bonus948/osatscoun139**

1. Characteristics of a crisis include all of the following EXCEPT:

a. Decision making may be impaired during the chronic phases of a crisis.
b. Problem solving may be limited or insufficient when one is faced with a crisis.
c. Developmental crises include leaving for college or retirement.
d. Situational crises include job loss or the sudden death of a family member.

Refer to the following for questions 2 - 5:

You work in an inner city school where students are subject to a number of risk factors. The rate of violent incidences is above average, as are the numbers of drug offensives and teen pregnancies. The school currently has various in-house prevention and intervention programs offered on a volunteer or referral basis to all students. However, even the most successful of these programs yield few positive results. As the counselor, you decide to restructure the programs in an attempt to increase their effectiveness by collaborating with the community.

2. Collaborations with the community will help provide students with more effective programs in what main way?

a. The number of support systems for students both during school and outside of school will increase.
b. Opportunities to keep a close eye on students when outside of school will be offered.
c. School programs will receive increased funding.
d. Volunteer opportunities for community members will grow.

3. You would like to enhance your school's drug prevention programs. Which community agency will you most likely collaborate with?

a. Local police department
b. Local courthouse
c. Local jail
d. Local AA group

4. It comes to your attention that some of the teachers in this school are treating students in drug intervention programs differently. As the school counselor, what should you do to stop this behavior?

a. Conduct training for the teachers on discrimination and diversity in the schools
b. Report these teachers to the proper superiors
c. Nothing, your job is to deal only with the students
d. Speak to each teacher individually about the effects of their negativity

Copyright © Mometrix Media. You have been licensed one copy of this document for personal use only. Any other reproduction or redistribution is strictly prohibited. All rights reserved.
This content is provided for test preparation purposes only and does not imply an endorsement by Mometrix of any particular political, scientific, or religious point of view.

5. Even after the restructuring of prevention and intervention programs, you feel the results could be better. What further action could you take to increase program effectiveness?

a. Change participation in the prevention programs from voluntary to mandatory
b. Increase the number of programs available
c. Bring in a consultant to review programs and brainstorm new ideas
d. Ask administration to increase funding for programs

6. A student goes into a counseling office at the end of the day wanting to speak to the counselor. What would be the best approach to this situation?

a. The counselor should stay late to speak to the student immediately.
b. The counselor should give the student her home phone and ask her to call when she gets home.
c. The secretary should state that the counselor is going home in 10 minutes and schedule an appointment during school hours.
d. The counselor should briefly speak to the student and schedule a meeting for the next day if possible.

7. How might a counselor serve a School Advisory Committee?

a. Provide general information about the state of the students
b. Lead the committee to make sure his or her recommendations are followed
c. Email reminders to members about upcoming meetings
d. Make sure the committee is following all bylaws when voting on student issues

8. A 14-year-old client is involved in a neighborhood gang, is truant, and is using drugs on a daily basis. Which treatment program would be most efficacious for this client?

a. The Incredible Years
b. Parent-implemented intervention
c. Self-help (e.g.,12-step groups)
d. Multisystemic therapy (MST)

Refer to the following for questions 9 - 11:

> At the beginning of a counseling relationship, the counselor informs the student of confidentiality, stating that he cannot revel anything that is discussed during the sessions no matter what. After a few sessions, the counselor feels that the student would benefit from extra sessions and offers to meet the student outside of school to talk over coffee. During these after school sessions, the student informs the counselor that she is considering suicide. Since the counselor does not think this student will follow through, he disregards the statement.

9. What exception relating to confidentiality did the counselor neglect to discuss with the student?

a. Pregnancy
b. Harm to self or others
c. Sexual relationships
d. Problems with self-esteem

Copyright © Mometrix Media. You have been licensed one copy of this document for personal use only. Any other reproduction or redistribution is strictly prohibited. All rights reserved.
This content is provided for test preparation purposes only and does not imply an endorsement by Mometrix of any particular political, scientific, or religious point of view.

10. What ethical consideration did this counselor violate with the sessions outside of school?

a. Professional Competence
b. Dual Relationship
c. Appropriate Referrals
d. Confidentiality

11. What ethical consideration did the counselor violate by disregarding the threat of suicide?

a. Appropriate referral
b. Danger to self
c. Danger to others
d. Dual relationships

12. A known bully in the school is referred to your office. In addition to providing intervention for his violent behavior, what common issue or risk factor should you take into consideration?

a. Pathology
b. Potential to drop out of school
c. Future self-esteem issues
d. Poor conflict management skills

13. Research studies using focus groups and case studies are known as:

a. Qualitative designs
b. Quantitative designs
c. Quasi-experimental designs
d. Ex post facto designs

14. According to Kohlberg's theory of moral development, a student will follow school rules in order to avoid receiving detention. This is an example of what stage of moral development?

a. Personal Reward
b. Law and Order
c. Good Boy-Nice Girl
d. Punishment-Obedience

15. There are a number of risk factors affecting children and adolescents. Which is not considered a risk factor?

a. Poverty
b. Uneducated parents
c. Single-parent family
d. One parent with a high school diploma and one with a bachelor's degree

16. Which of the following stress management techniques involves tensing and releasing muscle groups one by one?

a. Autogenic training
b. Biofeedback
c. Progressive relaxation
d. Guided imagery

Copyright © Mometrix Media. You have been licensed one copy of this document for personal use only. Any other reproduction or redistribution is strictly prohibited. All rights reserved.
This content is provided for test preparation purposes only and does not imply an endorsement by Mometrix of any particular political, scientific, or religious point of view.

17. Kohlberg proposes a developmental theory in which developmental domain?

a. Psychosexual
b. Vocational
c. Moral
d. Life-style systems

18. When developing a school's counseling programs, a counselor should consider what students would like to gain from the programs. Which of the following are factors important to students in regard to school counseling?

a. Academic counseling
b. Available resources and personnel
c. College-preparation assistance
d. All of the above

19. What is the purpose of demographic information on survey assessments?

a. No real purpose
b. This information should not be included.
c. Identify differences
d. Identify similarities

20. Communication and conflict resolution can be taught most effectively in what type of setting?

a. Primary prevention group
b. Structured intervention group
c. Individual counseling
d. Group detentions

21. It is important that school counselors manage their stress on a regular basis to avoid career burnout. What is one way to do this?

a. Take a vacation
b. Have daily "down time"
c. Schedule the most difficult students in the morning
d. Volunteer for school activities to spend non-counseling time with students

22. Some counselors give students assignments related to the problems and goals that have been identified in counseling sessions to complete in between sessions. What is this kind of an assignment called?

a. Homework
b. Counselor Tasking
c. Strategic Task
d. Goal-oriented Task

23. There is little parent involvement in many schools due to large numbers of working parents. What is one strategy to use to increase participation?

a. Offer incentives for participation
b. Focus on the unemployed parents to work with
c. Suggest holding meetings and events on the weekends
d. Offer opportunities at various times during the week

Copyright © Mometrix Media. You have been licensed one copy of this document for personal use only. Any other reproduction or redistribution is strictly prohibited. All rights reserved.
This content is provided for test preparation purposes only and does not imply an endorsement by Mometrix of any particular political, scientific, or religious point of view.

24. One major risk factor for students is having parents with little or no education or parents who do not speak English as a first language. As a counselor, how could you address this issue?

a. Offer educational opportunities for parents, such as reading and writing classes
b. Suggest to parents that they enroll in college and earn degrees
c. Develop educational programs that teach students to be independent of their families
d. Provide counseling services to all students who have uneducated parents

25. A counselor who assesses a student according to his or her microsystem, macrosystem, and exosystem will have a complete picture of the student's cultural and racial identity. What is this model called?

a. Systems model
b. Ecological model
c. Cultural assessment model
d. Full overview model

26. If a counselor witnesses unethical behavior from a colleague, what actions should she take?

a. Do nothing so that the colleague does not get in trouble
b. Let the colleague know she is aware of his or her behavior and inform the colleague that they must stop immediately or face the consequences
c. Inform the colleague of intentions to alert the proper authorities and follow school policy on such matters
d. Inform parents of the students who may be victims of the unethical behavior

27. A counselor initiates a home visiting program to be conducted when a student is at a transition point in school, such as moving from elementary to middle school. What would the goal of a home visit be?

a. To check up on the home environment and the parents
b. To provide supportive services and education to the parents
c. To make sure the home is suitable for studying
d. To inform the parents of their child's new teacher and classroom location

28. A counselor has developed a comprehensive developmental counseling program in a large school. This program consists of daily meetings and programs to address the various needs of students. In order to avoid burnout, how might the counselor effectively manage so many meetings and programs?

a. Schedule meetings a few hours after school ends so she or he can take a break
b. Recruit the help of teachers and peer mentors to assist with the programs
c. Try to combine groups so that there are not so many
d. Rely on consultants to run the programs that are scheduled for after school

29. If a school counselor has a private practice, why would she refer a student in need of intensive counseling to someone else rather than seeing the client at her private practice?

a. She cannot see a client more than once a week.
b. She does not offer the counseling that this student needs.
c. She must have a full case load with her private practice.
d. She cannot use her position within the school to benefit her private practice.

Copyright © Mometrix Media. You have been licensed one copy of this document for personal use only. Any other reproduction or redistribution is strictly prohibited. All rights reserved.
This content is provided for test preparation purposes only and does not imply an endorsement by Mometrix of any particular political, scientific, or religious point of view.

30. Solution-Focused Brief Counseling consists of what six steps?

a. Define problem, determine goals, develop intervention, assign strategic tasks, emphasize positive behavior, terminate counseling
b. Define problem, determine goals, develop intervention, revisit goals, develop a second intervention, terminate counseling
c. Conduct psychoanalysis, determine underlying problem, develop group intervention plan, reinforce behavior, assign strategic task, terminate counseling
d. Identify prevention steps, define problem, determine goals, develop intervention, assign strategic task, terminate counseling

31. A supervisor for a counseling program collects outcomes data for all clients who received services last year. When plotting the distribution, the supervisor notices that clients younger than age 12 have measures skewed to the left. Which of the following is true of distributions skewed to the left (i.e., negatively skewed)?

a. The mean is less than the median.
b. The mean is greater than the median.
c. The mean and the median are the same value.
d. The mode is the lowest value.

32. Rather than requiring students who disobey the rules on fighting to serve a silent detention, you suggest conducting a problem-centered, structured intervention group. What issues should you focus on during this group?

a. Self-actualization
b. Aggressive behaviors
c. Safety
d. Physiological issues

33. Collaboration with other teachers is a good way to incorporate positive behaviors and communication throughout the school. How can a teacher advisor program assist in this collaboration?

a. Provides all-around support to the students
b. Makes the teacher feel important and more willing to work with the counselor
c. Provides more watchful eyes for bad behavior
d. Gives students more opportunities to get help with their school work

Refer to the following for question 34:

A teacher approaches a school counselor complaining that her students tend to get into fights because of racial tensions. These fights typically begin with students yelling racial slurs at each other and often end up with one or more of the students being sent to the office because of violence or the threat of violence.

34. How might the implementation of human relations training be beneficial in this class?

a. This type of training teaches anger management techniques.
b. This type of training teaches students how to be friends.
c. This type of training promotes conflict resolution.
d. This type of training promotes an understanding of cultural differences.

Copyright © Mometrix Media. You have been licensed one copy of this document for personal use only. Any other reproduction or redistribution is strictly prohibited. All rights reserved.
This content is provided for test preparation purposes only and does not imply an endorsement by Mometrix of any particular political, scientific, or religious point of view.

35. A new counselor feels that it is necessary to help all students solve their problems as quickly as possible. Because of this she, routinely brings paperwork home. Why would this practice be frowned upon in the field of counseling?

a. Counselors are not paid to work at home.
b. Counselors should establish boundaries between their professional and personal lives.
c. Colleagues may become jealous because the counselor is more efficient then they are.
d. This practice could lead to dual relationships.

36. Members belonging to groups with which of the following characteristics experience transitions after there are vacancies or a group member leaves?

a. Ongoing groups with a fixed membership
b. Time-limited groups with a fixed membership
c. Ongoing groups with revolving membership
d. Time-limited groups with revolving membership

37. Why are evidence-based evaluations important in program management?

a. Evaluations contribute to training and an increase in professional knowledge.
b. Evaluations prove that counselors are conducting programs.
c. Evaluations that show positive change will receive state funding.
d. Evaluations provide a paper trail of the counselor's work.

38. How might training workshops be misperceived by parents?

a. Parents are uneducated.
b. Parents do not welcome additional training.
c. They see such programs as trying to change their core values and methods of raising their children.
d. They have problem children.

39. As a high school counselor, you observe that the numbers of pregnant teens on campus have been increasing over the past few years. What steps can you put into place to address this issue?

a. Continue to focus on student academics
b. Allow pregnant students to have a lighter course load in order to focus on their health and the pregnancy
c. Develop prevention and intervention programs to address this issue
d. Counsel students on the difficulties of having a child at this age and assist with federal aid paperwork

40. Counselors have a professional responsibility to provide parents with what type of information?

a. The details of sessions with their children
b. Objective reports with respect to ethical guidelines
c. Subjective reports on their child's progress
d. Positive parenting information

Copyright © Mometrix Media. You have been licensed one copy of this document for personal use only. Any other reproduction or redistribution is strictly prohibited. All rights reserved.
This content is provided for test preparation purposes only and does not imply an endorsement by Mometrix of any particular political, scientific, or religious point of view.

41. What is the benefit of continued assessments?

a. Student progress is monitored.
b. Areas of weakness are identified.
c. Learning styles and goals can be modified.
d. All of the above

42. Which is true of using telemental health services for crisis management?

a. Asynchronous communication helps treat the client in the present moment.
b. Emergency triage services can be put in place quickly for clients with suicidal ideation.
c. Telehealth decreases the validity of standardized suicide risk assessment instruments.
d. For suicidality, there are poorer treatment outcomes with telehealth than with face-to-face encounters.

43. When developing counseling programs, what type of outcomes are associated with success?

a. Counselor-activity outcomes
b. Community involvement outcomes
c. Parent involvement outcomes
d. Student outcomes

44. What is the main premise behind a developmental guidance program?

a. All students develop at different rates, so various programs must be designed.
b. Guidance programs are developmental in nature, beginning with simple concepts and progressing to more abstract concepts.
c. Developmental guidance programs are used for students with developmental disabilities to help them achieve their full potential.
d. Developmental guidance programs focus on human development and positive self-concepts.

Refer to the following for questions 45 - 46:

> A 5-year-old boy continues to attempt to play with children who openly ridicule him and leave him out of games. His persistence with this group of children has recently resulted in a number of fights on the playground. After being referred to your office, you learn that he has an unsupportive home life. His parents were divorced last year. He lives with his mother who works at night, and he does not see his father. He is often left at home alone; however, a neighbor watches him from time to time.

45. According to the Cognitive Behavior Theory, what developmental skills is this child lacking?

a. Interpersonal skills
b. Abstract thinking skills
c. Concrete thinking skills
d. Self-Identity

46. According to Pavlov's theory of development, what would you expect to occur in terms of this child's learning and behavior?

a. Nothing, he would naturally continue to try to fit in.
b. The child would become conditioned to the negative response and avoid the situation.
c. The child would take cues from his social environment and act accordingly.
d. The child would grow out of this stage and soon make friends.

Copyright © Mometrix Media. You have been licensed one copy of this document for personal use only. Any other reproduction or redistribution is strictly prohibited. All rights reserved.
This content is provided for test preparation purposes only and does not imply an endorsement by Mometrix of any particular political, scientific, or religious point of view.

47. A counselor develops a peer-mentoring program. What is the main responsibility of the counselor during the implementation of this program?

a. Overseeing all actions of the peer mentors
b. Training peer mentors in various counseling aspects
c. Meeting with mentees to make sure the mentors are doing their jobs
d. Monitoring progress and supporting the peer mentors

Refer to the following for questions 48 - 50:

In survey type assessments, a Likert-type scale is often used. These scales use either an even or an odd number of responses. For scales using an even number of responses, there is no neutral answer, and the individual must choose either a negative or a positive response. For scales using an odd number of responses, the individual has the opportunity to choose a neutral or undecided response.

48. As a counselor, you decide to use a 5-point Likert-type scale student survey to determine your students' knowledge and use of drugs and alcohol. What is one flaw of this method that you must be aware of?

a. Students might not understand the scale.
b. Students might choose the neutral selection to avoid committing to a positive or negative answer.
c. The method can produce unrealistic results due to social desirability factors.
d. None of the above

49. What is one downside to using a 4-point Likert-type scale?

a. It does not provide enough choices.
b. It forces a student to choose either positive or negatively.
c. Responses cannot be validated.
d. There are is no downside.

50. A student is given a 5-point Likert-type scale and selects all Neutral responses. What would a counselor determine from these results?

a. The student is laid back and easy going.
b. The student did not want to share his own thoughts and wanted to get the assessment done as quickly as possible.
c. The student did not understand the task.
d. The student is in need of intervention for indecisiveness.

51. What type of students are developmental guidance programs designed for?

a. Those with developmental delays
b. Those with learning disabilities
c. All students
d. Those with emotional issues

52. When conducting a program evaluation, what outcomes measure the intended effects of the program or intervention?

a. Immediate outcomes
b. Proximal outcomes
c. Distal outcomes
d. Intervention outcomes

Copyright © Mometrix Media. You have been licensed one copy of this document for personal use only. Any other reproduction or redistribution is strictly prohibited. All rights reserved.
This content is provided for test preparation purposes only and does not imply an endorsement by Mometrix of any particular political, scientific, or religious point of view.

53. According to Bloom's Taxonomy of Learning, what is the highest level of learning?

a. Evaluation
b. Comprehension
c. Application
d. Knowledge

Refer to the following for questions 54 - 55:

A counselor currently works in a school with a traditional counseling program that offers crisis counseling in times of need. Additionally, due to a lack of support programs, students who get into fights are often sent to the crisis-counseling program. After witnessing a number of students repeatedly getting into fights, a counselor sees that many fights are due to communication problems and simple misunderstandings, and the school's traditional counseling program is having little effect on students involved in fights. As a result, the counselor decides to change the current counseling model to a developmental counseling program.

54. In developing the new programs, the counselor decides to address essential skills with the students. What specific skills does he want to address?

a. Developmental skills
b. Social literacy skills
c. Cognitive skills
d. Emotional literacy skills

55. In terms of the crisis program, what can he do to adapt this program to fit a developmental counseling model?

a. Implement prevention and intervention programs
b. Discuss developmental issues during the crisis counseling sessions
c. Include family members in the counseling
d. Offer crisis counseling to younger students

56. Why are collaborations between teachers and the community important for a counselor?

a. Collaborations provide insight and information that might not otherwise be readily available.
b. Collaborations provide additional financial support for students.
c. Collaborations could be an additional funding source for programs.
d. With the community's assistance, a counselor's work load will be reduced.

57. When would a formative assessment be conducted?

a. Prior to an intervention
b. During an intervention
c. After an intervention
d. Only if the student refuses an intervention

Copyright © Mometrix Media. You have been licensed one copy of this document for personal use only. Any other reproduction or redistribution is strictly prohibited. All rights reserved.
This content is provided for test preparation purposes only and does not imply an endorsement by Mometrix of any particular political, scientific, or religious point of view.

58. A counselor finds that many of the parents of the students she works with do not speak English, and the counselor is not bilingual. What should the counselor do with regard to communication between the school and parents?

a. Send letters home and have the students translate them
b. Do not communicate with the families
c. Provide a translator for meetings
d. Require the parents take English courses

59. In group interventions, there are typically three stages involved in the group dynamics: group formation, group awareness, and group action. What is the focus of the Group Formation stage?

a. To facilitate cooperation
b. To introduce all participants
c. To find out why everyone is in the group
d. To ask what group members hope to gain from the group

60. A counselor in a predominately-white school does not feel that cultural diversity programs are important in the school. What is wrong with this belief?

a. Non-white students may feel left out of school activities.
b. White students might feel left out of school activities.
c. Cultural diversity involves more than just the color of one's skin.
d. A student may want to attend a college that is very diverse.

61. A counselor is a covered mental health provider under the Health Insurance Portability and Accountability Act of 1996 (HIPAA). As such, their clients have a right to:

a. Contest payment for services if records show that inadequate progress has been made
b. Request to have their protected electronic health records amended
c. Receive a copy of their diagnostic summary, treatment plan, and psychotherapy notes
d. Prevent the counselor from contacting family members in the event of a serious and imminent threat

62. The school you work in has a high rate of parent participation. You would like to use this information to further increase the success of your students. What can a counselor do to make sure parents have the opportunity to continue supporting the school?

a. Send notes home thanking them for their continued support
b. Develop programs that encourage parent participation
c. Offer parent education programs addressing the needs of their children in terms of success in the future
d. Provide students with mentoring programs so that they can gain the support of adults in the business community

63. Which of the following serves as an initial coping mechanism when experiencing grief and loss?

a. Anger
b. Depression
c. Denial
d. Bargaining

Copyright © Mometrix Media. You have been licensed one copy of this document for personal use only. Any other reproduction or redistribution is strictly prohibited. All rights reserved.
This content is provided for test preparation purposes only and does not imply an endorsement by Mometrix of any particular political, scientific, or religious point of view.

64. Parents can be involved in the school in a number of ways. You would like to increase parent participation in the career resource room at the school. In addition to contacting the PTA, how else might a counselor recruit parents to volunteer?

a. Distribute annual surveys for parents to identify their volunteer interests and abilities
b. The PTA is the only place to find volunteers.
c. Place an ad in the newspaper
d. Recruit teachers because they are easier to contact

65. Researchers examining teen dating and relationships consider peer influences, personal beliefs, and environmental factors. This is known as:

a. The zone of proximal development
b. The pleasure principle
c. Reciprocal determinism
d. Psychological hedonism

66. The DIRECT technique is a consulting method used in many school districts. What does DIRECT stand for?

a. District Initiative Regarding Educational Counseling Techniques
b. Dynamic Introspective Reasoning for Educational Counseling Theory
c. Direct Individual Response Educational Consulting Technique
d. Direct Individual Reaction to Educational Counseling Theories

67. A counselor wishing to increase students' ability to control feelings and understand their own feelings would develop what type of program?

a. Social literacy program
b. Cognitive literacy program
c. Emotional literacy program
d. Conflict resolution program

68. Elementary school counselors must have a strong understanding of what?

a. Child development
b. Continued education options
c. Relationship building
d. Adjustment and coping mechanisms

69. Studies have suggested that training in social skills benefits gifted and special needs students. What specific factor does such training address?

a. Self-esteem
b. Sociability
c. Attendance rates
d. Family risk factors

70. Beginning around the age of 11, children can think in logical, abstract terms. According to Piaget's theory of development, what stage does this represent?

a. Formal operational
b. Pre-operational
c. Concrete operational
d. Sensory-motor

Copyright © Mometrix Media. You have been licensed one copy of this document for personal use only. Any other reproduction or redistribution is strictly prohibited. All rights reserved.
This content is provided for test preparation purposes only and does not imply an endorsement by Mometrix of any particular political, scientific, or religious point of view.

71. A recent transfer student came from an inner city school to your rural school. She is having difficulty adjusting to the area and the school. As the counselor, what steps can you take to ease this student's transition?

a. Announce that there is a new student and ask volunteers to show her around the school
b. Create a support team with the help of other students, teachers, and the new student's parents
c. Provide Solution-Focused Brief Counseling to the student to find out the underlying problem
d. Provide information about making friends and offer this information to the student and her parents

72. What forms can professional development take?

a. Continued education
b. Evaluating and reporting on program outcomes
c. Presenting research at professional conferences
d. All of the above

73. Unrealistic demands on time and job duties refer to what?

a. Role ambiguity
b. Role conflict
c. Role mutations
d. Role confusion

74. Which of the following measures suicidal risk using four constructs: severity of ideation, intensity of ideation, behavior, and lethality?

a. The Suicidal Probability Scale (SPS)
b. The Columbia Suicide Severity Rating Scale (C-SSRS)
c. The Daily Living Activities 20 (DLA-20)
d. The Brief Psychiatric Rating Scale (BPRS)

75. Which of the following would be a barrier to a child's mental development?

a. Malnutrition
b. An abusive home
c. A lack of family support
d. All of the above

76. Counselors are often responsible for initiating a parent conference by making a phone call or sending a letter home. What should a counselor do in order to avoid an automatic negative reaction from parents?

a. State all the problems their child is having
b. Speak with a level of equality and openness
c. State that things at home must change
d. Suggest that their child seeks additional help

Copyright © Mometrix Media. You have been licensed one copy of this document for personal use only. Any other reproduction or redistribution is strictly prohibited. All rights reserved.
This content is provided for test preparation purposes only and does not imply an endorsement by Mometrix of any particular political, scientific, or religious point of view.

77. What is the main premise behind Solution-Focused Brief Counseling?

a. Serious underlying psychological problems must be addressed before counseling can take place.
b. Individuals have the ability to solve their own problems with the assistance of a counselor.
c. Individuals cannot understand their own issues and need a counselor to help them.
d. This counseling technique is effective after only three sessions.

78. A counselor from a small town begins working at urban school. What action should the counselor take to ensure that she is aware of the difference in cultures between herself and her students?

a. Refer those students of differing cultures to another counselor. Since their cultures are different, she will not be able to help them.
b. Educate herself on the diversity of the school and the community.
c. Counsel the students with the confidence that she can help them no matter what.
d. Offer cultural diversity programs so that students can learn about each other.

79. What is one of the primary reasons why counselors have a difficult time getting support from immigrant parents?

a. Immigrant parents do not challenge school authority.
b. Immigrant parents are oftentimes unfamiliar with American school systems.
c. Immigrant parents do not have time to talk with school counselors.
d. Immigrant parents have to work during the day.

80. A student comes into your office with a referral from her English teacher. This is typically a straight A student; however, her grades have been slipping lately. She states that she has been "stressed out" but that nothing serious is going on. What issues might you want to ask about in order to determine the reason for her lower grades?

a. Self-esteem issues
b. Problems with a friend or boyfriend
c. Difficulty level of her classes
d. Mental health history

81. All of the following accurately reflects the impact of divorce on families EXCEPT:

a. Rates of academic difficulties are higher for children of divorce.
b. Rates of emotional difficulties are higher for children of divorce.
c. Among children of divorce, boys have higher rates of maladjustment than girls.
d. Among divorced couples, divorced women report higher levels of life satisfaction than divorced men.

82. Teachers need basic safety training in school violence to learn how to keep themselves and students safe. In addition to this basic safety training, what other issues should be discussed to assist teachers in understanding problems in their schools?

a. Student dynamics
b. Basic psychology of the student involved in violence
c. Nonviolent reactions to student behavior
d. All of the above

Copyright © Mometrix Media. You have been licensed one copy of this document for personal use only. Any other reproduction or redistribution is strictly prohibited. All rights reserved.
This content is provided for test preparation purposes only and does not imply an endorsement by Mometrix of any particular political, scientific, or religious point of view.

83. Self-control procedures include all of the following EXCEPT:

a. Self-monitoring
b. Self-punishment
c. Response control
d. Stimulus control

84. Ego, esteem needs, confidence, sense of mastery, positive self-regard, self-respect, and self-extension refers to what developmental theory?

a. Erikson's Theory of Psychosocial Development
b. Maslow's Hierarchy of Human Needs
c. Sullivan's Interpersonal Theory
d. Havighurst's Stages of Childhood Development

85. What are three essential developmental skills?

a. Self-concept, self-esteem, self-respect
b. Ego, Id, Super-ego
c. Operational thinking, concrete thinking, abstract thinking
d. Thinking, feeling, relating

86. Professional counselors are expected to contribute to the profession of counseling. What is one way for counselors to participate and contribute?

a. Maintain an active case load
b. Hold group sessions for students
c. Participate in professional associations
d. Maintain their licensure regardless of whether they are currently providing counseling services

87. A counselor is reviewing a client's record and discovers an inaccuracy. Unless otherwise dictated by agency or institutional policy, the counselor should:

a. Destroy and replace the original document.
b. Add a clinical note explaining the inaccuracy.
c. Explain the inaccuracies to the client and obtain permission to destroy the documentation.
d. Seek consultation and have the consultant document any necessary changes.

88. There are generally six levels of parent participation. Which of the following is not considered a level of parent participation?

a. Parenting
b. Communication
c. Continued Education
d. Volunteering

Copyright © Mometrix Media. You have been licensed one copy of this document for personal use only. Any other reproduction or redistribution is strictly prohibited. All rights reserved.
This content is provided for test preparation purposes only and does not imply an endorsement by Mometrix of any particular political, scientific, or religious point of view.

89. Children learn their cultural identity by the time they are three years old. What implication does this have on a school counselor?

a. Counselors of a different culture should meet with parents to discuss their cultural beliefs before counseling a student.
b. This will not be an issue since cultural identity is already established by time the child begins school.
c. This established identity must be respected and taken into consideration when addressing students' issues.
d. Cultural identity can be discounted in young children but must be addressed in older children.

90. What type of skills will a counselor focus on if he wants to increase students' ability to think out problems and find positive solutions to such problems?

a. Basic academic skills
b. Relating skills
c. Conflict resolution skills
d. Cognitive literacy skills

91. Counselors may deny a client's request to view some or all their counseling records only when:

a. There is compelling evidence suggesting that access would cause harm to the client.
b. There is compelling evidence suggesting that the client would require extensive and timely assistance in interpreting the records.
c. The counselor providing services has experienced incapacitation, death, retirement, or has terminated their practice.
d. The situation involves multiple clients, and the requesting client cannot agree to keep the other clients' information confidential.

92. A local plant recently closed down, causing hundreds of adults in your community to lose their jobs. How might this affect the school district's community?

a. Schools may experience a drop in attendance and achievement.
b. Students will be able to spend more time with their parents and, as a result, do better in school.
c. The number of students in schools will decrease as families move to find work.
d. There may be an increase in participation in the school's on-the-job training program, as students need to work to help the family financially.

93. When developing an intervention, a counselor should state the problem in a positive way. What is this known as?

a. Positive problem statements
b. Utilization
c. Reframing
d. Rephrasing

Copyright © Mometrix Media. You have been licensed one copy of this document for personal use only. Any other reproduction or redistribution is strictly prohibited. All rights reserved.
This content is provided for test preparation purposes only and does not imply an endorsement by Mometrix of any particular political, scientific, or religious point of view.

94. Pre–post tests are important tools for assessments. What is the main thing to consider when developing a pre-post test?

a. Who will take the test
b. Key ideas and concepts
c. Number of questions
d. When to give the test

95. Edgar Schein used which of the following terms to explain an individual's perception of their own values, skills, abilities, and interests in regard to work?

a. Active adjustments
b. Career anchors
c. Career congruence
d. Life role salience

96. When beginning a program evaluation, what documentation will be necessary?

a. Satisfaction surveys from previous program sessions
b. A list of programs offered
c. The number of participants in last year's programs
d. Guidance curriculum guides

97. Which of the following is not considered a major developmental task of children and adolescents?

a. Sense of identity
b. Autonomy
c. Self-esteem
d. Knowledge acquisition

98. A counselor initiating a school-family curriculum program will probably structure the program in what way?

a. Take-home activities for students and their parents
b. Group discussions
c. Surveys for parents
d. Counseling sessions for those in need of cultural diversity education

99. What issues might a primary prevention group address for adolescent girls?

a. Grief and loss
b. Aggressive behaviors
c. Self esteem
d. Abuse

100. When a diagnostic assessment for learning needs is conducted, what factors are not considered?

a. Prior knowledge
b. Interests
c. Learning style preferences
d. Sociability

Copyright © Mometrix Media. You have been licensed one copy of this document for personal use only. Any other reproduction or redistribution is strictly prohibited. All rights reserved.
This content is provided for test preparation purposes only and does not imply an endorsement by Mometrix of any particular political, scientific, or religious point of view.

101. According to the Social Cognitive Theory, to what does the term "perspective taking" refer?

a. Internalizing another person's situation
b. Thinking cognitively about another person's situation
c. Role playing
d. Thinking cognitively about your own situation

102. According to Piaget, what is a schema?

a. Information that has been taught
b. A universal view of the world
c. An individual's representation of something
d. The visualization of a concept

103. When dealing with middle school students, it is important for a counselor to understand the developmental relationship between Industry and Inferiority. This is an example of a theory of development based on the work of what psychologist?

a. Freud
b. Piaget
c. Erikson
d. Bandura

104. What is the best strategy for choosing teacher advisors for students?

a. Divide the students alphabetically by last name
b. Obtain a list of students each teacher would like to advise
c. Obtain a list of preferred teacher advisors from the students
d. Obtain a list of preferred teacher advisors from the parents

105. Young girls who experience abuse in the home or in a relationship have increased risk factors including:

a. Drug abuse
b. Teen pregnancy
c. Poor grades
d. All of the above

106. What developmental theory describes an adolescent's ability to think abstractly?

a. Cognitive Development
b. Erikson's Theory of Development
c. Social Cognitive Theory
d. Dynamic Systems Theory

107. A school counselor begins at a new school and notices that there are few cultural diversity programs available. What might she do to increase cultural expression in the school?

a. Ask teachers to provide information on the ethnic demographics of their classes
b. Encourage families to discuss cultural diversity at home
c. Coordinate a field trip to a more diverse school
d. Develop programs and events that celebrate and educate students about cultural diversity

Copyright © Mometrix Media. You have been licensed one copy of this document for personal use only. Any other reproduction or redistribution is strictly prohibited. All rights reserved.
This content is provided for test preparation purposes only and does not imply an endorsement by Mometrix of any particular political, scientific, or religious point of view.

108. A school counselor would like to observe the social skills of a newly referred third grader. Prior to the intake, the counselor observes the student during physical education and later during lunchtime. This type of observation is advantageous over a formal observation because:

a. There is a decreased likelihood for the Hawthorne effect.
b. There is a decreased likelihood for confirmation bias.
c. Interrater reliability values are higher.
d. Threats to internal validity are minimized.

109. Cultural identity is:

a. Primarily influenced by race and ethnicity
b. Fully developed by early adulthood
c. Stable across changing contexts
d. Dynamic and constantly evolving

110. How are School Advisory Boards connected with parent collaboration?

a. They include the participation of parents and community in the decision-making process, which results in a feeling of ownership from these groups.
b. They are a way to get parents to volunteer and increase a school's parent participation rate.
c. Meetings are held at night so that working parents can attend.
d. They allow parents to see what is really going on with the school

111. What is Bandura's main argument concerning behavior development?

a. Behavior and environment affect each other.
b. The ego is affected by the id and superego.
c. Genetics is the sole cause of behavior.
d. Behavior has no effect on the environment.

112. A counselor begins seeing a student who has issues with low self-esteem. This student is of Chinese descent but was adopted by an African American family as a baby. What responsibility does the counselor have toward the student regarding culture?

a. Provide the student with information on her Chinese heritage and encourage her to embrace it
b. Suggest she join the Chinese American Club at school
c. Question her feelings of being of Chinese descent but being raised in an African American home
d. Respect the student's cultural identity as it is and assist her instead with the problems she brought to the attention of the counselor

113. What is one strategy that a high school counselor can implement to increase parent participation in their children's academics?

a. Provide training sessions that teach parents to be tutors for their children
b. Require parents to sign a form confirming that students have completed outside reading assignments
c. Suggest that parents help students with home work every night
d. Offer regular reports and information on student performance, as well as school events and programs

Copyright © Mometrix Media. You have been licensed one copy of this document for personal use only. Any other reproduction or redistribution is strictly prohibited. All rights reserved.
This content is provided for test preparation purposes only and does not imply an endorsement by Mometrix of any particular political, scientific, or religious point of view.

114. Why should cultural identity be integrated into early interventions for developmental issues?

a. Culture will affect how children and parents view the learning environment and respond to various programs or interventions.
b. Interventions should focus on a student's culture, as the child may not understand concepts that are otherwise unrelated.
c. Students within the same area should learn the same information, and culture should not be taken into consideration.
d. Each group deals with issues differently; therefore, there may be confusion between the student and the counselor if these issues are considered when developing the intervention.

115. Conferences with parents and the school can come in many forms. What is one type of conference that will promote communication between parents and students, as well as the school?

a. Parent-teacher
b. Student led
c. Teacher-student
d. Counselor-student

116. Which of the following serves as the foundation for short- and long-term treatment plan goals?

a. The student's diagnosis
b. The student's desire to change
c. The student's insurance coverage
d. The student's collateral information

117. What is one strategy a counselor can use to increase job experience and skills that would require community collaboration?

a. Creating an on-the-job training program
b. Finding part time jobs for students
c. Offering more career-based or skill-improvement courses, such as auto shop and computer applications
d. Offering programs that focus on resume writing and interviewing skills

118. A 16-year-old female with an intellectual disability reports chewing up her food, regurgitating it, and then rechewing it, reswallowing it, or spitting it out. Her symptoms are likely to meet the diagnostic criteria for:

a. Bulimia nervosa
b. Pica
c. Binge eating disorder
d. Rumination disorder

119. You have implemented a new teacher-advising program for students in the school. What do the teachers need to know about their new role?

a. They should both provide support and serve as advocates for their students.
b. They need to meet with students only once a year.
c. They should provide tutoring services to the students when necessary.
d. They will be required to report all interactions with the students on a monthly basis.

Copyright © Mometrix Media. You have been licensed one copy of this document for personal use only. Any other reproduction or redistribution is strictly prohibited. All rights reserved.
This content is provided for test preparation purposes only and does not imply an endorsement by Mometrix of any particular political, scientific, or religious point of view.

120. What is one explanation if a student continues to perform poorly on Summative Assessments?

a. Formative assessments were not properly conducted.
b. The intervention was successful.
c. The student is bored and is not trying.
d. The assessment is too difficult.

Copyright © Mometrix Media. You have been licensed one copy of this document for personal use only. Any other reproduction or redistribution is strictly prohibited. All rights reserved.
This content is provided for test preparation purposes only and does not imply an endorsement by Mometrix of any particular political, scientific, or religious point of view.

Answer Key and Explanations

1. A: During a crisis, decision making is impaired during the acute rather than chronic phase. The very nature of a crisis makes it acute rather than chronic. During this time, problem solving may be limited or impaired. Developmental crises include those associated with a specific developmental stage, such as leaving for college, retirement, having a child, or getting married. Situational crises are unanticipated events that disrupt normal psychological functioning.

2. A: Community support provides schools, staff, and students with a sense of connectedness, which in turn enhances the learning environment. This support works to provide individuals with clear expectations. These factors serve to provide staff and students with a healthy learning environment with reduced stressors and less burn out. Additionally, when students have numerous avenues of support, they typically perform better academically, and schools experience a lower dropout rate. Having the community as a support system for a school also helps reduce some risk factors that students often experience. For example, links to financial aid resources and parenting education classes can serve to reduce child abuse and poverty.

3. A: Students may benefit from speaking to representatives from all of these organizations. However, a representative from the local police department would be the best option. These individuals are usually trained in drug education for school-aged children. Additionally, most police departments have drug prevention programs in place that have been proven to have positive outcomes. By bringing in individuals from the community, students get a different perspective of the issue at hand. Students will be able to ask questions and receive life experience answers from the presenter. This helps to show students the reality of the problem, as well as its consequences.

4. A: Students in drug intervention programs may be experience a number of feelings and barriers as they attempt to stop using drugs. Teachers must be aware of these issues, along with the recovery process. It will be important for those students in intervention programs to receive support from all staff members to ensure success. As a counselor, you may offer training for teachers and other staff members. This training can include information about the specific intervention programs offered at your school, the recovery process, and sensitivity training specific to this population of students.

5. C: Consultation is one way to improve school programs and involve the community. Consultants provide assessments and evaluations of programs, as well as suggestions for improvements. When schools and the community work together, there will be certain expectations that reduce stressors caused by unclear roles and responsibilities. Also, having an unbiased professionals evaluate school programs is the accepted way to report on school programs. Using a consultant on a regular basis for programs and services also serves as a system of checks and balances. These measures allow both the school and the community to view school programs on an outcomes-based perspective with little to no underlying agendas being intermingled.

6. D: It is important that the counselor set appropriate boundaries for herself and the students. In this situation, the counselor will want to speak briefly to the student to make sure that there is no immediate threat of danger. After a quick assessment, the counselor may want to schedule an appointment with the student to discuss the problem in more detail the next day. By addressing this situation in this manner, the counselor has shown concern for the student's needs and safety and addressed her own need for boundaries. It would be inappropriate to give a student the counselor's home phone number, and staying late would eventually cause the counselor to experience burnout

Copyright © Mometrix Media. You have been licensed one copy of this document for personal use only. Any other reproduction or redistribution is strictly prohibited. All rights reserved.
This content is provided for test preparation purposes only and does not imply an endorsement by Mometrix of any particular political, scientific, or religious point of view.

in her job. Finally, not addressing the student at all does not show concern for the student and does not assess any potential danger the student may be in.

7. A: School Advisory Committees are run by parents, members of the community, and teachers. Oftentimes, the school counselor, principal, or vice principal may attend these meetings in order to serve as a resource for information and assistance. The role of the school counselor is to provide the committee with objective information about the state of the school and its students. This information will often be in the form of reports from program evaluations. The advisory board will use this information to make decisions about such matters as the school's education improvement plan and allocation of funds.

8. D: MST is an evidence-based practice (EBP) for adolescent substance abuse and associated issues. MST addresses severe behavioral issues, including community influences, school issues, and family factors. Family involvement is a critical element for adolescent substance use disorder treatment. The Incredible Years is an early childhood EBP for children with challenging behaviors, including symptoms of ADHD and ODD. The parent-implemented intervention is an EBP for children with ASD. Finally, self-help groups, including Alcoholics Anonymous and Narcotics Anonymous, are not EBPs for adolescent substance use and antisocial behaviors.

9. B: Although counselors have a responsibility to their clients, they are also ethically accountable for the safety of others; this must be disclosed at the beginning of a counseling relationship. If a client ever threatens to harm himself or someone or something else, the rules of confidentiality do not apply. It is up to the counselor to make a professional judgment about any threatening statements a client might make to determine if alerting authorities and breaking confidentiality is necessary. Many counselors will consult with another professional if a situation is ambiguous. After determining the validity of a threat to do harm, counselors must inform their clients of their intent to notify the proper authorities.

10. B: Dual relationships occur when a counselor and client know each other prior to beginning a counseling relationship. In the school setting, this may occur if the counselor has family members in the same school. In these cases, the counselor should refer their family members to another counselor if possible. In the situation described above, inviting a student to talk outside of school creates a dual relationship and violates professional guidelines against using a school to promote or benefit any private practice or nonschool counseling activities. This situation also illustrates that the counselor is crossing professional boundaries by suggesting that they meet over coffee.

11. B: The third leading cause of death among 15-24 year olds is suicide. Actions should be taken to include individual therapy, group therapy, and appropriate referral for students displaying risk factors of suicide. Counselors can develop prevention and intervention programs for this issue. Gaining the support of the school and the community is one way to help prevent this tragedy. However, any threat of danger to self should be fully investigated. When a student threatens suicide, the counselor has a responsibility to alert the proper authorities and refer the client to appropriate help.

12. B: Bullies are at risk for a number of negative outcomes, including the increased potential to drop out of school. Counselors can implement a many intervention strategies for bullying. School wide interventions can include posted rules, announcements, and programs. Classroom interventions can involve the same intervention strategies as those implemented school wide, except on a smaller level. Individual interventions will address the student bully specifically. This type of intervention should be tailored to the individual and aim to define the root problem while

Copyright © Mometrix Media. You have been licensed one copy of this document for personal use only. Any other reproduction or redistribution is strictly prohibited. All rights reserved.
This content is provided for test preparation purposes only and does not imply an endorsement by Mometrix of any particular political, scientific, or religious point of view.

providing education and intervention to change the negative behaviors. Referrals can also be made to anger management, communication, and conflict resolution programs.

13. A: Qualitative designs use data that cannot be assigned a numeric value, including focus groups, case studies, interviews, and observations. Quantitative designs are numeric and measurable. Experimental and quasi-experimental studies are examples of quantitative research designs. Experimental designs use statistical methods to measure the effects of the independent variable on the dependent variable. True experimental researchers manipulate the independent variable hypothesized to bring about change in the dependent variable. Quasi-experimental studies set out to identify support of a causal relationship between the independent and dependent variables; they differ from true experimental designs in that the independent variable is not manipulated nor is the assignment of treatment groups controlled by the researcher. Ex post facto (i.e., after the fact), or causal-comparative, designs study the effects of the independent variable on the dependent variable. Ex post facto designs differ from true experimental designs in that subjects are not randomly assigned and the qualities being measured already exist (e.g., age, weight).

14. D: In Kohlberg's Punishment/Obedience stage, an individual will not distinguish between doing right and simply avoiding punishment. This stage applies directly in this situation as the student would comply with rules solely as a means to avoid the negative consequence of receiving detention. Answer A, Personal Reward, refers primarily to instances in which an individual is motivated to attain or achieve something. Answer B, Law and Order, refers to an appeal to maintain the social order and supersedes individual interests. Answer C, Good Boy-Nice Girl refers to a stage in which intention is taken into account above action alone. In this stage, being liked or having a good reason is a motivating factor, even in an otherwise morally wrong situation. The student in this situation is only described as avoiding a negative consequence rather than having any pleasing rewards or societal devotion for following the rules, leaving answer D as the only possible correct answer.

15. D: Having only one educated parent is typically not considered a risk factor for students. Often, parents with some education can provide their children with academic support that uneducated parents cannot. However, if a student is from a single-parent family, then that child may be at risk. Additionally, students with parents with no education and those who live in poverty are also at risk for problems in school. These risk factors can be addressed by the counselor in a number of ways. These include providing support for both the family and the student, referrals to community social service agencies, and offering free educational programs to parents.

16. C: Progressive relaxation (i.e., progressive muscle relaxation) involves tensing and releasing muscle groups one by one. Autogenic training is used to promote relaxation by "telling" one's body to relax using verbal prompts (e.g., "Your arms are becoming heavy"). Biofeedback uses an electronic device to measure body functions (e.g., heart rate and blood pressure). Finally, guided imagery is a visualization technique used to guide another person or oneself through a series of positive, relaxing images.

17. C: Kohlberg's Theory of Moral Development involves the development of an individual's ethics, values, and principles. This theory consists of three stages: pre-conventional, conventional, and post conventional. In the pre-conventional stage, children learn morals and values though obedience and punishment. For instance, children learn that it is not acceptable to hit others when they are punished for hitting a sibling. In the conventional stage, youth learn through conformity and social order. Individuals learn by observing the world around them and understanding social norms. Finally, in the post-conventional stage, individuals learn through universally accepted ethical considerations.

Copyright © Mometrix Media. You have been licensed one copy of this document for personal use only. Any other reproduction or redistribution is strictly prohibited. All rights reserved.
This content is provided for test preparation purposes only and does not imply an endorsement by Mometrix of any particular political, scientific, or religious point of view.

18. D: When developing a counseling program, the counselor should take a number of factors into consideration, including what the students would like to gain from the programs. One factor that students often consider is academic counseling. This type of counseling provides students with additional support as they progress through their courses, as well as support during transitional periods such as moving from high school to college. In addition to this, students are often interested in counseling programs pertaining to career and self-awareness. Many students would also like to know the availability of counselors and the frequency of planning sessions they have with the counselor. Finally, visibility of counselors and their ability and availability to answer questions and assist with problems is often listed as a student concern for counseling programs.

19. C: Typically, a counselor will conduct a student survey in order to gain an overall view of the student body. By collecting demographic information, the counselor can determine important differences in the student body. This information will assist in developing additional programs, activities, or interventions. When conducted as a formative assessment, demographic information can provide an indication of whether different groups of students are finding more benefit in a particular program or intervention. Again, this information will allow the counselor to modify a program or add programs to better fit the needs of all students involved.

20. A: Primary prevention groups are most beneficial for dealing with potential issues. School counselors should be cognizant of the school environment. This awareness will allow the counselor to determine main areas in which students are struggling. A counselor who notices a lot of bickering and fighting in the hallways in between classes may decide that school-wide prevention groups are necessary. A school-wide prevention program in communication and conflict intervention will serve to educate the students about these basic skills. On the other hand, if the counselor provides only individual counseling or problem-centered counseling, the focus is likely to be on a specific problem rather than on education on how to avoid or resolve a conflict.

21. B: Daily down time is one way to manage stress in the counseling profession. By giving herself 5-10 minutes during the day or 30-40 minutes after work, a counselor is able to calm down and refocus. While taking a vacation is a way to manage stress, this is not a long-term solution to the daily stressors faced in the counseling profession. Additionally, volunteering for additional school activities could increase a counselor's workload and cause unnecessary stress. Managing stress must be an essential part of someone's daily routine in order for that person to maintain mental, emotional, and physical health.

22. C: The strategic task is the intervention treatment. This can be an actual task, such as completing one hour of homework a night, or a behavior change, such as taking a deep breath when angry. It is the student's responsibility to act according to the intervention plan in situations related to the problem and the goals of the counseling. These tasks will be discussed during the counseling sessions. Depending on the success or failure of the tasks, the counselor may decide to introduce different tasks throughout the counseling period. Doing so would be beneficial in a case in which the student is having difficulty controlling his anger. One week, for example, the counselor's task for the student may involve counting to ten. If this strategy is successful, the counselor may assign a breathing exercise as a task. This method would provide the student with a number of strategies for dealing with anger.

23. D: Oftentimes, schools get into the habit of holding meetings at the same times year after year. In the case of parent-teacher conferences, which are often held during the day, working parents may have to take off work to attend. Additionally, many school council and PTA meetings are held in the evening. While this may be more convenient for working parents, busy families often find it

Copyright © Mometrix Media. You have been licensed one copy of this document for personal use only. Any other reproduction or redistribution is strictly prohibited. All rights reserved.
This content is provided for test preparation purposes only and does not imply an endorsement by Mometrix of any particular political, scientific, or religious point of view.

difficult to participate in these events. By offering various times and days of these meeting and events, a school can maximize the participation of the parents.

24. A: As communities become more diverse, counselors are seeing an increase in the number of parents who do not speak English as a first language. Because this dynamic often creates a barrier between these parents and their children's schools, a lack of participation from these parents is common. In these cases, counselors can provide information or opportunities for parents to increase their English skills through free or low cost programs. Additionally, adult education programs in basic reading, writing, and GED preparation can be offered to parents who wish to increase their skills or earn their GED. Educated parents are able to offer more academic assistance to their children.

25. B: The ecological model consists of the microsystem, macrosystem, and excosystem. The microsystem encompasses the students' immediate family and support systems. This will include parents, siblings, extended family, and friends. The macrosystem is defined by the students' culture. This will vary from student to student and often may include various subcultures. The exosystem refers to students' social support systems, such as their community. Understanding these three aspects of students' support systems will assist in developing appropriate programs and interventions, as the counselor will be able to incorporate the students' beliefs, morals, and values into counseling programs.

26. C: Any unethical behaviors should not be tolerated in this profession. When these situations occur, the integrity of the profession is threatened. When one professional witnesses unethical behaviors or practices from another, he should make his intention to report the action clear. All schools have policies on unethical behaviors and reporting guidelines for staff and administrators. In order to ensure proper protocol when reporting unethical behaviors, a thorough review and consultation with another professional, most likely the principal of the school, should be conducted.

27. B: This is a good strategy to use in lower income school districts. In these areas, transportation is often an issue, and parents are typically less able to participate in school activities because traveling to the school is difficult. In these situations, counselors must find alternative options for including parents in the academic lives of their children, especially during times of transition. Home visits can be used for regular parent-teacher conferences if a counselor feels participation would increase with this additional option. Prior to initiating any home visiting program, a counselor must ensure that all individuals conducting these visits have received the proper safety training.

28. B: Proper delegation of responsibilities will lead to more effective counseling programs. There are many opportunities for teachers and students to participate in leading programs. For example, developing a teacher advisor program increases participation from teachers and offers students a larger support system. Peer mentoring programs allow mentors the ability to increase their leadership skills and allow mentees the opportunity to widen their network of support systems. Counselors who encourage the assistance of teachers and students with various programs will foster a cohesive school that works together toward a common goal. This cohesiveness will provide all students with the best possible learning environment.

29. D: It is considered an unethical professional practice for a counselor to use the school as a place to gain private practice clients. While many issues can be resolved within the capacity of a school counseling program, there may be times when a counselor feels a student needs additional therapy or support. In these cases, the counselor should discuss these options with the student and the parents while keeping in mind rules of confidentiality. Additionally, after a referral is made, the school counselor does not have a right to information that the new counselor and student share. In

Copyright © Mometrix Media. You have been licensed one copy of this document for personal use only. Any other reproduction or redistribution is strictly prohibited. All rights reserved.
This content is provided for test preparation purposes only and does not imply an endorsement by Mometrix of any particular political, scientific, or religious point of view.

certain circumstances, the school counselor may be asked to consult on various issues. If this occurs, the school counselor and the private practice professional must discuss the case only in factual, objective ways.

30. A: Beginning a Solution-Focused Brief Counseling session involves having the student define the problem and determine his desired goals of the counseling. With the assistance of the counselor, the intervention or behavior change is both determined and initiated by the student. Strategic tasks are assigned by the counselor and involve a direct behavior change. For example, if a student is having difficulty with academics and has a goal to raise his grades, then a strategic task would be for him to study for one hour every night. In subsequent counseling sessions, the counselor would offer support and positive feedback in order to encourage the student to reach his academic goals. Once the goals for that particular problem have been reached, the sessions are no longer required and counseling is terminated.

31. A: Generally speaking, the mean is less than the median in distributions with data skewed to the left. The mean, median, and mode (i.e., measures of central tendency) are all the same values in a normal distribution. When distributions are skewed to the right, the mode is the lowest value. In distributions skewed right (i.e., positive distributions), the mode is less than the median and the median is less than the mean.

32. B: Problem-centered, structured counseling groups allow students to share their experiences and hear similar experiences from their peers in a safe environment. This type of group setting also allows students to gain the support of their peers as well as receive feedback. Counselors conducting these groups should focus on changing deviant behaviors and encouraging participants to try out new behaviors during the week. These exercises can be discussed during sessions, and students can learn how to brainstorm appropriate behaviors together by sharing their experiences. While it is possible to conduct a problem-centered group for a number of different issues, topics such as self-actualization, safety, and physiological issues are typically the focus of primary prevention groups.

33. A: Teacher advisors cooperate with school counselors to provide students all-around support. These advisors help students adjust to a new school by offering orientation and support. Additionally, teacher advisors provide students with a sounding board when resolving disputes or misunderstandings with faculty members or other students. Oftentimes, advisors will initiate student work groups for various issues students may experience. These groups may focus on communication, conflict resolution, or general adjustment strategies. Overall, teacher advisors serve as advocates for students in order to make school and the educational experience both pleasant and rewarding.

34. D: Human relations training offers students the opportunity to see each other as individuals. This type of training serves to increase students' understanding of one another. In the given situation, there appears to be a lot of racial tension, which is leading to regular fighting. When a school offers students human relations training, they will learn to view each other as human beings rather than racial stereotypes. This training should serve to increase cultural understanding and decrease the current level of fighting in the classroom. This situation may prompt a counselor to study the school overall to see if this behavior is occurring elsewhere. If so, a school-wide human relations training program may be appropriate.

35. B: Counselors must establish boundaries between their professional and personal lives. It is a very common characteristic in this field for a counselor to want to help or fix all students in need. However, this is not practical and will eventually cause counselors to experience burnout.

Copyright © Mometrix Media. You have been licensed one copy of this document for personal use only. Any other reproduction or redistribution is strictly prohibited. All rights reserved.
This content is provided for test preparation purposes only and does not imply an endorsement by Mometrix of any particular political, scientific, or religious point of view.

Counselors can avoid this by managing their work time properly and not taking work home. Additionally, counselors should schedule short breaks throughout the day where they can focus on something not related to counseling. These professionals should have down time every day and try to spend quality time with their friends and family when not at work.

36. A: Members of ongoing groups with a fixed membership experience transition after there are vacancies or when group members leave. Groups that are ongoing do not have an end date. In contrast, groups that are time limited have a set number of sessions. Membership can either be revolving or fixed, with revolving groups admitting new members when they become ready and fixed groups that begin and end with the same members. Interpersonal process groups are generally ongoing with a fixed membership. Psychoeducational groups tend to be time limited with a fixed membership. Inpatient milieu therapy groups are considered ongoing groups with a revolving membership. Finally, art therapy (e.g., expressive) groups are an example of time-limited groups with revolving membership.

37. A: All counselors have a professional responsibility to contribute to the counseling profession. One way of doing this is to report on the success or failure of various school counseling programs. In doing so, the reporting counselor can make visible various strategies for addressing student needs. This also allows other counseling and educational professionals to learn from their successes and failures alike. Opportunities to present program outcomes can range from school advisory meetings, PTA meetings, professional conferences, publication in professional journals, and attending professional association meetings.

38. C: Counselors must be careful when conducting training programs involving parents. Parents may be sensitive and misinterpret these trainings as the school's trying to change their core values and methods in raising their children. Schools can offer other types of support to increase parent involvement. Some suggestions include providing parents with information on effective study skills, recommending time limits for homework, or babysitting during PTA meetings and parent-teacher conferences. The goal of offering parents these various services is to increase participation and develop strong parent support for the school. Counselors should also keep in mind that parents do not necessarily have to be at the school to be active with the school. When parents help their children with homework or participate in a phone tree, they are offering much needed support.

39. C: Programs addressing teen pregnancy are designed to offer students education and support for various issues. As a counselor, regardless of your personal beliefs, you must be sensitive to the needs and views of your students. Prevention programs can provide education about safe sex, as well as information about the reality of being pregnant and a teenage parent. These prevention programs should be geared toward those who are not pregnant but may currently be or thinking about being sexually active. Intervention programs should be geared toward those who are currently pregnant or recently had a child. These programs should provide supportive services along with education about being a teenage parent. Whenever possible, involving the student's parents in the programs will help increase the student's support system.

40. B: Students have the right to seek confidential counseling. Counselors should inform parents of this confidentiality, as well as the roles, responsibilities, and expectations of the counselor and the student being counseled. Counselors should also work to provide parents with objective information regarding their children within the scope of confidentiality. At times, it may be necessary to inform the parents of certain issues pertaining to safety. This information will be provided only after the counselor has made a professional judgment that the client is in danger or intends to inflict harm on another and after telling the client of their intention to inform their

Copyright © Mometrix Media. You have been licensed one copy of this document for personal use only. Any other reproduction or redistribution is strictly prohibited. All rights reserved.
This content is provided for test preparation purposes only and does not imply an endorsement by Mometrix of any particular political, scientific, or religious point of view.

parents. Finally, the counselor also has a responsibility to keep conversations he has with the parents confidential.

41. D: Continued monitoring and assessment of the learning environment can be beneficial in many ways. This process provides the counselor, teacher, student, and parents an ongoing progress report. Additionally, regular assessments allow problems to be identified sooner rather than later. This will ensure that the student is not falling behind his classmates or his intervention goals. Ongoing monitoring and assessment also allow the counselor to update and to modify goals and target dates. When considered a fluid process, assessments, goal monitoring, intervention modification, and encouragement will ensure that students are progressing at a comfortable and successful rate.

42. B: One benefit of telemental health services is the immediate availability of emergency triage for clients with suicidal ideation. Telemental health allows the client to be treated in the present moment. Synchronous rather than asynchronous communication is conducted in real time, making it possible to use standardized suicide risk assessment instruments. The Ask Suicide-Screening Questions toolkit, the Collaborative Assessment and Management of Suicidality approach, and the Columbia Suicide Severity Rating Scale (also known as the Columbia protocol) have demonstrated effectiveness as alternative modalities to in-person screening and assessment (Substance Abuse and Mental Health Services Administration, 2021). Finally, treatment outcomes for suicidality using telehealth do not differ from treating suicidality through face-to-face encounters.

43. D: Ultimately, counseling programs are designed for students. Accordingly, student outcomes will determine the success of a program. As a counselor, it is important to conduct regular evaluation measures on each program offered. These measures will show the success of a program by including information about student improvement and students' ratings of satisfaction with the programs. For example, if a program is intended to improve a student's grades in a math course, outcome measures will include the student's final grades compared to her grades when she began the program. Additionally, conducting student surveys to find out how the students enjoyed the program is beneficial in creating future programs that both engage students and increase their performance.

44. D: Developmental guidance programs offer schools a full service guidance program. These programs take all factors of a student's life into consideration: academics, developmental growth, social skills, and emotional maturity. By focusing on developmental stages as well as positive self-esteem, counselors can assist students in reaching their full potential as human beings rather than succeeding only academically. When creating this type of guidance program, counselors are aware of human development in various aspects including, social, emotional, and cognitive growth and development. Developmental guidance programs often rely on the support and participation of the school, families, and communities in order to offer students support and opportunities for learning and personal growth.

45. A: Interpersonal skills are the skills necessary to relate to and understand peer interactions. These skills begin developing at an early age and are reinforced by responses from others. Typically, a child with adequate interpersonal skills has the ability to understand if he is not liked or welcomed by his peers. This situation would result in the child's becoming withdrawn and possibly depressed. However, in this case, the child does not seem to possess this ability. While his interpersonal skills are so stunted that he does not recognize when he is not liked, there may be a deeper physiological explanation for his problems. It will be important for the counselor to gain as much information as possible from the family and others in contact with this child, and a referral to a specialist may be necessary.

Copyright © Mometrix Media. You have been licensed one copy of this document for personal use only. Any other reproduction or redistribution is strictly prohibited. All rights reserved.
This content is provided for test preparation purposes only and does not imply an endorsement by Mometrix of any particular political, scientific, or religious point of view.

46. B: Pavlov's theory of conditioning responses states that when an action is repeatedly followed by a response, the one performing the action will either continue or stop doing so depending on the response. In this case, the child continually receives a negative response from his peers. Theoretically, the child would begin to relate his actions to this negative response and cease the action. However, this is not occurring and may be an indication of developmental delays. As seen in the vignette, the child has little social support at home, and there is a clear indication of other interpersonal issues with his parents. To help this child, a counselor could explore social development delays he has and propose some type of intervention.

47. D: Peer mentoring programs are beneficial for many students and can address a number of issues. These programs give students the opportunity to guide and lead other students. Counselors spearheading peer mentoring programs are responsible for overseeing these programs and being available when questions or problems arise. Since the focus of these programs is students helping students, micromanagement of peer mentors by a counselor would result in an ineffective and potentially unfulfilling experience for the students. Also, it is not necessary that peer mentors know all aspects of counseling, as their responsibilities in the program will not deal directly with counseling another students. Peer mentors should receive training in leadership and sensitivity to other student's needs.

48. C: When taking an assessment relating to topics that may be socially undesirable, individuals have a tendency to report answers that conform to mainstream society. In this case, students may be afraid of getting in trouble if they answer positively in response to questions about drug or alcohol use. Conversely, if this assessment is given in a group setting, students may want to "show off" to their peers by giving a greater number of positive answers. While this type of assessment may provide the counselor with preliminary results, the results may be skewed. This type of assessment should always include a variety of questions in different forms in order to validate findings and to control for false answers.

49. B: This type of scaling can be beneficial for a preliminary view of a student's thoughts on a topic. However, providing only four choices means that the student must choose in a positive or negative direction. This can produce skewed results and lead the counselor to believe that a majority of students are for or against a topic. What may be the case is that students are neutral on some topics but are required to make a decision. For example, consider the following statement: "Morning announcements are a waste of time." This statement may elicit a natural response for students; however, they are forced to agree or disagree. If students choose a negative answer, does this necessarily indicate that they would like more announcements in the morning? Conversely, if students respond positively, does this indicate that they want no morning announcements?

50. B: Although using this type of assessment may result in more neutral responses, most individuals will provide their true thoughts. Receiving an assessment with all neutral responses should be considered as an outlier. Depending on the purpose of the assessment, the counselor may consider disregarding it in the results and providing an explanation in any required report. Depending on the nature of the assessment, the counselor can conduct additional assessments with the student to determine any difficulties this student may be having. Regardless, when giving students surveys, it must be indicated that all responses are confidential, and the students should respond as honestly as possible.

51. C: Developmental guidance programs are geared toward all students. These programs focus on understanding and assisting the students with their academic needs by offering services such as tutoring or peer mentoring. In order to meet the social needs of students, developmental programs embrace the cultural identities of students and aim to provide programs, increase student support

Copyright © Mometrix Media. You have been licensed one copy of this document for personal use only. Any other reproduction or redistribution is strictly prohibited. All rights reserved.
This content is provided for test preparation purposes only and does not imply an endorsement by Mometrix of any particular political, scientific, or religious point of view.

systems, and offer opportunities for students to express their individuality. This type of program will also enhance students' cognitive development and provide opportunities to increase their understanding of themselves and the world around them. Because programs developed as part of a comprehensive developmental guidance program offer positive opportunities for growth and development, they are appropriate for all students.

52. B: Immediate outcomes will occur during the program or intervention. These outcomes could include members of an anger management group being nicer to each other or students in a study skills group utilizing different study strategies. Proximal outcomes are specific to an intervention and are often observed after the intervention. For example, a member of an anger management group has a confrontation with teacher. The reaction of the student will be the proximal outcome of the group. Finally, distal outcomes are long-term effects of the intervention which the intervention was not necessarily designed to address. For example, the student in the anger management group reacted positivity to the teacher confrontation because he applied a calming strategy learned during the group. A few months later, he witnesses a friend yelling at another student for bumping into him. The group participant teaches his friend a calming strategy to better deal with confrontations.

53. A: Bloom's Taxonomy of Knowledge describes six levels of knowledge. At the lowest level, *Knowledge* is the ability to name and identify things. *Comprehension* occurs when a student can explain a topic or concept. *Application* refers to a student's ability to use information in the real world. *Analysis* is the ability to analyze and make comparisons. *Synthesis* is the ability to develop hypotheses and produce results. Finally, the highest level in Bloom's Taxonomy is *Evaluation*, which refers to the ability to assess and critique an idea or concept. Assessments should touch on all six levels of learning. By making sure all levels in Bloom's Taxonomy are covered, the counselor will have an indication of areas that need improvement and what level of understanding to focus on. For example, a student may be able to identify parts of a sentence but not understand how to analyze that sentence. The intervention would then focus more on sentence analysis and less on defining parts of the sentence.

54. B: Social literacy skills are also known as interpersonal skills. These skills refer to how individuals relate to one another. The level of these skills also determines an individual's self-esteem, peer acceptance, and self-efficacy. In this situation, it appears that these students are having a difficult time relating to and communicating with each other. A group on crisis intervention will not offer these students the appropriate social skills, as a crisis group is typically geared toward students who are affected by issues such as a death in the family, a natural disaster, or another large crisis. A group that focuses on social literacy skills can help students understand themselves as well as others. This type of group teaches students appropriate social behaviors, communication skills, and techniques for dealing with conflict.

55. A: Traditional counseling programs tend to focus on issues after something has occurred. In the given situation, this crisis intervention program is probably reserved for students who have recently experienced some type of personal crisis. In a developmental counseling model, the counselor will develop programs to meet the needs of students by using a full-service approach. This counselor may implement crisis prevention as well as intervention programs. By including a crisis prevention program, the counselor is meeting the needs of at-risk students. This program will assist these students in avoiding potential crisis situations by offering various emotional and cognitive skills that these students may not already possess.

56. A: School counselors may oftentimes feel overworked and can easily become burned out. This is typically due to a high client load and few resources. If a school counselor can enlist the help of

Copyright © Mometrix Media. You have been licensed one copy of this document for personal use only. Any other reproduction or redistribution is strictly prohibited. All rights reserved.
This content is provided for test preparation purposes only and does not imply an endorsement by Mometrix of any particular political, scientific, or religious point of view.

teachers and community members, his or her burden is lightened. These outside individuals can offer the counselor new ideas and information about students or community programs that might not otherwise be available to the counselor. This additional support will result in more services for students and their families. Additionally, when communities and schools are strong and able to offer a supportive environment, students' academic performance tends to increase.

57. B: Formative assessments are used to determine the effectiveness of an intervention and can be used to modify the treatment. This is an important step in the intervention process, as a student's rate of learning is not always apparent. This type of assessment can be in the form of informal questions to determine if the student understands the topic. The goal of a formative assessment is to provide the best possible setting for the student in order to increase learning and understanding. When done at regular intervals, the counselor can determine if the goals of the intervention are being met in a timely manner. A formative assessment will also provide an indication of an ineffective intervention strategy.

58. C: A counselor must always take into consideration the cultural barriers and needs of students and their families. In situations where language barriers are present, a counselor should offer a translator during any meeting. This will ensure that the parents receive the correct information. This will also show the parents that they are welcome and accepted into the school. By offering translation services, parents may become more comfortable, which means that their participation with the school and their children's education will increase. Another effective strategy is to offer free or low cost English courses. While a counselor cannot require anyone to take these courses, making them available to those who are interested will be beneficial to families.

59. A: A group setting in counseling can be very effective when a counselor takes time to develop positive group dynamics. During the group formation phase, participants are getting to know one another. Because of personal reasons, participants may be resistant to the group, be uncomfortable sharing, or not trust others in the group. It is important to focus the first session or sessions on developing guidelines for cooperation within the group. This process includes encouraging the participation of all group members and agreeing on group rules, goals, and objectives. A common technique during this stage is to allow group members themselves to develop their own rules, goals, and objectives. This activity encourages participation and gives the participants a sense of ownership and belonging within the group.

60. C: Cultural diversity education is important in all schools, regardless of demographics. In this situation, it could be argued that the counselor is acting in an unprofessional and possibly unethical manner. What this counselor is failing to understand is that culture expands beyond the color of someone's skin. Culture includes various lifestyles, family types, religious beliefs, and ethnicities. Even in a predominantly white school, many cultures may be observable. If the counselor in this situation were aware of her own culture as well as that of others, she may realize the importance of offering these programs to all students.

61. B: HIPAA grants clients the right to request that a "covered entity" amend their electronic healthcare record. Professional counselors who use electronic health records to transmit health information in a transactional capacity (e.g., to bill insurance) qualify as a covered entity under HIPAA. Counselors have the right to deny the amendment if they determine that the client's healthcare record is accurate and complete. Payment for services must be agreed upon at the onset of treatment and cannot be contested based on the client's inadequate progress. Under HIPAA, clients may receive a copy of their records, including diagnostic summaries and treatment plans. However, psychotherapy notes are considered to be an exemption. Psychotherapy notes are a counselor's personal notes and are typically not a part of the client's medical record. When the

Copyright © Mometrix Media. You have been licensed one copy of this document for personal use only. Any other reproduction or redistribution is strictly prohibited. All rights reserved.
This content is provided for test preparation purposes only and does not imply an endorsement by Mometrix of any particular political, scientific, or religious point of view.

client poses a serious and imminent threat to themselves or others, counselors can contact family members without client authorization.

62. B: Parent participation is the key to developing physically, emotionally, and academically healthy children. When a school already has a high parent interest, it is important to foster that interest. By developing programs for parents to participate in, a school can keep these parents excited and motivated. Parent programs such as the PTA or school advisory councils are good ways for parents to take an active role in their children's schools. Additionally, offering one-time volunteer activities will allow working parents to participate in some school functions. Counselors should also encourage regular meetings with parents and teachers to keep all parties informed about the students both in and out of school.

63. C: Denial occurs when individuals experience shock and disbelief over the loss of a loved one. The experience is so overwhelming that it cannot be experienced all at once. Denial serves as a protective or coping mechanism during the initial stage of grief and loss. Elizabeth Kubler-Ross's five stages of grief are denial, anger, bargaining, depression, and acceptance. Individuals in the anger stage of grief may blame others or believe that the circumstances surrounding the death were unfair. The depression stage of development involves sadness and loss. Finally, individuals in the bargaining stage may try to make a deal with a higher power to have a better or different outcome

64. A: Annual surveys are an easy and effective way to learn about the level of participation, interests, and abilities of parents. These surveys can be sent to parents at the beginning of the year and offer parents the opportunity to volunteer for long or short-term projects. Surveys should include information about the parents' willingness to participate, their availability, and any special skills they may have. A preliminary list of volunteer events or projects should also be included in these surveys so that parents can select opportunities that correspond with their schedules and interests. By reaching beyond the PTA for support and assistance, schools will develop lasting partnerships with parents and improve the learning environment for the students.

65. C: The influence of peer relationships, personal beliefs, and environmental factors is known as reciprocal determinism. Reciprocal determinism is the foundational concept of Bandura's social learning theory, or social cognitive theory (SCT). SCT has been used along with attachment theory, interpersonal theory, and feminist theory to study factors related to adolescent dating and relationships. Lev Semyonovich Vygotsky used the term zone of proximal development to describe the difference between what a child does independently and what they can do with help. This concept is used to explore ways to teach reading, writing, and other language skills. Sigmund Freud used the term pleasure principle when explaining the role of the id in personality development. Psychological hedonism states that all human behavior is dictated by actions directed toward attaining pleasure or avoiding pain.

66. C: This training method is intended to increase consulting and interview skills for the counselor. This model is comprised of seven steps. *Establishing a Consulting Relationship* involves relationship building and goal setting with the client. *Identifying and Clarifying the Problem Situation* requires a counselor to hear beyond what is being said in order to uncover any underlying problems. *Determine Desired Outcome* is a simple restatement of the problem and goals. *Develop Ideas and Strategies* requires the client and counselor to set objectives for achieving the goals. *Developing a Plan* requires the counselor and client to determine the best course of action for implementing objectives and achieving goals. *Specify the Plan* serves to further determine the specific steps for success. Finally, *Confirming the Consulting Relationship* will be complete when the student understands the problem-solving process and is comfortable with the plan of action developed with the counselor.

Copyright © Mometrix Media. You have been licensed one copy of this document for personal use only. Any other reproduction or redistribution is strictly prohibited. All rights reserved.
This content is provided for test preparation purposes only and does not imply an endorsement by Mometrix of any particular political, scientific, or religious point of view.

67. C: Emotional literacy is also referred to as intrapersonal skills. Individuals with good intrapersonal skills are aware of their own feelings and have an understanding of how these emotions affect their actions. This understanding helps individuals cope with emotional personal situations as well as display empathy for others. Additionally, understanding emotions also helps students manage and control their emotions. This type of program also helps students understand the importance and value of teamwork and cooperation with others. Developing a program that addresses intrapersonal skills serves to increase students' self-awareness and self-esteem.

68. A: Elementary School is the time when children are learning the most and developing important motor skills and mental functions. Counselors must be able to recognize developmental delays, as well as advanced learners. School counselors will be major advocates for students who may experience developmental delays. While the other options may be important, these issues are more likely seen at the junior high and high school levels. Knowledge in continued education will be important for high school students who wish to pursue a college education; counselors with students in these age groups will need to educate students and offer assistance in applying to colleges and obtaining financial aid and scholarships. Additionally, relationship building, adjustment, and coping mechanisms are issues most often seen in junior high school, as these years are a time of many changes physically, emotionally, and educationally.

69. B: Researchers have studied the effects of providing social skills training to gifted and special needs students. These trainings often take a cognitive-behavioral approach to learning new behaviors. The results of these studies show that these students demonstrate a significant increase in their sociability. This includes their willingness to participate in social situations, such as on the playground. Social skills trainings often focus on listening skills, empathy, building rapport, self-disclosure, and appropriate eye contact. This training typically does not affect a student's self-esteem or other school related issues, such as attendance or grades.

70. A: Children begin in the sensory-motor stage. During this time, a child acts and learns based on senses and reflexes. An infant who receives a laugh from his mother when he makes a face will continue to make the face. The reflex of making a face slowly becomes a voluntary learned expression. In the pre-operational stage, children can use representative language. For example, they begin to understand that a round toy is a ball. This is also the time when the concept of conversation is understood. During the concrete operational stage, children begin to think logically. For example, children in this stage begin to understand mathematical concepts. The formal operational stage refers to the time when children master abstract thinking. Concepts such as death become easier to understand during this time.

71. B: Making a broad announcement about the student's arrival is likely to embarrass the student and possibly create more alienation from the general student body. As this student does not necessarily have a problem, direct counseling and education may not beneficial. School counselors who offer the student, as well as her family, supportive services will be the most beneficial in easing the transition from one school to the next. Counselors can enlist the support and assistance from other students by providing the new student a peer guide for the first couple of days. The guide will show them around the school and make sure the student knows where her classes are. This guide can also provide information about the school, such as the various clubs and sports available and upcoming events. Additional support from the school and the community will provide the student and her family with important information about the school and the new area.

72. D: Continued education is required for professional licenses. Depending on the state board of education, a counselor will have a specific number of hours in continued education to complete. This education is intended to provide the counselor with the latest counseling information and

Copyright © Mometrix Media. You have been licensed one copy of this document for personal use only. Any other reproduction or redistribution is strictly prohibited. All rights reserved.
This content is provided for test preparation purposes only and does not imply an endorsement by Mometrix of any particular political, scientific, or religious point of view.

practices. Additionally, by evaluating and reporting on programs, counselors are able to learn about the success of specific programs as well as areas of improvement. By reporting on the outcomes, counselors are educating the community about the school and its counseling programs. Giving presentations at professional conferences allows the counselor the opportunity to share different counseling practices and strategies with other professionals. The sharing of information promotes professional development and is highly recommended in the counseling profession.

73. B: Role conflict refers to unrealistic demands on the counselor. This often occurs when counselors does not establish appropriate boundaries between themselves and the students. In addition, not establishing boundaries with teachers can lead to unrealistic expectations of the counselor. Role conflict often leads to counselor burnout because the counselor tries to help everyone. On the other hand, role ambiguity occurs when an individual is unclear about his role within a particular occupation. Role mutations occur when counselors serve in roles not intended for those in the counseling profession, which often leads to inconsistent counseling practices and programs. Schools and counselors must be clear on the expectations and responsibilities of the school counselor in order to provide effective programs for the students.

74. B: C-SSRS measures suicidal risk in the following four constructs: the severity of ideation, the intensity of ideation, suicidal behavior, and lethality. C-SSRS also assesses protective factors. SPS is a 36-item self-report inventory measuring suicidal ideation, hopelessness, hostility, and negative self-evaluation. DLA-20 is a functional assessment instrument measuring multiple domains, including time management, safety, and communication. BPRS measures psychosis and psychosis-related symptoms of schizophrenia or major psychotic disorders.

75. D: All of the above problems can affect a child's mental development. Without proper nutrition, children will not receive the vitamins and minerals necessary for both physical and mental development. Abuse can also cause many mental issues that will oftentimes manifest in the form of poor grades and poor social skills. Finally, all children need support and encouragement to develop into healthy adults. Without this support, counselors may see developmental problems in the form of delays. As a counselor, one should always be mindful of the family dynamics of students. With proper interventions and family education, issues related to these factors may be corrected or avoided altogether.

76. B: Almost all parents believe that they have well-behaved, intelligent children; therefore, some parents are quick to become defensive and be unwilling to listen when schools call regarding problems with their children. As a counselor, it often falls on you to set up parent conferences. It is important to keep in mind the feelings and beliefs of the parents as well as the policies of the school. By speaking to parents with openness and allowing them to be a part of decision-making processes, a partnership can develop. By creating this sense of partnership and cooperation, the student's best interest will remain the focus.

77. B: Solution-Focused Brief Counseling has recently become a popular counseling method due to time and budget constraints on schools and students. This method is based on the premise that individuals can solve their own problems with assistance and prompting from a counselor. Students play an active role in deciding the goals of their counseling with focused attention on a specific problem. Additionally, the counselor will assist the student in identifying the appropriate behavioral changes that are needed in order to reach the state's educational goals. With Solution-Focused Brief Counseling, the counselor plays a supportive role as the student identifies his strengths and determines alternative solutions to the problem.

Copyright © Mometrix Media. You have been licensed one copy of this document for personal use only. Any other reproduction or redistribution is strictly prohibited. All rights reserved.
This content is provided for test preparation purposes only and does not imply an endorsement by Mometrix of any particular political, scientific, or religious point of view.

78. B: While there may be times when a counselor will refer a student to a different counselor, this is not an effective alternative to a lack of cultural diversity education. Additionally, a counselor cannot effectively treat students based on the counselor's belief system. When offering programs for cultural diversity education within the school, the counselor must have education in this area in order to create effective programs. Therefore, counselor education is the best way to ensure that students' needs are met. Most counselor training programs today offer multicultural training and education. Additionally, there are many opportunities for continued education in this area.

79. B: Immigrant parents have many challenges when sending their children to school in America. Oftentimes, the parents do not speak English and are unfamiliar with the American school system. While language barriers often result in parents not participating in their children's education, a counselor can easily offer translators and other educational opportunities to overcome these barriers. However, if parents continue to be unclear about the needs and expectations of the school system, immigrant parents will continue to be inactive. This can be overcome by providing a supportive environment for both the parents and the students. Counselors in school systems with a high immigrant population will need to serve as "school-home-community liaisons" in order to promote the needs of the students and their families.

80. B: There are a number of factors that can affect students, especially during middle and high school. In this case, it would be wise to discuss problems with friends or a boyfriend with this student. Social problems are often a cause of problems in school, including a marked drop in grades. If this student is having problems with a boyfriend, it may be important to determine the seriousness of the problems, as abusive relationships in schools do occur. Since this student typically does well in school, the difficulty level of the classes would not be the major concern, unless she recently began new advanced courses. Additionally, there is nothing in this student's history to indicate that she may have problems with self-esteem or mental health issues.

81. D: Among divorced couples, divorced men (rather than divorced women) report higher levels of life satisfaction than divorced women. For children of divorce, rates of academic and emotional difficulties are higher than those of children with married parents. Additionally, among children of divorce, boys are found to have higher rates of maladjustment than girls.

82. D: Teachers need to understand some of the basic psychology of their students and their students' behaviors. Counselors can help provide teachers with such information in a number of a ways, including offering discussion and training sessions throughout the school year. These sessions should provide teachers with a basic understanding of student dynamics and the psychology of student violence. When teachers are aware of these aspects of their students, they will be more aware of what is going on and may be able to respond to issues before a situation escalates to violence. Additionally, teachers need to be aware of their own emotions when dealing with angry or upset students. In order to control a situation that is or may become violent, teachers will need to remain calm and react in non-violent ways: for example, trying to separate fighting students and talking calmly to them vs. pushing a student out of the way and yelling at him.

83. C: Self-control procedures do not include response control. Self-control procedures include self-monitoring, self-punishment, stimulus control, and self-reinforcement. Counselors using self-monitoring encourage clients to record information about the frequency and duration of specified symptoms. Self-punishment and self-reinforcement help clients self-administer the consequences of the targeted behavior, so that it can be modified. Stimulus control includes behavior that is controlled by associated consequences. Stimulus control techniques include narrowing, cue strengthening, and fading.

Copyright © Mometrix Media. You have been licensed one copy of this document for personal use only. Any other reproduction or redistribution is strictly prohibited. All rights reserved.
This content is provided for test preparation purposes only and does not imply an endorsement by Mometrix of any particular political, scientific, or religious point of view.

84. B: Maslow's Hierarchy of Human Needs suggests that human needs can be divided into five levels. The most basic level is the physiological level, which includes the necessities of life: food, breathing, water, etc. At the next level is safety, which includes an individual's sense of security, availability of resources, employment, etc. Love and belonging comprise the next level, which also includes a person's support systems. Esteem is the next level and includes a person's self-concept and respect of self and others. Finally, the top level is self-actualization, which includes one's morality and acceptance. Maslow indicates that the lower levels of human needs must be met in order for an individual to meet the needs of the higher levels.

85. D: Thinking, feeling, and relating are considered a modern model of human development. Thinking begins at home and consists of the values, thoughts, and beliefs imposed by parents. These thoughts are further supported by social interactions. Cognitive skills training assists students in further developing these abilities. Feelings can also be associated with the development of self-concept and self-esteem. Emotional literacy skills training and programs help students become more aware of their own feelings. Finally, relating involves an individual's interpersonal skills. Social literacy skills programs will assist students in relating to other students and adults.

86. C: There are a number of professional associations available for counselors to participate in at the local, state, and national levels. For example, the American School Counselor Association is a national organization made up of professionals from various backgrounds, from child development to clinical training. These associations provide professionals with current information on counseling practices, opportunities to attend conferences, and continued education. Additionally, professional associations offer a network of other professionals who are available to discuss counseling strategies and other issues a counselor may face. Counselors must keep in mind the ethical practices of sharing confidential information with colleagues.

87. B: The counselor should add a clinical note explaining the inaccuracy unless otherwise dictated by agency or institutional policy. The ACA Code of Ethics (2014) states, "Counselors take reasonable steps to ensure that documentation accurately reflects client progress and services provided. If amendments are made to records and documentation, counselors take steps to properly note the amendments according to agency or institutional policies." Destroying and replacing the original document or asking the client for permission to do so are unethical practices. Consultation may be sought; however, correcting the inaccuracy is ultimately the responsibility of the counselor.

88. C: While students with educated parents are not a risk factor, this is not considered a type of parent involvement. Involvement begins at the parenting level. Schools cannot tell individuals how to parent; however, they can provide information for parents about encouraging good academic practices while at home. For example, informing parents about the appropriate amount of time their child should spend on homework is one strategy. Communication is the next level of participation. Sending home progress reports and holding conferences both increase communication between schools and parents. The third level involves volunteering, which can include one-time projects or long-term participation. The last three levels include learning at home. Examples of this are providing information on the skills their children will learn throughout the school year, decision-making by encouraging participating on a school advisory board, and collaboration with the community.

89. C: One crucial role of the school counselor is to assist students when they face problems. Counselors must be sensitive to students' needs, beliefs, and values, including their established cultural identity. A student's cultural identity will affect the way he learns and responds to counseling. Understanding cultural diversity and identity will also be important for counselors when developing working relationships with the student's parents. Those who are insensitive to

Copyright © Mometrix Media. You have been licensed one copy of this document for personal use only. Any other reproduction or redistribution is strictly prohibited. All rights reserved.
This content is provided for test preparation purposes only and does not imply an endorsement by Mometrix of any particular political, scientific, or religious point of view.

culture identity will find it difficult to gain student and parent trust and cooperation. In order to do this, school counselors must fully educate themselves on cultural diversity in general, as well as learning the specific demographics of the school they work in.

90. D: Cognitive literacy skills teach students how to problem solve and make decisions. Programs designed to address cognitive skills focus on critical thinking, analysis, evaluation, classification, and conceptualization. According to Bloom's Taxonomy of Learning, these skills are essential in the education process. Schools can use organizational planners for homework and schools events in order to teach some of these skills. As students develop their cognitive skills, their study skills will also improve. Finally, cognitive skills development can also focus on self-regulation and self-monitoring. These abilities allow the student to think about their actions and the consequences of those actions.

91. A: According to the ACA Code of Ethics (2014), "Counselors limit the total or partial access of clients to their records only when there is compelling evidence that such access would cause harm to the client." If a client requires assistance with interpreting their records, counselors take the necessary time to provide that assistance. Counselors "prepare a plan for the transfer of clients and the dissemination of records to an identified colleague or records custodian in the case of the counselor's incapacitation, death, retirement, or termination of practice" (ACA, 2014). In situations involving multiple clients, counselors must "provide individual clients with only those parts of records that relate directly to them and do not include confidential information related to any other client" (ACA, 2014).

92. A: Poverty is one of the main risk factors for students. Often, those children who live in poverty do not eat properly or get enough sleep. Some students may be homeless or living with multiple families. Additionally, the strain of a sudden loss of income can cause fighting or tension in the household. As a result, students may not be prepared for school, as they may be too tired or hungry to participate. As a counselor, keen attention to the dynamics of a community will be beneficial in assisting students. In this case, the counselor can encourage families to participate in free or reduced-price breakfast or lunch plans at school. Additionally, the counselor can provide families with community resources to assist with financial emergencies.

93. C: Reframing is the restatement of a problem or issue in a positive light. This is the first step when developing an intervention for Solution-Focused Brief Counseling. Utilization is the second step in this process. Utilization involves taking a student's values and belief system into consideration. Also at this stage, the counselor must consider the student's motivations in applying the intervention. This information will be gathered from the student during initial discussions. By reframing the question and determining the student's beliefs and motivations, the counselor can assign the appropriate strategic tasks. This process is important to the success of the counseling.

94. B: Naturally, all of the answer choices are important to consider when administering pre-post tests. A counselor would not want to give a posttest designed for a first grader to kindergarten students. Also, an assessment for first graders is not likely to have 100 questions. However, during the development of this type of test, key ideas and concepts are important to consider. These key ideas and concepts will be the basis for all questions on the pre-post tests. This information must be related to the content being learned and be linked to state curriculum standards. These key ideas also must be grade appropriate. Pre-post tests will fail when this information is not appropriately presented.

95. B: Edgar Schein used the term career anchor to explain an individual's perception of their own values, skills, abilities, and interests in regard to work. Schein's eight career anchors include

Copyright © Mometrix Media. You have been licensed one copy of this document for personal use only. Any other reproduction or redistribution is strictly prohibited. All rights reserved.
This content is provided for test preparation purposes only and does not imply an endorsement by Mometrix of any particular political, scientific, or religious point of view.

technical competence, general managerial competence, autonomy/independence, security/stability, entrepreneurial, service/dedication to a cause, challenge, and lifestyle. Active adjustment is a concept in the theory of work adjustment. Active adjustment refers to an employee's effort to change jobs or occupations if one's ability is not reflected in their current role. Career congruence, a concept developed by John Holland, describes the positioning of career types on a hexagon. Careers that are congruent are similar and are located near one another. Finally, life role salience is defined by Donald Super as the importance or meaning given to one's career and life role, including roles in which an individual derives the most meaning.

96. D: Program evaluations are essential for guidance counseling programs. These evaluations will provide information on the effectiveness of a program and allow the counselor to make adjustments and improvements to these programs as necessary. When beginning an evaluation, the counselor should compile various forms of documentation about the program. This will include curriculum guides, unit lesson plans, and the school's master schedule for the counseling programs. This information will help give the counselor a picture of the school's current programs, which will allow the counselor to determine if the guidance curriculum is meeting the students' academic, emotional, and social needs.

97. D: Knowledge acquisition will occur throughout a person's life through formal education and life experiences; however this is not considered a developmental task or milestone. A child's sense of identity is a developmental task that is developed in the early stages of life. Self-identity tells the child who they are and what that means to others. Delays or deficiencies in this process can lead to insecurities or confusion for a child. Autonomy, or the sense of independence, is typically developed during adolescence. This developmental milestone provides youth with a sense of purpose and self-ability. Finally, self-esteem is continuously developed throughout life. These developmental tasks are essential for a healthy emotional mind set.

98. B: Discussion groups are effective ways to get parents and students involved in learning about cultural diversity. These discussion groups can offer participants the opportunity to talk about their particular cultures. Additionally, these groups offer a nonthreatening venue for others to ask questions and work out misunderstandings about various cultures that have been perpetuated by stereotypes. These groups also offer parents and students the chance to celebrate different cultures though activities. In addition to group discussions about participants' cultures, discussions about various types of families and lifestyles are beneficial. For example, biracial families, families with adopted or foster children, and families with stepparents are increasingly common in American society, and education about these various types of families is just as important as learning about other cultures.

99. C: Primary prevention groups aim at providing education and preventative counseling for a variety of problems. This type of group is beneficial for students who may have risk factors for future issues. These groups should focus on developing healthy lifestyles and center on the student's social, emotional, and cognitive abilities. Typically, a primary prevention group will discuss issues such as self-esteem, self-concept, listening skills, academic achievement, and methods of effective communication. Issues such as grief and loss, aggressive behaviors, and abuse are more often the focus of a problem-centered, structured intervention-counseling group. School counselors may conduct this type of group with students who have recently experienced a loss, have repeatedly violated school rules for fighting, or are known to have an abusive relationship.

100. D: A diagnostic assessment for learning needs focuses on four main factors: prior knowledge, misconceptions, interests, and learning style preferences. The purpose of this type of assessment is to determine the student's strengths and weaknesses in order to develop an effective intervention

Copyright © Mometrix Media. You have been licensed one copy of this document for personal use only. Any other reproduction or redistribution is strictly prohibited. All rights reserved.
This content is provided for test preparation purposes only and does not imply an endorsement by Mometrix of any particular political, scientific, or religious point of view.

strategy. Diagnostic assessments can be done in either formal or informal settings and in either individual or group settings. In the case of a formal setting, counselors can conduct a student survey or skills test. For informal settings, the counselor can simply ask a student or groups of students various questions pertaining to each factor. For example, a counselor may ask, "Do you like to learn by reading a book or seeing material presented in picture form?"

101. B: Perspective taking is similar to empathy; however, it involves different mental processes. While a person can be empathic toward another, this function involves only an attempt to understand another person's feelings based on previous experience. Perspective taking involves more complex cognition. The individual involved in perspective taking will attempt to understand another's situation, analyze this situation, and gain an understanding of and respect for different points of view. Perspective taking is a useful activity for children requiring conflict resolution. By asking children to look at a situation from another person's point of view, they can begin to understand why there was conflict and possibly begin to formulate their own ideas for a resolution.

102. C: As information is learned, individuals develop their own thoughts, beliefs, and representations about that information. These schemas are abstract and unique and assist the individual in understanding the world around them. Individuals also use schema to determine how they will act and respond to the world around them. For example, a common schema is how individuals perceive different cultures. Often in the form of stereotypes, these schemas are difficult to reverse once in place. Because of this, an individual with a negative schema about a certain type of ethnic group will react negatively to all individuals in that group.

103. C: Erikson suggests that children begin to associate with either industry or inferiority in early adolescence. Industry refers to a person's ability to succeed and feel worthy. Typically, healthy children who receive the appropriate support and encouragement at home and at school will feel a sense of industry. This identification is important, as it can be the basis of future educational, social, and coping skills. For example, a child who has a strong sense of industry will be more likely to cope with a low grade on a test. He will understand that he may need to study harder for the next test or seek assistance. On the other hand, a child with a poor school, family, or peer support system may experience feelings of inferiority. In this case, he is likely to have insufficient coping mechanisms and not perform well in school.

104. C: Teacher advisors serve as advocates for students. They are respected adults whom students can turn to for support when problems arise. Therefore, it is important for students to be comfortable with their teacher advisors. While it is not practical to allow students to make a final decision on the advisor, schools should include students in the decision making process. It is suggested that students be able to choose three to five teachers they would like to work with. Based on this information, counselors and teachers can then assign teacher advisors while keeping the student's wishes in mind.

105. D: Regardless of the type of abuse a girl may experience, there will be deep psychological effects that may last much longer than the actual abuse. Oftentimes, these girls will have low self-esteem and look for ways to make themselves feel better. Additionally, those children who are abused may turn to drugs and alcohol to numb the effects of the abuse. Teenage girls who experience abuse are also more likely to become pregnant than those girls who do not experience abuse. Finally, those experiencing abuse will often lose interest in school and their futures, and counselors will see a decline in their grades. Since the idea of abuse if often thought of taboo and embarrassing, counselors should be aware of these risk factors and outcomes when assessing students.

Copyright © Mometrix Media. You have been licensed one copy of this document for personal use only. Any other reproduction or redistribution is strictly prohibited. All rights reserved.
This content is provided for test preparation purposes only and does not imply an endorsement by Mometrix of any particular political, scientific, or religious point of view.

106. A: The Cognitive Behavior Theory suggests that as children grow into adolescents, they begin to form abstract thought. This is the ability to think about things that cannot be seen. This is an important part of youth development because as abstract thought develops, moral thought increases. For example, a young child may not understand consequences, because thought at this point is concrete. In order to fully understand consequences, one must be able to understand right from wrong, as well as be able to visualize what future consequences will come about by present actions. In most cases, an adolescent will understand these consequences because of their ability to think abstractly.

107. D: Education is the key to increasing tolerance and understanding between various cultures. Developing educational programs for students as well as teachers can offer a venue for these individuals to ask questions and gain a clear understanding of cultural diversity. It is also an opportunity to eliminate negative stereotypes. Additionally, offering programs or opportunities for students to celebrate their cultures will serve to provide education about other cultures to students from all backgrounds. These opportunities can be as simple as announcing various holidays celebrated by the different cultures in the school or allowing students to display pictures or information about their cultures in the halls of the school.

108. A: This type of observation (i.e., an informal observation) is advantageous over a formal observation because it decreases the likelihood of the Hawthorne effect. The Hawthorne effect presumes that a subject is more likely to modify their behavior based on knowing that they are being observed. Because the student was not a current client, the student lacked an awareness of being observed. Confirmation bias occurs when a counselor seeks information to confirm an initial hypothesis despite encountering information that may refute that hypothesis. Unstructured observations are at greater risk for confirmation bias than formal observations. Interrater reliability values are likely to be lower rather than higher. Likewise, threats to internal validity are not minimized.

109. D: Cultural identity is dynamic and constantly evolving. Cultural identity is multifaceted and is impacted by race, ethnicity, gender, religion, spirituality, socioeconomic status, profession, and sexual orientation. One's cultural identity is a social construct and continues to be formed through social interactions and is impacted by historical and political contexts.

110. A: School Advisory Boards consist of teachers, administrators, parents, and members of the business community. The makeup of this type of council is often directly related to the makeup of the school and the community at large. These boards discuss issues related to the general management of the school, along with district wide policies and procedures. School Advisory Boards are also responsible for developing school improvement and safety plans. These types of advisory boards are also responsible for delegating financial resources to various school programs. Parent involvement is necessary, as parents provide a voice for the parent community as a whole with students' best interests in mind.

111. A: Bandura proposed a social behavioral theory of development. This theory combines behaviorism and social psychology and suggests that each one affects the other. More specifically, a child's environment may dictate what behaviors he displays, but the behaviors displayed will also affect his environment. The environment that an individual lives in may present certain opportunities that elicit certain behaviors. A child with two parents who are highly supportive of education may be more inclined to study more. At the same time, the behaviors presented will determine the environments. The child who studies and gets good grades has a greater likelihood of being accepted into a good college and getting a good job. In this scenario, we can see that the

Copyright © Mometrix Media. You have been licensed one copy of this document for personal use only. Any other reproduction or redistribution is strictly prohibited. All rights reserved.
This content is provided for test preparation purposes only and does not imply an endorsement by Mometrix of any particular political, scientific, or religious point of view.

supportive environment affected the behavior (studying) and that this behavior affected the environment (good college and job).

112. D: Counselors must respect the cultural identity of their students. Since the student is not seeing the counselor because of cultural identity issues, it would be considered professionally unethical for the counselor to address her Chinese heritage. It is, however, the counselor's responsibility to understand this student's cultural identity in order to develop effective interventions for this student's presenting problem. The counselor must also have a clear understanding of her own beliefs and stereotypes in this situation that may cause bias when treating this student. Counselors who are unaware of these issues may inadvertently treat a student of another culture with negativity or less support than she would a student of her own culture.

113. D: Keeping parents informed about their students' academic progress is one important factor in the success of a student. These reports are useful in tracking a student's progress and identifying when intervention is necessary. By including the parents in these reports, counselors can take a step in gaining the parents' participation and cooperation if problems do arise. These reports also allow parents to send comments to the teachers, as well as request conferences. Additionally, providing parents' with information about school events and activities will allow parents opportunities to volunteer with the school and stay up-to-date on the extracurricular programs offered at a school.

114. A: Developing a comprehensive intervention program will offer students support from a number of sources and increase their chances of success. By understanding a student's culture, the counselor can optimize participation from the student, parents, and the community. Every culture views child development in a slightly different way; therefore, it is important to understand that what is classified as a developmental delay in one culture may not be considered so in another. This discrepancy can lean to resistance from students and parents, and the counselor must handle these situations with care in order to provide effective services to the student. It is not the counselor's responsibility to change the parents' and students' views; rather, the counselor must work with these cultural outlooks in order to offer the student the best environment for success.

115. B: A student-led conference is one in which the student participates in the preparation and presentation of the conference. This is a good strategy to encourage student-parent communication. This is also a good strategy to use to show parents the capabilities of their children. Student-led conferences offer students a number of advantages. By preparing a presentation for the conference, the student develops a sense of ownership. Additionally, this strategy holds the student accountable for school work that is presented during the meeting. Finally, this type of conference gives the student the opportunity to improve on oral and visual presentation skills in a nonthreatening environment.

116. A: The client's diagnosis serves as the foundation for treatment goals. The assessment, diagnosis, and case conceptualization should form the basis for a client's treatment plan. Treatment planning is a collaborative effort between the client and counselor, naturally incorporating a client's desire to change. The number of sessions may be influenced by insurance coverage; however, the goals themselves do not rely on that information. Collateral information is part of the assessment process rather than treatment planning.

117. A: Counselors can be responsible for more than just the mental and emotional well-being of students. When a school offers various career development programs, students who participate gain valuable skills for the future. On-the-job training programs are an excellent way to increase job skills. Additionally, these programs often help students decide what career path to follow. These

Copyright © Mometrix Media. You have been licensed one copy of this document for personal use only. Any other reproduction or redistribution is strictly prohibited. All rights reserved.
This content is provided for test preparation purposes only and does not imply an endorsement by Mometrix of any particular political, scientific, or religious point of view.

programs allow students to go to school and work while earning school credits and gaining practical business experience. Counselors must understand that cooperation and communication with the community and leaders in the business community can be the key to success for these types of programs.

118. D: Rumination disorder is characterized by repeated regurgitation of food for at least 1 month. Individuals with rumination disorder engage in rechewing, reswallowing, and spitting their food out. Infants and older individuals with intellectual disabilities are more likely to be diagnosed with rumination disorder. Individuals with bulimia nervosa discreetly consume amounts of food that are larger than most individuals would eat in the same time period. This is followed by inappropriate compensatory behaviors (e.g., excessive exercise, self-induced vomiting, refusing to eat, or misusing diuretics). Individuals with pica ingest nonnutritive substances (e.g., paint, plaster, or clay). Finally, binge eating disorder includes recurrent episodes of binge eating, eating until uncomfortably full, or socially isolating when eating.

119. A: The primary role of the teacher advisor is to provide support and serve as advocates for their students. In addition to this, advisors can assist the student when he is experiencing academic or personal problems. This added support system provides students with the opportunity to seek help before problems escalate. While regular meetings are encouraged, each school can determine specific meeting requirements based on the school environment and the needs of the student body. Aside from the primary role of the advisors, specific tasks will depend on the needs of the student and the number of students a teacher has.

120. A: Summative assessments are designed to determine the effectiveness of an intervention. These outcome measures should show at least some improvement if the intervention was properly done, and formative assessments were conducted throughout the intervention time. When improvement is not found, it is an indication that the intervention was not meeting the needs of the student. It is the responsibility of the counselor to monitor progress during this time carefully in order to modify interventions to meet the student's needs. Failure to do so will result in no improvement and may cause frustration in the student, counselor, and parents.

Copyright © Mometrix Media. You have been licensed one copy of this document for personal use only. Any other reproduction or redistribution is strictly prohibited. All rights reserved.
This content is provided for test preparation purposes only and does not imply an endorsement by Mometrix of any particular political, scientific, or religious point of view.

How to Overcome Test Anxiety

Just the thought of taking a test is enough to make most people a little nervous. A test is an important event that can have a long-term impact on your future, so it's important to take it seriously and it's natural to feel anxious about performing well. But just because anxiety is normal, that doesn't mean that it's helpful in test taking, or that you should simply accept it as part of your life. Anxiety can have a variety of effects. These effects can be mild, like making you feel slightly nervous, or severe, like blocking your ability to focus or remember even a simple detail.

If you experience test anxiety—whether severe or mild—it's important to know how to beat it. To discover this, first you need to understand what causes test anxiety.

Causes of Test Anxiety

While we often think of anxiety as an uncontrollable emotional state, it can actually be caused by simple, practical things. One of the most common causes of test anxiety is that a person does not feel adequately prepared for their test. This feeling can be the result of many different issues such as poor study habits or lack of organization, but the most common culprit is time management. Starting to study too late, failing to organize your study time to cover all of the material, or being distracted while you study will mean that you're not well prepared for the test. This may lead to cramming the night before, which will cause you to be physically and mentally exhausted for the test. Poor time management also contributes to feelings of stress, fear, and hopelessness as you realize you are not well prepared but don't know what to do about it.

Other times, test anxiety is not related to your preparation for the test but comes from unresolved fear. This may be a past failure on a test, or poor performance on tests in general. It may come from comparing yourself to others who seem to be performing better or from the stress of living up to expectations. Anxiety may be driven by fears of the future—how failure on this test would affect your educational and career goals. These fears are often completely irrational, but they can still negatively impact your test performance.

Elements of Test Anxiety

As mentioned earlier, test anxiety is considered to be an emotional state, but it has physical and mental components as well. Sometimes you may not even realize that you are suffering from test anxiety until you notice the physical symptoms. These can include trembling hands, rapid heartbeat, sweating, nausea, and tense muscles. Extreme anxiety may lead to fainting or vomiting. Obviously, any of these symptoms can have a negative impact on testing. It is important to recognize them as soon as they begin to occur so that you can address the problem before it damages your performance.

The mental components of test anxiety include trouble focusing and inability to remember learned information. During a test, your mind is on high alert, which can help you recall information and stay focused for an extended period of time. However, anxiety interferes with your mind's natural processes, causing you to blank out, even on the questions you know well. The strain of testing during anxiety makes it difficult to stay focused, especially on a test that may take several hours. Extreme anxiety can take a huge mental toll, making it difficult not only to recall test information but even to understand the test questions or pull your thoughts together.

Copyright © Mometrix Media. You have been licensed one copy of this document for personal use only. Any other reproduction or redistribution is strictly prohibited. All rights reserved.
This content is provided for test preparation purposes only and does not imply an endorsement by Mometrix of any particular political, scientific, or religious point of view.

Effects of Test Anxiety

Test anxiety is like a disease—if left untreated, it will get progressively worse. Anxiety leads to poor performance, and this reinforces the feelings of fear and failure, which in turn lead to poor performances on subsequent tests. It can grow from a mild nervousness to a crippling condition. If allowed to progress, test anxiety can have a big impact on your schooling, and consequently on your future.

Test anxiety can spread to other parts of your life. Anxiety on tests can become anxiety in any stressful situation, and blanking on a test can turn into panicking in a job situation. But fortunately, you don't have to let anxiety rule your testing and determine your grades. There are a number of relatively simple steps you can take to move past anxiety and function normally on a test and in the rest of life.

Physical Steps for Beating Test Anxiety

While test anxiety is a serious problem, the good news is that it can be overcome. It doesn't have to control your ability to think and remember information. While it may take time, you can begin taking steps today to beat anxiety.

Just as your first hint that you may be struggling with anxiety comes from the physical symptoms, the first step to treating it is also physical. Rest is crucial for having a clear, strong mind. If you are tired, it is much easier to give in to anxiety. But if you establish good sleep habits, your body and mind will be ready to perform optimally, without the strain of exhaustion. Additionally, sleeping well helps you to retain information better, so you're more likely to recall the answers when you see the test questions.

Getting good sleep means more than going to bed on time. It's important to allow your brain time to relax. Take study breaks from time to time so it doesn't get overworked, and don't study right before bed. Take time to rest your mind before trying to rest your body, or you may find it difficult to fall asleep.

Along with sleep, other aspects of physical health are important in preparing for a test. Good nutrition is vital for good brain function. Sugary foods and drinks may give a burst of energy but this burst is followed by a crash, both physically and emotionally. Instead, fuel your body with protein and vitamin-rich foods.

Also, drink plenty of water. Dehydration can lead to headaches and exhaustion, especially if your brain is already under stress from the rigors of the test. Particularly if your test is a long one, drink water during the breaks. And if possible, take an energy-boosting snack to eat between sections.

Along with sleep and diet, a third important part of physical health is exercise. Maintaining a steady workout schedule is helpful, but even taking 5-minute study breaks to walk can help get your blood pumping faster and clear your head. Exercise also releases endorphins, which contribute to a positive feeling and can help combat test anxiety.

When you nurture your physical health, you are also contributing to your mental health. If your body is healthy, your mind is much more likely to be healthy as well. So take time to rest, nourish your body with healthy food and water, and get moving as much as possible. Taking these physical steps will make you stronger and more able to take the mental steps necessary to overcome test anxiety.

Copyright © Mometrix Media. You have been licensed one copy of this document for personal use only. Any other reproduction or redistribution is strictly prohibited. All rights reserved.
This content is provided for test preparation purposes only and does not imply an endorsement by Mometrix of any particular political, scientific, or religious point of view.

Mental Steps for Beating Test Anxiety

Working on the mental side of test anxiety can be more challenging, but as with the physical side, there are clear steps you can take to overcome it. As mentioned earlier, test anxiety often stems from lack of preparation, so the obvious solution is to prepare for the test. Effective studying may be the most important weapon you have for beating test anxiety, but you can and should employ several other mental tools to combat fear.

First, boost your confidence by reminding yourself of past success—tests or projects that you aced. If you're putting as much effort into preparing for this test as you did for those, there's no reason you should expect to fail here. Work hard to prepare; then trust your preparation.

Second, surround yourself with encouraging people. It can be helpful to find a study group, but be sure that the people you're around will encourage a positive attitude. If you spend time with others who are anxious or cynical, this will only contribute to your own anxiety. Look for others who are motivated to study hard from a desire to succeed, not from a fear of failure.

Third, reward yourself. A test is physically and mentally tiring, even without anxiety, and it can be helpful to have something to look forward to. Plan an activity following the test, regardless of the outcome, such as going to a movie or getting ice cream.

When you are taking the test, if you find yourself beginning to feel anxious, remind yourself that you know the material. Visualize successfully completing the test. Then take a few deep, relaxing breaths and return to it. Work through the questions carefully but with confidence, knowing that you are capable of succeeding.

Developing a healthy mental approach to test taking will also aid in other areas of life. Test anxiety affects more than just the actual test—it can be damaging to your mental health and even contribute to depression. It's important to beat test anxiety before it becomes a problem for more than testing.

Study Strategy

Being prepared for the test is necessary to combat anxiety, but what does being prepared look like? You may study for hours on end and still not feel prepared. What you need is a strategy for test prep. The next few pages outline our recommended steps to help you plan out and conquer the challenge of preparation.

Step 1: Scope Out the Test

Learn everything you can about the format (multiple choice, essay, etc.) and what will be on the test. Gather any study materials, course outlines, or sample exams that may be available. Not only will this help you to prepare, but knowing what to expect can help to alleviate test anxiety.

Step 2: Map Out the Material

Look through the textbook or study guide and make note of how many chapters or sections it has. Then divide these over the time you have. For example, if a book has 15 chapters and you have five days to study, you need to cover three chapters each day. Even better, if you have the time, leave an extra day at the end for overall review after you have gone through the material in depth.

If time is limited, you may need to prioritize the material. Look through it and make note of which sections you think you already have a good grasp on, and which need review. While you are studying, skim quickly through the familiar sections and take more time on the challenging parts.

Copyright © Mometrix Media. You have been licensed one copy of this document for personal use only. Any other reproduction or redistribution is strictly prohibited. All rights reserved.
This content is provided for test preparation purposes only and does not imply an endorsement by Mometrix of any particular political, scientific, or religious point of view.

Write out your plan so you don't get lost as you go. Having a written plan also helps you feel more in control of the study, so anxiety is less likely to arise from feeling overwhelmed at the amount to cover.

Step 3: Gather Your Tools

Decide what study method works best for you. Do you prefer to highlight in the book as you study and then go back over the highlighted portions? Or do you type out notes of the important information? Or is it helpful to make flashcards that you can carry with you? Assemble the pens, index cards, highlighters, post-it notes, and any other materials you may need so you won't be distracted by getting up to find things while you study.

If you're having a hard time retaining the information or organizing your notes, experiment with different methods. For example, try color-coding by subject with colored pens, highlighters, or post-it notes. If you learn better by hearing, try recording yourself reading your notes so you can listen while in the car, working out, or simply sitting at your desk. Ask a friend to quiz you from your flashcards, or try teaching someone the material to solidify it in your mind.

Step 4: Create Your Environment

It's important to avoid distractions while you study. This includes both the obvious distractions like visitors and the subtle distractions like an uncomfortable chair (or a too-comfortable couch that makes you want to fall asleep). Set up the best study environment possible: good lighting and a comfortable work area. If background music helps you focus, you may want to turn it on, but otherwise keep the room quiet. If you are using a computer to take notes, be sure you don't have any other windows open, especially applications like social media, games, or anything else that could distract you. Silence your phone and turn off notifications. Be sure to keep water close by so you stay hydrated while you study (but avoid unhealthy drinks and snacks).

Also, take into account the best time of day to study. Are you freshest first thing in the morning? Try to set aside some time then to work through the material. Is your mind clearer in the afternoon or evening? Schedule your study session then. Another method is to study at the same time of day that you will take the test, so that your brain gets used to working on the material at that time and will be ready to focus at test time.

Step 5: Study!

Once you have done all the study preparation, it's time to settle into the actual studying. Sit down, take a few moments to settle your mind so you can focus, and begin to follow your study plan. Don't give in to distractions or let yourself procrastinate. This is your time to prepare so you'll be ready to fearlessly approach the test. Make the most of the time and stay focused.

Of course, you don't want to burn out. If you study too long you may find that you're not retaining the information very well. Take regular study breaks. For example, taking five minutes out of every hour to walk briskly, breathing deeply and swinging your arms, can help your mind stay fresh.

As you get to the end of each chapter or section, it's a good idea to do a quick review. Remind yourself of what you learned and work on any difficult parts. When you feel that you've mastered the material, move on to the next part. At the end of your study session, briefly skim through your notes again.

But while review is helpful, cramming last minute is NOT. If at all possible, work ahead so that you won't need to fit all your study into the last day. Cramming overloads your brain with more information than it can process and retain, and your tired mind may struggle to recall even

Copyright © Mometrix Media. You have been licensed one copy of this document for personal use only. Any other reproduction or redistribution is strictly prohibited. All rights reserved.
This content is provided for test preparation purposes only and does not imply an endorsement by Mometrix of any particular political, scientific, or religious point of view.

previously learned information when it is overwhelmed with last-minute study. Also, the urgent nature of cramming and the stress placed on your brain contribute to anxiety. You'll be more likely to go to the test feeling unprepared and having trouble thinking clearly.

So don't cram, and don't stay up late before the test, even just to review your notes at a leisurely pace. Your brain needs rest more than it needs to go over the information again. In fact, plan to finish your studies by noon or early afternoon the day before the test. Give your brain the rest of the day to relax or focus on other things, and get a good night's sleep. Then you will be fresh for the test and better able to recall what you've studied.

Step 6: Take a Practice Test

Many courses offer sample tests, either online or in the study materials. This is an excellent resource to check whether you have mastered the material, as well as to prepare for the test format and environment.

Check the test format ahead of time: the number of questions, the type (multiple choice, free response, etc.), and the time limit. Then create a plan for working through them. For example, if you have 30 minutes to take a 60-question test, your limit is 30 seconds per question. Spend less time on the questions you know well so that you can take more time on the difficult ones.

If you have time to take several practice tests, take the first one open book, with no time limit. Work through the questions at your own pace and make sure you fully understand them. Gradually work up to taking a test under test conditions: sit at a desk with all study materials put away and set a timer. Pace yourself to make sure you finish the test with time to spare and go back to check your answers if you have time.

After each test, check your answers. On the questions you missed, be sure you understand why you missed them. Did you misread the question (tests can use tricky wording)? Did you forget the information? Or was it something you hadn't learned? Go back and study any shaky areas that the practice tests reveal.

Taking these tests not only helps with your grade, but also aids in combating test anxiety. If you're already used to the test conditions, you're less likely to worry about it, and working through tests until you're scoring well gives you a confidence boost. Go through the practice tests until you feel comfortable, and then you can go into the test knowing that you're ready for it.

Test Tips

On test day, you should be confident, knowing that you've prepared well and are ready to answer the questions. But aside from preparation, there are several test day strategies you can employ to maximize your performance.

First, as stated before, get a good night's sleep the night before the test (and for several nights before that, if possible). Go into the test with a fresh, alert mind rather than staying up late to study.

Try not to change too much about your normal routine on the day of the test. It's important to eat a nutritious breakfast, but if you normally don't eat breakfast at all, consider eating just a protein bar. If you're a coffee drinker, go ahead and have your normal coffee. Just make sure you time it so that the caffeine doesn't wear off right in the middle of your test. Avoid sugary beverages, and drink enough water to stay hydrated but not so much that you need a restroom break 10 minutes into the

Copyright © Mometrix Media. You have been licensed one copy of this document for personal use only. Any other reproduction or redistribution is strictly prohibited. All rights reserved.
This content is provided for test preparation purposes only and does not imply an endorsement by Mometrix of any particular political, scientific, or religious point of view.

test. If your test isn't first thing in the morning, consider going for a walk or doing a light workout before the test to get your blood flowing.

Allow yourself enough time to get ready, and leave for the test with plenty of time to spare so you won't have the anxiety of scrambling to arrive in time. Another reason to be early is to select a good seat. It's helpful to sit away from doors and windows, which can be distracting. Find a good seat, get out your supplies, and settle your mind before the test begins.

When the test begins, start by going over the instructions carefully, even if you already know what to expect. Make sure you avoid any careless mistakes by following the directions.

Then begin working through the questions, pacing yourself as you've practiced. If you're not sure on an answer, don't spend too much time on it, and don't let it shake your confidence. Either skip it and come back later, or eliminate as many wrong answers as possible and guess among the remaining ones. Don't dwell on these questions as you continue—put them out of your mind and focus on what lies ahead.

Be sure to read all of the answer choices, even if you're sure the first one is the right answer. Sometimes you'll find a better one if you keep reading. But don't second-guess yourself if you do immediately know the answer. Your gut instinct is usually right. Don't let test anxiety rob you of the information you know.

If you have time at the end of the test (and if the test format allows), go back and review your answers. Be cautious about changing any, since your first instinct tends to be correct, but make sure you didn't misread any of the questions or accidentally mark the wrong answer choice. Look over any you skipped and make an educated guess.

At the end, leave the test feeling confident. You've done your best, so don't waste time worrying about your performance or wishing you could change anything. Instead, celebrate the successful completion of this test. And finally, use this test to learn how to deal with anxiety even better next time.

Review Video: Test Anxiety
Visit mometrix.com/academy and enter code: 100340

Important Qualification

Not all anxiety is created equal. If your test anxiety is causing major issues in your life beyond the classroom or testing center, or if you are experiencing troubling physical symptoms related to your anxiety, it may be a sign of a serious physiological or psychological condition. If this sounds like your situation, we strongly encourage you to seek professional help.

Copyright © Mometrix Media. You have been licensed one copy of this document for personal use only. Any other reproduction or redistribution is strictly prohibited. All rights reserved.
This content is provided for test preparation purposes only and does not imply an endorsement by Mometrix of any particular political, scientific, or religious point of view.

Thank You

We at Mometrix would like to extend our heartfelt thanks to you, our friend and patron, for allowing us to play a part in your journey. It is a privilege to serve people from all walks of life who are unified in their commitment to building the best future they can for themselves.

The preparation you devote to these important testing milestones may be the most valuable educational opportunity you have for making a real difference in your life. We encourage you to put your heart into it—that feeling of succeeding, overcoming, and yes, conquering will be well worth the hours you've invested.

We want to hear your story, your struggles and your successes, and if you see any opportunities for us to improve our materials so we can help others even more effectively in the future, please share that with us as well. **The team at Mometrix would be absolutely thrilled to hear from you!** So please, send us an email (support@mometrix.com) and let's stay in touch.

Copyright © Mometrix Media. You have been licensed one copy of this document for personal use only. Any other reproduction or redistribution is strictly prohibited. All rights reserved.
This content is provided for test preparation purposes only and does not imply an endorsement by Mometrix of any particular political, scientific, or religious point of view.

Additional Bonus Material

Due to our efforts to try to keep this book to a manageable length, we've created a link that will give you access to all of your additional bonus material:

mometrix.com/acfw/vi/428468

Copyright © Mometrix Media. You have been licensed one copy of this document for personal use only. Any other reproduction or redistribution is strictly prohibited. All rights reserved.
This content is provided for test preparation purposes only and does not imply an endorsement by Mometrix of any particular political, scientific, or religious point of view.